CHRISTMAS
WITH
MORMON HANDICRAFT

Deseret Book Company
Salt Lake City, Utah

We gratefully acknowledge the talents and assistance of all those who have contributed in any way to the publication of this book. In addition to the individual contributors and creators of the patterns included, we are indebted to the following:

Ann Danzig, Mormon Handicraft Project Coordinator
Cathy Finnegan, Assistant Coordinator
Carole Cole, Editor
Shauna Gibby, Designer and Illustrator
Vicky Clarke, Illustrator
Steve Bunderson, Photographer
Melanie Shumway, Photo Stylist

Every effort has been made to ensure that these instructions and recipes are accurate and complete. We cannot, however, be responsible for human error, typographical mistakes, or variations in individual work.

Materials are available from Mormon Handicraft. Within Utah call 801-355-2141. Outside of Utah call 1-800-843-1480.

Library of Congress Cataloging-in-Publication Data

Christmas with Mormon handicraft.
       p. cm.
  ISBN 0-87579-535-8 (HB)
  1. Christmas decorations. 2. Arts, Mormon. 3. Christmas cookery.
4. Cookery, Mormon. I. Deseret Book Company.
TT900.C4C486 1992
745.594'12—dc20   92-15016
                                   CIP

Printed in the United States of America
10 9 8 7 6 5 4 3 2 1

CONTENTS

ENTERTAINMENT

FOREWORD

The Christmas season speaks to giving and sharing more than any other time of the year. We decorate our homes and workplaces with fragrant pine boughs, gaily colored ribbons, and traditional as well as unique trimmings to reflect the abundant spirit of the season. We cook special dishes, spend hours to make or find just the right gifts, and share our bounty with those less fortunate than ourselves.

Mormon Handicraft has long been known for its tradition of beautiful, handmade gifts. More than 2,000 contributors bring their crafts to our store in the heart of downtown Salt Lake City each season. We are often asked for the pattern to "that darling doll" or the "lovely quilt" or that "cute toy" featured in our windows--sometimes from years-old displays.

Christmas with Mormon Handicraft is a collection of patterns, ideas, and recipes from contributors, friends, and the staff of Mormon Handicraft. More than 100 ideas from 50 different sources fill these pages. We know you'll find herein a fun project to do with your child, just the right item to decorate your home, or the perfect keepsake gift to make for your family or to be given with joy. Here too you will delight in numerous delicious recipes and entertaining ideas for a wonderful holiday party.

Our thanks to all who so generously shared their ideas and talents.

DECORATIONS

FOR THE TREE

FOR THE WALL

FOR HERE AND THERE

ANGEL GARLAND OR HANGING ANGEL

Liz Hansen
See picture on p. 97

1/3 yd. muslin
1/8 yd. or scraps of Christmas print
1 yd. of 1/2" wide gathered lace
Raffia
Polyester fiber filling
Hot-glue gun
Brown acrylic paint
Red ribbon bow

Read all instructions before you begin. Trace patterns onto tracing or typing paper, then cut out. All seams are 1/8".

Cut out head, dress-body, and small arms from muslin. Cut feet and heart out of Christmas print scraps.

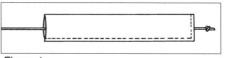

Figure 1

Sew feet and turn right side out. Sew arms after folding in half lengthwise. Cut a piece of yarn 2" longer than arms. Put a knot in one end. Insert to inside of fold (see Fig. 1), machine stitch (backstitching across yarn), and leave end open. Pull gently on yarn to help turn right side out. Tie a knot in middle of arms.

Baste arms in place on one piece of dress-body. Baste a 3-1/4" piece of lace at bottom of dress. Baste feet on top of that. (See Fig. 2.)

Place top piece of dress-body on other piece, right sides together and sew through all thicknesses.

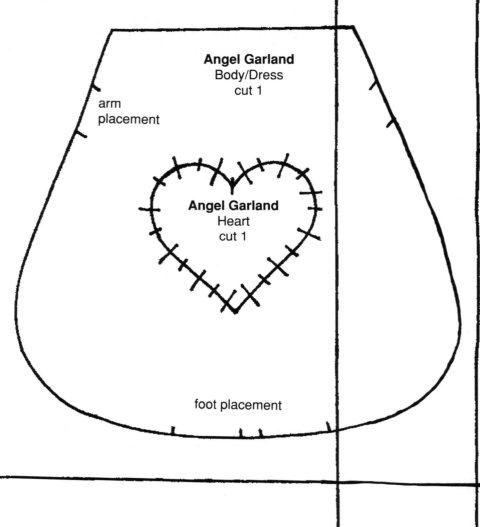

Hanging Angel
Arms
cut 1

Angel Garland
Body/Dress
cut 1

arm
placement

Angel Garland
Heart
cut 1

foot placement

Angel Garland
Head
cut 2

Angel Garland
Foot
cut 4

Angel Garland
Arms cut 1

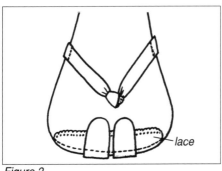

Figure 2

Turn right side out and stuff. Turn neck edge under 1/4" and sew a piece of lace around it.

Sew head. Turn right side out and stuff. Run a gathering stitch around neck of dress-body. Place neck end of head into dress-body. Pull gathering stitch tight; take one stitch through to back and secure.

Hand stitch heart to dress-body with crochet thread making uneven stitches.

Braid six strands of raffia for hair. Knot at each end for desired length. Hot glue small pieces of raffia for bangs; then glue braid over that.

Make bow of 10-12 strands of raffia for wings. Hot glue to back of neck. Using a needle, split strands of raffia hanging down.

Paint on eyes with dots of brown paint. Make freckles with fine liner brush or toothpick. When paint is dry, brush blush on cheeks.

Tie bow with red ribbon. Put red ribbon bow at angel's neck. When making a garland, tie together with a red bow.

ANGEL AND HEART GARLAND

Trudy Nydegger
See picture on p. 100

Scraps of muslin
2 tea bags to make tea dye
Scraps of brown fabric
Scraps of red fabric
Scraps of patchwork fabric
White felt
Pellon fleece
Hot-glue gun
Jute twine

Figure 1   Figure 2

DOLL
Cut doll out of muslin. Sew all around. Cut a slit in back of doll. Clip corners and curves. Turn right side out.

Dye with tea water (2 tea bags to 1 cup boiling water). Allow to dry. Stuff the doll and whipstitch slit closed.

DOLL HAIR
Cut three 1/2"x12" strips of brown fabric. Cut three 1/2"x2" strips of red print fabric.

For one tuft of hair, fold brown fabric back and forth until there are

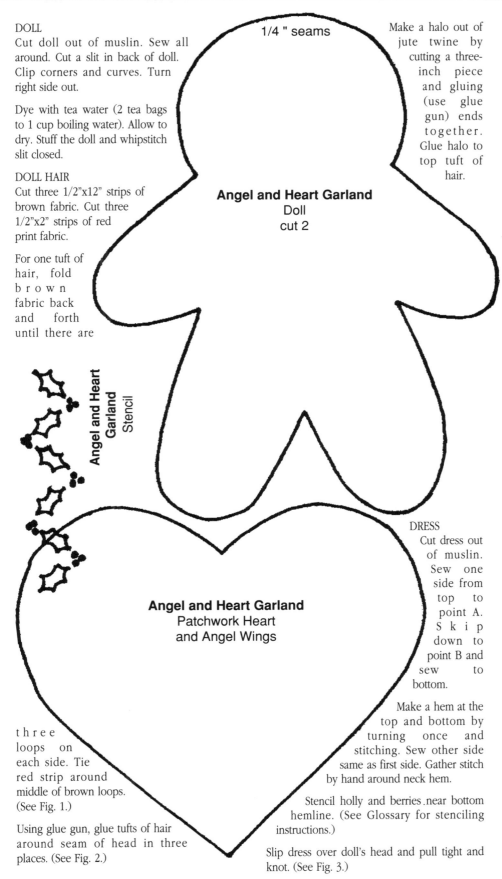

1/4 " seams

Angel and Heart Garland
Doll
cut 2

Angel and Heart Garland Stencil

Angel and Heart Garland
Patchwork Heart
and Angel Wings

three loops on each side. Tie red strip around middle of brown loops. (See Fig. 1.)

Using glue gun, glue tufts of hair around seam of head in three places. (See Fig. 2.)

Make a halo out of jute twine by cutting a three-inch piece and gluing (use glue gun) ends together. Glue halo to top tuft of hair.

DRESS
Cut dress out of muslin. Sew one side from top to point A. Skip down to point B and sew to bottom.

Make a hem at the top and bottom by turning once and stitching. Sew other side same as first side. Gather stitch by hand around neck hem.

Stencil holly and berries near bottom hemline. (See Glossary for stenciling instructions.)

Slip dress over doll's head and pull tight and knot. (See Fig. 3.)

Figure 3

Figure 4

WINGS

Cut one heart out of white felt. Glue to back.

PATCHWORK HEART

Cut two patchwork hearts (make your own crazy patch or buy preprinted patchwork). Cut two hearts of Pellon fleece and two of backing fabric (muslin). Make a sandwich with fleece heart on bottom, then patchwork, right sides together, then backing. Repeat for second heart. Stitch all around Cut slit in top layer, clip curves and corners, turn inside out. Whipstitch slit closed.

TIES

Cut four 30" pieces of jute twine. Tie knots in ends. Make a loop with one piece of twine. Hold tight while tying second piece of twine around middle of loop. After making initial tie, make a bow. (See Fig. 4.)

Glue swag together with angel in middle, hearts on either side of angel, ties on ends of hearts.

CHRISTMAS BALL WITH DOILY

See picture p. 63

3" glass Christmas ball in desired color or colors
1 yd. 1/4" wide ribbon in desired color
3" or 4" crocheted doily in white or ecru
Tacky glue

Cut out center of doily large enough to fit over cap of ornament.

Glue points of doily to ball using Tacky glue. Decorate with moss, baby's breath, dried or silk flowers and ribbon in that order.

Make 4" ribbon loop to hang the ornament.

CHRISTMAS BEAR ORNAMENT

Shar Nelson

See picture on p. 100

One 6-inch circle of Christmas fabric
6" of narrow (1/2" wide) gathered lace
One 1-1/2" tan pompon (head)
Four 3/4" tan pompons (ears and hands)
One 1/4" tan pompon (nose)
Three 4mm whole black beads (eyes and nose)
Small scrap of red felt (tongue)
Small bow made from 1/8" wide ribbon
Small Christmas wreath
Gold cord

Tacky glue or glue gun (or both)
Polyester fiber filling
Blush
Needle and thread
Tweezers
Scissors

Cut a six-inch circle from fabric. Sew two rows of gathering stitches around outer edge of circle.

Place a handful of fiber filling in center and pull gathering threads as tight as possible without breaking thread. Tie off gathering threads.

Glue gathered lace around top of gathering stitches, gathering a little more fullness as you go.

Glue 1-1/2" pompon on top of gathers (covering top edge of lace) for head. Determine which side is front and trim pile where eyes will go. When gluing pompons together, separate pile and glue down in, not just on top.

Glue two 3/4" pompons for ears. With small scissors, clip small indentation in middle of front of each ear.

Glue the 1/4" pompon on front of face for nose. While glue is wet, glue tiny red felt circle 2/3"under nose.

Glue two 4mm black beads (separating pile with tweezers) down into pile. (Do not glue just to top of pile.) Glue remaining black bead on top of nose. Using regular make-up brush, apply blush to bear's cheeks.

Glue two 3/4" pompons under head for hands. Glue wreath onto both hands.

Make bow from 1/8" ribbon. Make a loop for hanging out of 7" of gold cord, tying both ends in knot. Separate pile between ears and glue knot of gold cord down into pile. Glue bow just in front of cord loop.

SPRING BEAR VARIATION

Use spring-type fabric. Use wooden heart or dried flowers for bear to hold. If using dried flowers, make another small bow (with 1/8" ribbon) with longer streamers and glue on stems of flowers.

If using heart, paint wooden heart with base coat of white or off-white acrylic paint. When dry, dot-paint flowers on top of heart. Hearts can be personalized.

Angel and Heart Garland
Dress
cut 2

top

A

A

B

B

1/4" seams

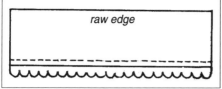

BUNNY STOCKING

Liz Hansen

See picture on p. 61

1/4 yd. or scraps of Christmas fabric
Scraps of muslin
1/2 yd. of 1" gathered lace
Red ribbon
Twine (for bow on front)
Polyester fiber filling
Acrylic paint: Brown, Mauve
Excelsior
Hot glue gun

From fabric, cut number and shape of pieces shown on pattern.

BUNNIES
Stitch around bunnies leaving bottom edge open. Turn right side out. (It will be hard to turn ears. Try using tweezers).

Stuff. Hand stitch bottom closed. Tie red ribbon around ears. Paint on face.

STOCKING
With right sides together stitch around stocking leaving top edge open. Turn right side out.

Fold under 1/4" on one lengthwise side of cuff. Press. Top stitch lace on. (See Fig. 1.)

Fold cuff in half with right sides together. Stitch side seam. Stitch lace also. Turn right side out. With right side of cuff against wrong side of stocking, stitch raw edges together. Turn cuff to outside of stocking.

To make the hanger, cut a piece of fabric 1-3/4"x5". Fold long edges in to meet in middle, then fold in half lengthwise. Stitch close to edge. Fold in half to make loop. Tack raw edges to inside of stocking.

Figure 1

Stuff stocking with polyester fiber filling. Stuff top part with excelsior leaving some of it exposed. Dot hot glue on bottom of bunnies and arrange in stocking. Glue twine bow to front.

CLOWN ORNAMENT

Terry Leonard

See picture on p. 99

Approximate finished size: 6-1/2"

1/4" red pompon for nose
1/2" red (or green) pompon (hat)
Two 7mm wiggly eyes
6"x12" piece of Christmas print fabric
3"x6" piece of light pink felt (head)
1"x2" piece of dark pink felt (cheeks)
2"x3" piece of red (or green) felt
4" piece of piping for hat trim
2" piece of red cord for mouth
4" curly chenille for hair
6" elastic cord for hanger
12" red (or green) grosgrain ribbon, 3/8" wide
Sewing thread to match fabric and light pink felt
Polyester fiber filling

Cut out pieces as marked.

Sew piping to curved edge of hat, then fold hat (right sides together) and sew up the back. Turn right side out. Glue pompon to tip of hat. Tie elastic cord ends together and glue knot down into

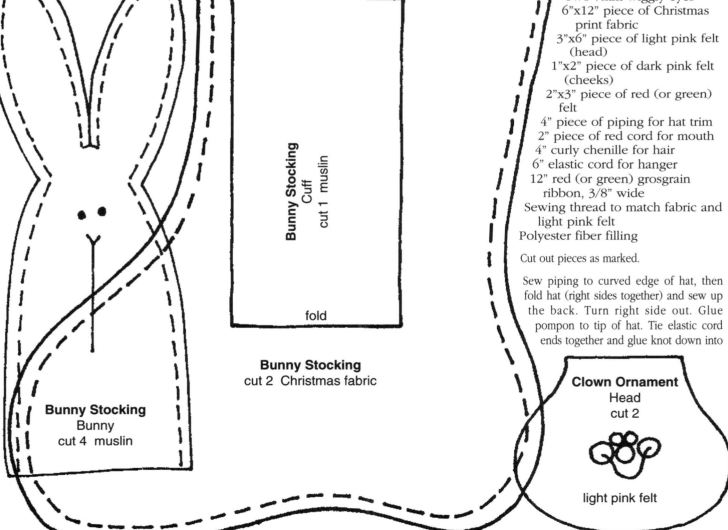

Bunny Stocking
Cuff
cut 1 muslin

fold

Bunny Stocking
cut 2 Christmas fabric

Bunny Stocking
Bunny
cut 4 muslin

Clown Ornament
Head
cut 2

light pink felt

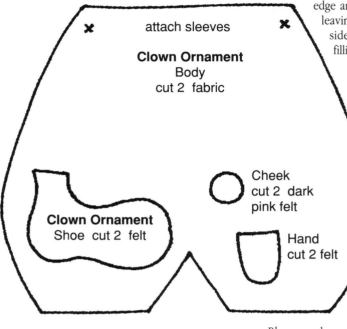

attach sleeves ✕ ✕

Clown Ornament
Body
cut 2 fabric

Clown Ornament
Shoe cut 2 felt

Cheek
cut 2 dark
pink felt

Hand
cut 2 felt

fold here

Clown Ornament
Sleeve
cut 2 fabric

hand ✕

Clown Ornament
Hat
cut 1 fabric

sew piping here

pompon on hat. Set aside. This is the ornament hanger.

Pin shoes to right side of one body piece (fold toe out of the way of stitching area). Pin the two body pieces right sides together. Stitch with 1/4" seam across bottom of both legs in long machine stitch. Pull basting thread to gather both legs tightly. Stitch along curved

edge and inseam, catching in shoes, leaving top end open. Turn right side out. Stuff body with fiber filling. Set aside.

Fold each sleeve in half along line, right sides together. Insert one hand inside sleeve, having straight side close to folded edge. Stitch across bottom of sleeve in long stitch, catching in hand. Pull up basting thread to gather. Stitch around curved edge of sleeve and across bottom (to reinforce gathers). Turn right side out and stuff with fiber filling. Repeat for other sleeve.

Place a sleeve on both sides of body, overlapping body just a little. Stitch across the entire top in long machine stitch. Pull up basting thread to gather, then tie off. Set aside.

Baste bottom part of one head to top of body section. Then pin the heads together. Stitch around curved edges catching in the body section. Stuff through the top of the head, then stitch it closed.

Put a little fiber filling in hat and glue to head.

Cut 4" curly chenille in half. Fold each piece in half and glue to sides of head.

Glue eyes, cheeks, mouth and nose onto head.

Tie ribbon into a bow and glue where head meets the body.

CHRISTMAS TREE ORNAMENT ANGEL

Jeen Brown
See picture p. 98

Fabric and Battenburg 4" square doily (6" for large ornament)
Fabric and Battenburg 6" square doily (8" for large ornament)
24" of 1/8" wide white satin ribbon (30" for large ornament)
3/4" styrofoam ball and a fine crochet 4" doily or a 3/4" white satin-covered tree ornament or pick
10" of gold-wired ribbon
6" of gold elastic thread for hanger (optional)

Tacky glue
Large-eyed needle to thread 1/8" wide ribbon

Press a 1" fold across one side of a 6" square fabric and Battenburg doily (8" for large ornament).

Using 15" of 1/8" wide white satin ribbon (18" for large ornament) and a large-eyed needle, run a 1/2" basting stitch 3/4" down from the folded edge. The satin ribbon will run through the tape of Battenburg lace. (See Fig. 1.) Pulling the satin ribbon through the fabric is difficult. It will help to take no more than one or two stitches at a time. You may consider using a rubber disk, called a grabber (sold in notions departments) to help pull the ribbon and needle through the fabric more easily.

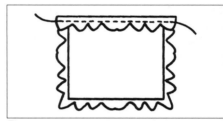

Figure 1

Tighten the ribbon as firmly as possible and tie a square knot in the center front on top of the folded part of the doily. Tie a bow on top of the knot. Fluff the folded edge to create a front collar for the angel's head.

Using 9" of 1/8" satin ribbon (11" for the large ornament), make one vertical 1/2" stitch slightly above the gathered ribbon line on the back side of the gathered doily. The folded edge is on the underneath side. Leave at least 4" of ribbon extending from the bottom stitch. (See Fig. 2.)

Figure 2

Keeping the ribbon intact in the large doily and using the center crease as a guideline, pinch the small square doily in the center to form wings. Lay the gathered doily on top of the ribbon. Tie a bow on top of the knot. (See Fig. 3.)

Figure 3

Center the 3/4" styrofoam ball on a 4" round fine crochet lace doily. You may need to trim the outer edge of the doily so there is no overlap when the doily is wrapped to cover the styrofoam ball. Tack the edges of the doily to the ball with Tacky glue.

Wrap 10" of 1/4" gold-wired ribbon around a pen, leaving 1" on each end of the ribbon straight. Slip the pen out from the ribbon without disturbing the spiral in the ribbon. Satin ribbon may be used if it is soaked in fabric stiffener and then allowed to dry on the pen. If a smaller spiral is desired, wrap the ribbon around a knitting needle. (See Fig. 4.)

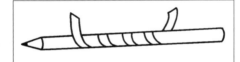

Figure 4

Place the covered styrofoam ball, raw edges down, just above the center of the wings on the opposite side where the wings have been attached. Glue in place with Tacky glue.

At the back of the angel's head, pierce the doily and ball deep enough to create a hole to insert the ribbon ends. Circle the spiral ribbon and put the ends together. Dip the ends in glue and insert in the hole at the back of the head.

A hanger (optional) may be made out of 8" of gold metallic thread or 1/8" white satin ribbon. Loop the thread or ribbon under the wings. Form a circle and tie a knot at the top above the angel's head.

VICTORIAN CANDLE ORNAMENTS

See picture on p. 64

Clothes pin doll stand rings
Candles small enough to fit in stand
   (1/2" dia.)
Standard sized clothes pins
One 4" doily per candle
3/8" red beads

Tacky glue
Baby eucalyptus leaves, dried

Glue the flat surface of the doll stand to one of the flat sides of the clothes pin, centering stand over the metal spring clip. Center base of candle in middle of right side of 4" doily. Place doily and candle in the hole of the stand and gently push to secure. (Dab a bit of glue in the center of the doll stand just before inserting candle and doily to keep it secure.) Glue eucalyptus leaves and beads around candle to finish.

YO-YO TREE ORNAMENT

See picture on p. 61

One star bead, 3/4" to 1"
One pipe cleaner, brown
Six different green fabric scraps
One cork (for stand of tree), approx.
   3/4"x1/2"
Fishing line

Yo-yo's

Cut one green fabric circle for each template.

Using a running stitch, stitch 1/8" away from edge on all circles. Pull tight and knot. Cut a small hole in the center bottom of each circle (large enough to slide pipe cleaner through).

Run pipe cleaner through middle of star bead and secure by folding the pipe cleaner down about 1/4".

Starting with smallest yo-yo, slide it up the pipe cleaner close to star bead. Repeat with rest of yo-yos.

Cut off the pipe cleaner, leaving 3/4" of it exposed at bottom. With sharp object, poke a hole in top of cork. Put a dab of glue on end of pipe cleaner and push into cork.

Arrange yo-yos so pipe cleaner cannot be seen.

Thread fishing line through center of star bead, tie knot in ends to form loop to hang ornament.

ADVENT CALENDAR

Susan Petersen
See picture on p. 99

1 yd. Christmas fabric for calendar
1/2 yd. heavy-weight Pellon
24 squares of contrasting fabric for pockets on calendar. Cut them 2-3/4"x2-1/4". Make four rows with six pockets in each row. Finish edges with pinking shears or Fray-check.
   Dowel, 1/4" or 3/8"
   1 yd. of 1/4" wide ribbon
   Scraps of fabric for pictures
   1/8 yd. "Wonder Under"
   1/2 yd. of green fabric for tree
   2 yds. of 1/4" wide green ribbon
   7" of 1/2" wide Velcro
   Small piece of brown fabric for trunk
   Polyester fiber filling
   Thread
   Tacky glue
   Hot-glue gun
   Black permanent marker

With selvages together, cut fabric in half. Attach Pellon to back of one piece.

With right sides together, sew 1/4" around edges, leaving a 2" opening at top for turning. Turn right side out. Press. Number pocket squares from 1 to 24.

Center squares for pockets on bottom background piece and sew in place. Sew two sides and bottom leaving top open to form pocket. Turn top of background piece under enough to make a casing for dowel. Stitch. Tie ribbon on each end of dowel.

Make 14 ornaments. Sew a 1/2" piece of Velcro to the back of each ornament (to attach to tree) at Xs indicated on pattern pieces. Do this before sewing tree pieces together.

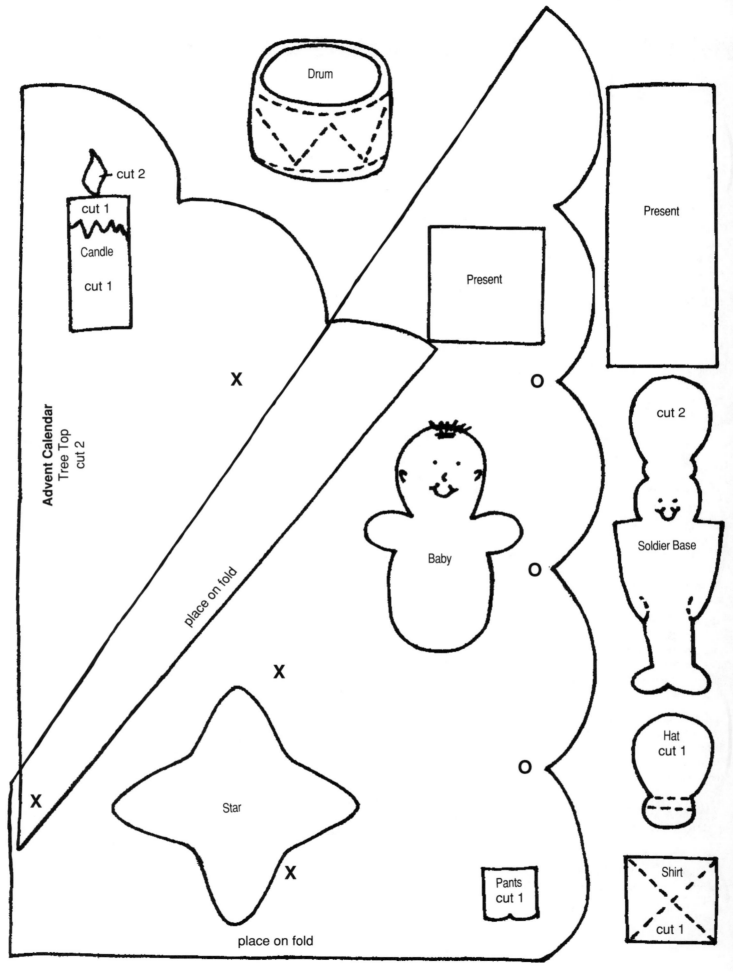

Drum

cut 2

cut 1

Candle

cut 1

Advent Calendar
Tree Top
cut 2

X

place on fold

X

X

X

Star

place on fold

Present

Present

O

cut 2

Soldier Base

O

Baby

O

Hat
cut 1

Shirt

cut 1

Pants
cut 1

8

Stocking

place on fold

Bear

dvent Calendar
Tree Middle
cut 2

X

O

Bell

X

cut 2
Reindeer

Present

O

Santa cut 2

Advent Calendar
Tree Trunk
cut 2

X   X

Elf cut 2

Santa Hat
cut 2

Elf Hat

X

9

Attach the 10 pieces of candy to the tree with ribbon. Cut the 1/4" wide ribbon into 7" lengths. Sew middle of length to tree in spots indicated by Os on the patterns. Attach star at top of tree and the 3 presents on the tree trunk. Place all other ornaments as desired.

TREE

Cut tree pieces on fold line. On back piece, make a 2" slit in the center for turning. With right sides together, sew 1/4" around all sides.

Turn through back slits. Stuff with fiber filling. Stitch opening closed. Attach to calendar with glue gun.

FIGURES

Make these figures from scraps of material or felt. Using two pieces with Wonder Under in between makes them stronger. Use contrasting colors. (Example: Drum: red base with flesh top). Or make mock stitches with black, permanent-ink marker. Attach tiny pieces (such as holly on bell) with Tacky glue.

SANTA

Before putting hat together, put head inside of hat. Redden cheeks and nose with crayon.

BABY

Use a square of white fabric for a blanket. Take a stitch of yellow embroidery floss in the middle to attach blanket to baby. Tie stitch in a bow.

ELF

Before putting hat together, put head in between hat pieces to dotted line.

REINDEER

Before putting head together, insert antlers into head pieces to dotted line.

Number the backs of pieces so you know which day to use them. For the days that are not represented by a figure, use candy canes, or other candy as desired.

ANGEL BANNER

Cathy Finnegan

See picture on p. 27

Two 22" squares of muslin
One 22" square of Pellon fleece
3/8 yd. Christmas print fabric
1/8 yd. light print fabric (wings)

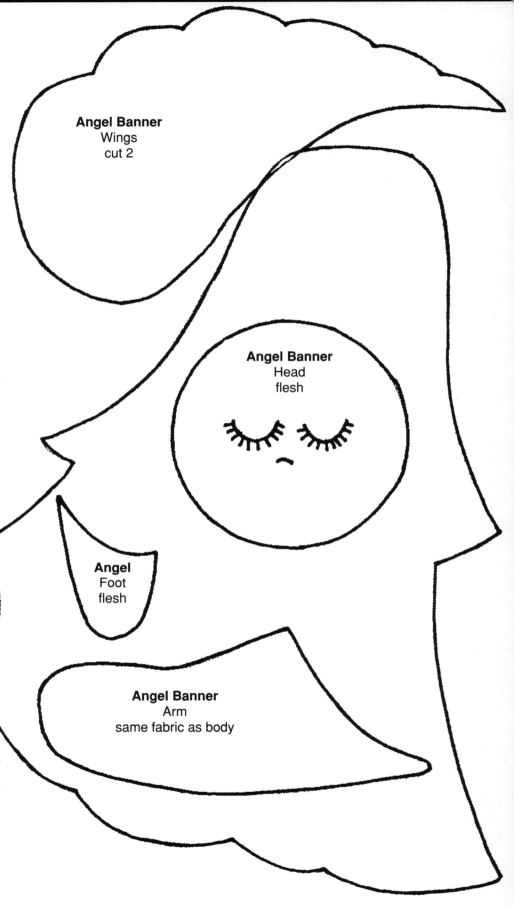

Angel Banner
Wings
cut 2

Angel Banner
Head
flesh

Angel
Foot
flesh

hand
flesh

Angel Banner
Arm
same fabric as body

One 14"x20" sheet of Mylar or material for templates
Scrap of flesh-colored fabric
1/4 yd. "Wonder Under"
18" piece of 1/4" satin ribbon
1 pkg. wool crepe hair
Permanent, fine-point marker
Christmas stencil (example: Noel)
Baby's breath and dried flowers or ribbon roses
Thread to match fabrics of choice

On one of the 22" squares of muslin, stencil the word *Noel* about 3" from the bottom in the center. Follow the instructions included in Glossary. Let dry.

Trace all template patterns onto Mylar and cut out. Label all pieces.

Turn all templates writing side down. Place templates on Wonder Under and trace around each. (See Wonder Under instructions in Glossary.) Iron pieces to wrong sides of selected fabrics and cut out.

Draw eyes onto face using the permanent marker.

Peel off paper and place Wonder Under side down onto the center of the muslin square. Arrange as shown in photograph on p. 27, then iron in place. Overlap where needed.

Place other square of muslin, then the fleece, then top, right side up, to form sandwich. Baste all three layers together to keep in place while machine appliquéing.

Machine appliqué in place with 1/8" wide satin stitch, using thread that closely matches the part of the angel you are doing. (Loosen upper tension of sewing machine to make satin stitch smooth. Do not let bobbin thread pull to surface.) Appliqué all unfinished edges of angel.

Cut two 23"x2" and two 22"x2" strips of Christmas print for binding.

Fold strip in half lengthwise, wrong sides together, and press.

On right side of banner, place the folded strip, raw edge against raw edge of banner and sew with 1/4" seam allowance.

Fold to back and slip stitch. Do the same to parallel edge, leaving 1/2" overlap of binding at each end of remaining two sides.

Stitch two sides. As you slip stitch closed, tuck in overlap at corners to finish.

For finishing touches, glue wool hair onto head. Decorate with dried flowers and ribbon bows. For flowers in hand, glue together and tie ribbon around them. Glue at hand. To add life to angel, blush her cheeks.

Sew hooks to back and hang up.

CANDY WREATH

Cathlene Caras

See picture on p. 133

Approx. 3 lbs. of twist-wrapped candy (paper twisted at both ends of candy)
10" wood hoop
Heavy crochet cotton or yarn
Curly ribbon

Cut crochet cotton in five or six 24-inch pieces. With one piece and starting at the top of the hoop, tie a square knot around the hoop.

Take one candy and starting at the knot, place one end of the wrapper on the hoop and wrap string over to secure. (See Fig. 1.)

Figure 1

Continue to add candy until hoop is full.

Pull tight after each addition. To add to string, just tie a square knot in string and keep wrapping.

To end, wrap string around several times and tie a knot to secure.

As a finishing touch, take curly ribbon and make a bow at the top. Then tie curly ribbon randomly and as often as desired throughout wreath and curl. Hang a pair of children's scissors from a piece of curly ribbon. Hang wreath on door and allow all visitors to cut off a sweet treat.

NOEL BANNER

See picture on p. 61

1/2 yd. muslin or other background fabric
1/4 yd. red border fabric
1/8 yd. red fabric for lettering
1/8 yd. dark green for holly

Scraps of red for holly berries
1 yd. Pellon fleece
1/4 yd. "Wonder Under"

Trace letters and holly onto paper side of Wonder Under. (Remember to reverse the letters.) Cut out roughly around traced pieces.

Iron pieces onto the wrong side of selected fabrics. Cut out, peel off paper backing, and set aside.

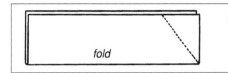

Figure 1

Cut background fabric 6-1/2" wide by 18-1/2" long. Fold in half lengthwise, press lightly, and draw a line at an angle from the folded edge of fabric to open edge, about 3" from end. (See Fig. l.) Cut along this line to form a point.

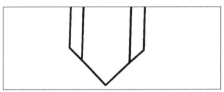

Figure 2

Starting about 1-1/2" from top of background piece, center the letters using the fold line as a guide. Leave about 1/2" between letters. Iron in place.

Cut two 45"x3" strips of fabric chosen for borders. Sew border down straight sides of background piece, right sides together. Using a straight edge, trim the border to match the angle of the point. (See Fig. 2.)

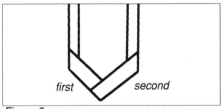

Figure 3

Sew the border on one side of the point and trim; do the same to the other side and trim. (See Fig. 3.) Sew border across the top and trim. (See Fig. 4.)

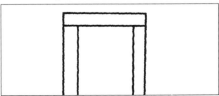

Figure 4

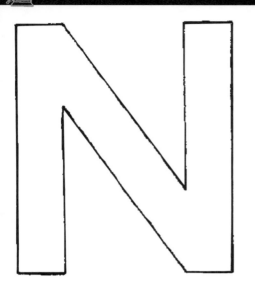

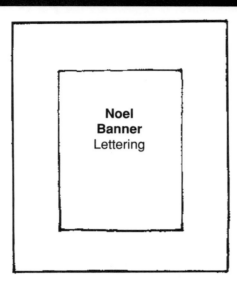

Noel Banner Lettering

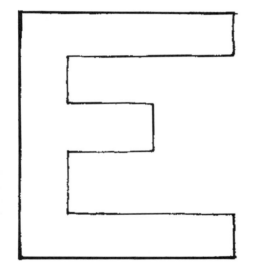

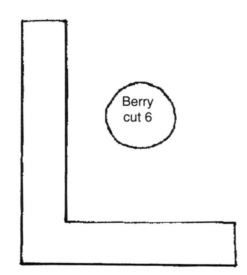

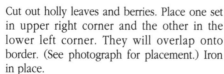

Berry cut 6

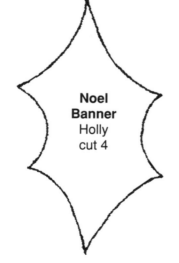

Noel Banner Holly cut 4

FOR HEAD
1/4 yd. Flesh-toned broadcloth
(Optional: Apply blush to cheeks for rosy look)

FOR BOOTS
1/4 yd. Black double knit or broadcloth

FOR BAG
1/3 yd. Green Christmas cloth

FOR TRIM
White fur: 1/4 yd.
Extra loft batting: 3/4 yd.
Small scrap of Pellon fleece for mustache
Small scrap for nose (same as suit material or red pin dot)
One 2" red pompon
Six 1/2" bells for boots
One 1-inch ring to hang finished Santa
1 yd. 1/2" wide red ribbon
One or two large bells to hang from bag
Two 1/2" round black buttons for eyes
Assorted Christmas toys (small bear, sleigh, brass horn, or packages)
Hot-glue gun and glue sticks
Red, black and white thread

Cut out Santa's suit pointing arrows on pattern in direction of nap. Cut out all other pieces; 1/4" seam allowance is included.

BODY
On front of Santa's body, on arms, and on hat, mark where fur must go. With right side of fur to right side of body, sew fur to body using 1/4" seam allowance. Turn fur down. On other edge, turn seam allowance under and top-stitch fur to body. Pin batting to wrong side of Santa's front. Pin back to front of body with right sides together, leaving an opening. Stitch. Turn right sides out. Turn seam under and hand-stitch opening closed. Top stitch (on machine) center of legs.

ARMS
Sew fur on arms in same manner as on body. With wrong sides together stitch around arm, leaving an opening. Turn right sides out; stuff firmly with fiber filling. Do not overstuff—pieces should be somewhat flat. Turn seam under and hand-stitch opening closed.

HAT
Sew fur band to front of hat in same manner as on Santa front. With wrong sides together, sew front and back of hat together, leaving brim open. The back will have a seam allowance left over. This will be turned under when sewn onto head.

Cut out holly leaves and berries. Place one set in upper right corner and the other in the lower left corner. They will overlap onto border. (See photograph for placement.) Iron in place.

Cut a piece of background fabric and Pellon fleece the same size as banner.

Put banner and back right sides together. Place Pellon fleece on top and stitch all three layers together leaving a six-inch opening at top. Turn right side out and slip stitch closed.

SANTA HANGING

Alana Winegar
See picture on p. 98
FOR SUIT
Red velour: 1-1/2 yd. (45" wide) or 1-1/4 yd. (60" wide)
FOR BEARD AND MUSTACHE
White: 1/3 yd. (45" wide)

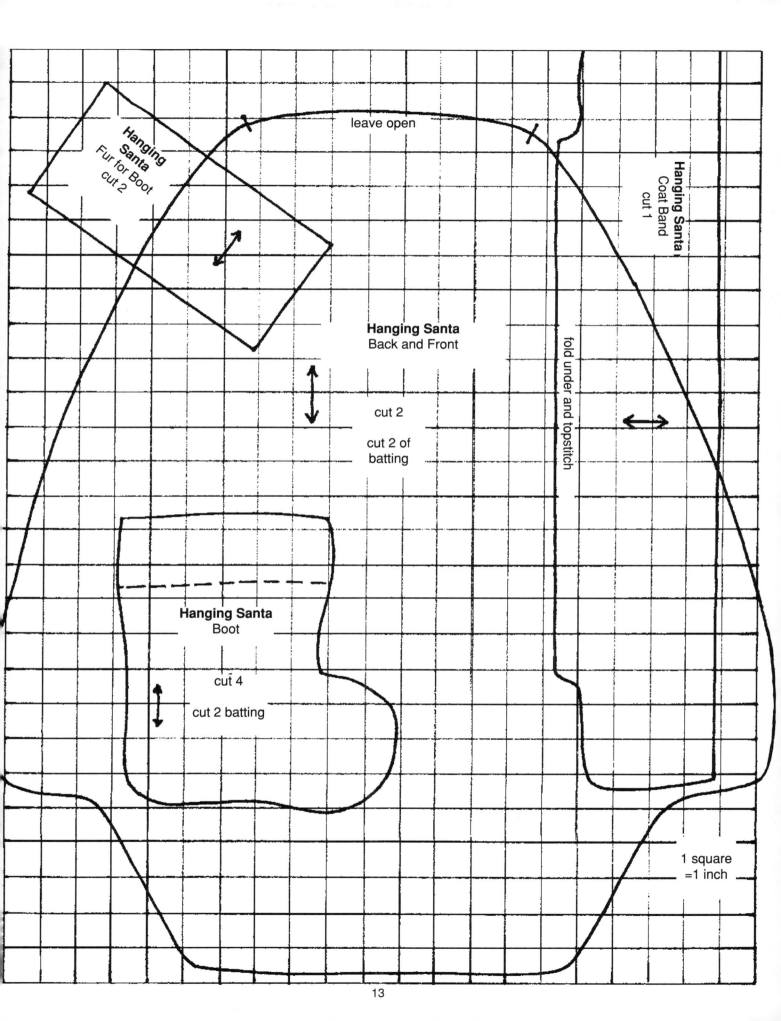

Hanging Santa
Fur for Boot
cut 2

leave open

Hanging Santa
Coat Band
cut 1

fold under and topstitch

Hanging Santa
Back and Front

cut 2

cut 2 of
batting

Hanging Santa
Boot

cut 4

cut 2 batting

1 square
=1 inch

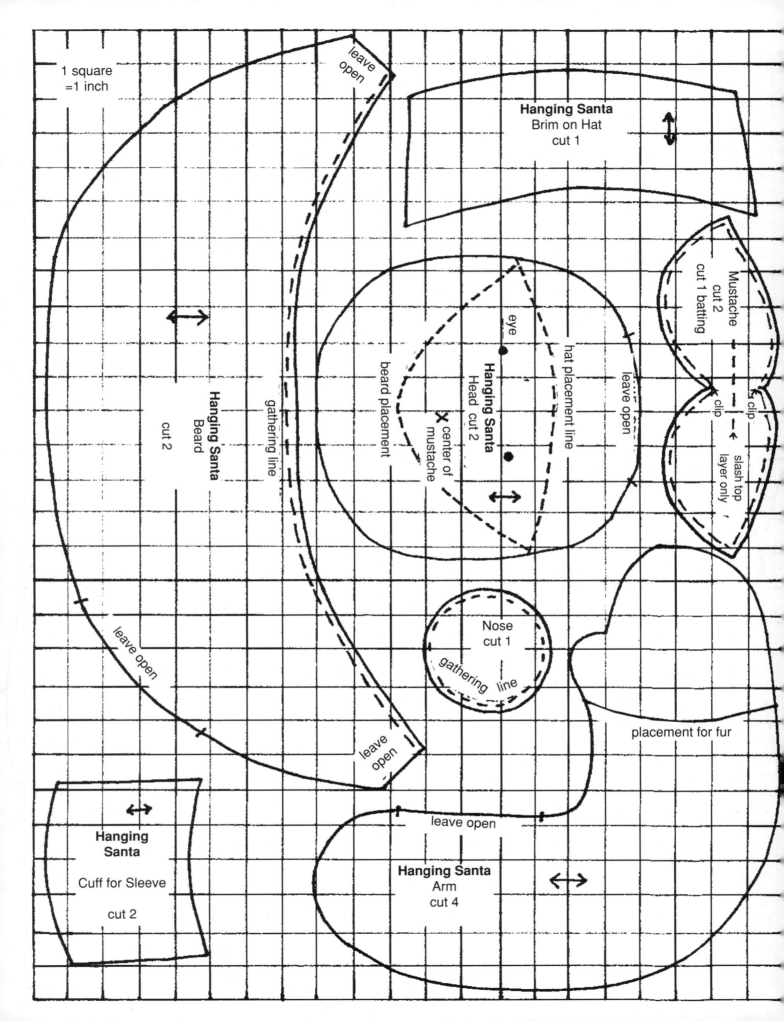

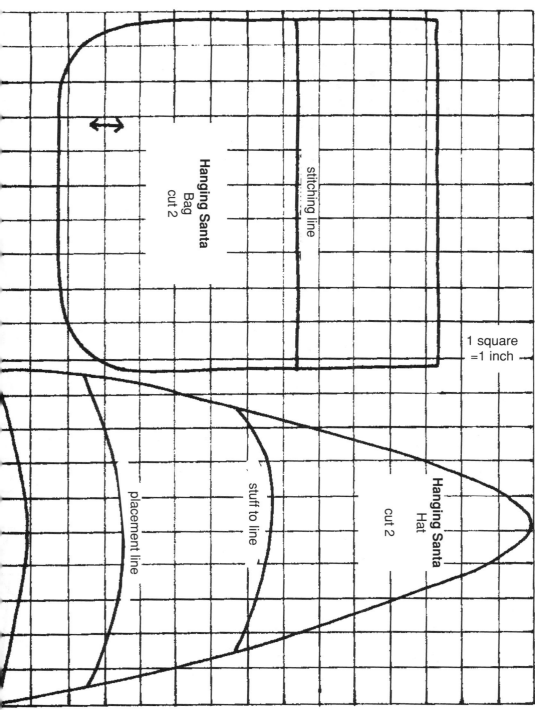

Hanging Santa
Bag
cut 2

stitching line

1 square
=1 inch

placement line

stuff to line

Hanging Santa
Hat

cut 2

mustache right side out. Hand-stitch slash closed. With double thread, hand-stitch center of mustache and gather. Knot thread. Attach mustache to face by hand on under side of mustache.

NOSE
Hand-stitch a gathering stitch around outside edge of nose. Using a small ball of fiber filling, stuff nose and pull thread tight, making a ball. Sew closed and knot thread. Sew nose to center of mustache.

EYES
Sew black button eyes onto face.

HAT
Stuff hat so only partially filled head will fill the end of hat. Place on head and hand-stitch front of hat onto face. Turn seam allowance under and hand-stitch to back of head.

HANGER
Center ring on back of head and hand-stitch many times to secure. Glue point of hat down to fur at an angle. Hot glue pompon on point of hat.

BAG
With right sides together, sew around bag leaving top open. Turn right sides out. Turn under top and hand-stitch with a gathering stitch. Stuff lightly, leaving space at top for toys. Arrange toys in top of bag. Pull gathering stitch tight and knot. Hot glue toys in place, making sure front of bag is glued to toys also. Tie ribbon around gathering line and tie in a bow. With bow in front, hang bells from bow. Hot glue bow securely to bag so it will be strong enough to support bells.

BODY ASSEMBLY
Place head and arms on body and glue in place, but glue arms only at shoulders. Put bag under Santa's hands, so Santa is holding bag. Glue bag in place. Glue hands onto bag.

BOOTS
With right sides together (and batting next to feed dog), sew around boots, leaving an opening at top. Clip curve. Turn right sides out. With right side of fur to right side of boot, stitch fur to boot. Turn fur up to cover top of boot. Hot glue fur edges to back side of boots. Do same thing to top edge. Hot glue boots to legs with toes pointing out, about 1" from end of legs. Hot glue bells in place.

Hang Santa from wall or door and enjoy him and your handiwork!

BEARD
With right sides together, sew bottom of beard together, leaving an opening. Sew top of beard together with a gathering stitch. Turn right sides out. Gather top of beard with thread to measure 11-1/2". Use same thread on both sides to gather so thread won't break. Tie knots in gathering thread. Place beard on head. Pin in place. Raw edges near gathering threads should fit under hat when hat is on. Hand-stitch beard to face. Stuff beard lightly

but don't leave any air pockets. Hand-stitch opening closed. Lift beard and on underside, hot glue beard to face for added strength.

MUSTACHE
Cut a slash in one of the mustache pieces as pattern shows. This becomes the back piece. Place front piece of mustache on top of Pellon fleece, wrong side next to fleece. On top of front piece put back piece, right sides together. Sew around entire mustache. Clip curves and trim point. Using slash, turn

"JOY" WALL HANGING

See picture on p. 64

1/2 yd. muslin
1/4 yd. Christmas print for borders
Scraps of 9 to 18 different Christmas fabrics for hearts
1/3 yd. "Wonder Under"
1/2 yd. Pellon fleece
Permanent fine-point black marker
     or
Black floss to embroider stitches
Calligraphy fabric pen

Cut six 3-1/2" muslin squares. Cut Mylar or card stock templates for heart and patchwork parts. Trace six hearts on the paper side of the Wonder Under. Also trace the patchwork pieces on the paper side of the Wonder Under. (These templates are not reversible so make sure you do them all the same way—either face up or face down.)

Cut around traced pieces to separate. Choose fabric for hearts and patchwork pieces and iron Wonder Under to the wrong side of chosen fabrics (paper side up). Carefully cut hearts and patchwork pieces out along the traced line. Remove the paper back and center the heart on the muslin square, fitting patchwork pieces into place. Then iron them on.

Using the black marker, draw buttonhole stitch around each heart. Then use assorted stitch marks for outlining patchwork pieces. (See Glossary for diagrams of buttonhole and other decorative stitches.)

Cut a 1-1/4" strip of border fabric for the stripping between the hearts. Using 1/4" seam allowance sew the hearts together with

stripping in between. Add stripping to the bottom of one row of hearts and to the top of the other.

Cut a 2-1/2"x11" piece of muslin for the words JOY, JOY, JOY. Use a felt tip calligraphy pen and write the words on the fabric. Ironing Wonder Under to the back side of the piece will stabilize the fabric so that you can write on it easier. Be sure to take the paper off the Wonder Under when you are through. (Peel the paper off and iron it to another piece of muslin.) You may also choose to embroider the words using a satin stitch.

Sew the word strip to the top row of hearts, bottom of heart strip to top of word strip, and top of the bottom row of hearts to the bottom of the word strip.

Cut two 2-1/2" strips of border. Add top and bottom and two sides, trimming to fit.

Cut Pellon fleece and muslin backing the size of the piece and pin together in the following order: pieced top (right side out); Pellon fleece; muslin backing. Stitch down all edges to secure the three layers and bind with border fabric or similar colored bias tape.

Machine or hand quilt if desired.

COUNTRY BELLS

Fayette Skinner
See picture on p. 61

1/2" thick wood
150-grit sandpaper
1 38mm bell
51" of 5-ply natural jute
1-1/2 yds. Creative Twist ribbon

6 berry picks (Mylar star garland, or other decoration of your choice)
26-gauge paddle wire
Acrylic paints, as desired
Hot-glue gun

Draw bell pattern onto 1/2" thick wood. Cut out. Sand wooden cutouts. Drill a 3/8" hole in the top of each bell.

Paint bells with acrylic paint on all sides. After paint has dried, sand front edges of bells with 150-grit sandpaper to give them a "worn country" look.

Using the twist ribbon, make a large bow. (If the ribbon is wider than 5 inches when untwisted, cut it in half lengthwise and get two bows out of the 1-1/2 yds.)

Attach the 38mm bell to the bow using paddle wire.

drill 3/8" hole

Country Bells
cut 2

Glue the berry picks, star garland, or other

decoration of your choice into the bow with hot glue.

Fold jute in half and wrap the cut ends with a short piece of paddle wire. Glue this end into the top of a bell with hot glue. Wrap the folded end with wire the same way and insert it into the other bell with hot glue.

Lay the bells out on a flat surface, folding the jute so that one bell sits just above the other. Wrap a piece of paddle wire around all 4 thicknesses of jute 4 inches down from the top so you have a loop from which to hang the bells.

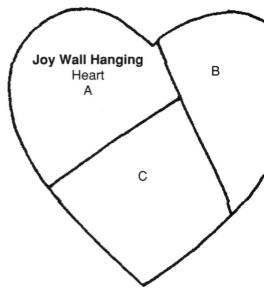

Joy Wall Hanging
Heart
A

B

C

Hot glue the bow to the jute over the last piece of wire.

CROSS-STITCH WALL HANGING

Susan Boden

See picture on p. 98

1/8 yd. each of three lightly colored fabrics, three dark fabrics, and a plain color for center
5"x7-1/2" piece 14-count white Aida cloth
DMC embroidery floss, Green 321
DMC embroidery floss, Red 319
2/3 yd. print for border and back
1/3 yd. Pellon fleece
1/4" to 3/8" dowel
Two wooden balls to fit ends of dowel

Following Merry Christmas pattern, finish cross-stitch piece.

Cut two plain 1-1/2" squares. Cut one 1-1/2" strip of each light and each dark fabric.

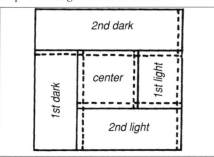

Figure 1

Cut three 2-1/4" strips of the border print.

Following drawings, strip-piece two log cabin blocks. (See Fig. 1.)

NOTE: Press all seams away from the center.

Continue adding second strip of second light, strips of second dark, then third light, followed by third dark in same manner as above.

Sew 2-1/4" strips to squares as shown in Figs. 2 and 3. (Trim even with sides of square.)

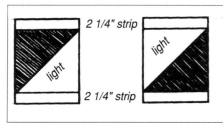

Figure 2

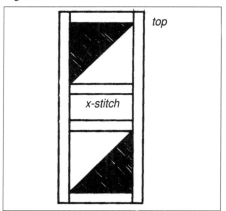

Figure 3

Attach log cabin blocks to top and bottom of cross-stitch piece.

Sew 2-1/4" strips down each side. (See Fig. 3.)

Cut 4"x7" piece of border print. Fold lengthwise and sew long edges together, right sides together. Sew, turn, press. Cut in half to make two 3-1/2" sections.
Fold in half with open edges at top. Pin one on each side next to inner seams on top.
Border: Cut backing and fleece to same size as front. Place top and bottom sections, right sides together, on top of fleece. Pin and sew, leaving a 6" opening on side to turn.

Turn. Press. Blind stitch opening closed.

Tie in corners of each block and center of log cabin with six strands of embroidery floss.

Cut dowel to 11". Slide wall hanging onto dowel and cover ends with wooden balls.

CHRISTMAS FLAG

John M. Hartvigsen

See picture on p. 27

2 yds. of 100% cotton fabric in red Christmas print
2/3 yd. white cloth
2/3 yd. solid green material
2-2/3 yds. "Wonder Under"
Scrap of bright red material
2 yds. of belt interfacing, 1" wide
2 "D" rings, 1-inch size
2 yds. colorful Christmas ribbon (optional)
Red and green cotton thread

Lay out material as shown in Fig. 1. Thread the two "D" rings on the belt interfacing. Fold the interfacing to form a flattened continuous loop with the join in the middle and the rings at each end. (See Fig. 2.)

Using fabric glue or fusible Pellon, secure flattened loop. This loop will become the flag's heading. It will be fastened to the halyard or string of the flag pole by the "D" rings at each end of this heading strip.

Fuse a piece of backed Wonder Under (22-1/2"x36") to one half of a piece of the red material (45" by 36"). Remove the backing and make a 1/4" hem on the top and bottom edges (the 45" side).

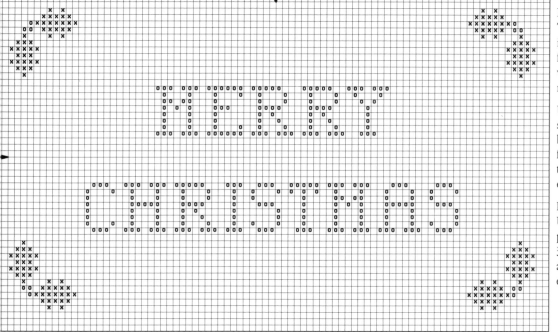

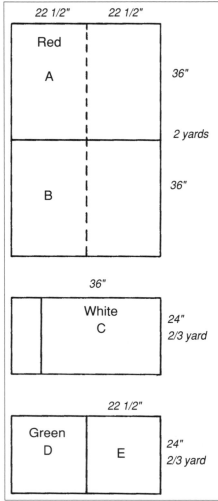

Figure 1

Position the heading strip in the middle of the piece and fold the half without the Wonder Under over the top. (See Fig. 3.) With a hot iron, fuse the folded material together. Sew along the edge of the heading strip.

Figure 2

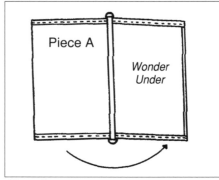

Figure 3

Repeat with the second half of red material eliminating insertion of heading strip. Fold the material in half (see Fig. 4) and fuse together.

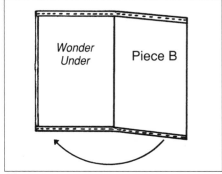

Figure 4

Fuse a 22-1/2"x24" piece of backed fusible Pellon to a piece of green material (D). Transfer the holly design to it. Carefully cut out the three green leaves.

Remove the backing from the leaves, but not from the background. Using the background as a stencil, position the three green leaves in the center of the white material (C). Fuse the leaves to the white material with a hot iron and then remove the background stencil.

Fuse a piece of backed Wonder Under to a red scrap of material. Trace three 2"-diameter circles on the backing and cut them out. Remove the backing and position them as the holly berries. Fuse in place with a hot iron.

Pin or baste the second piece of green material (E) to the back of the white material (C). Using a satin zigzag stitch, sew around the edges of each holly leaf. Cut away the excess green material (E) from the back of the white piece. This produces exact appliquéd leaves on the front and back of the white material.

Lay out the three pieces of material as shown in Fig. 5. Hem the white material (C) top and bottom so it is exactly the same height as the two red pieces that flank it.

Join pieces A and C with a 1/2" seam.

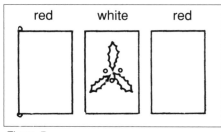

Figure 5

Trim the white material back to 1/4". Fold the red material over the white and pin it down to the white material. Sew along the red edge and you have joined the two pieces with a flat felled seam. Repeat the process to join piece B to pieces A and C.

Straight stitch along the top and bottom edge of the flag about 1/4" from the edge. Sew a double seam at the end of the flag and triple stitch along the seam (Fig. 6.)

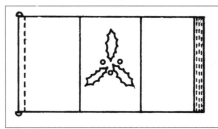

Figure 6

Loop the Christmas ribbon through the top "D" ring and secure.

Raise your Christmas flag on a two-piece aluminum pole that fits in an angled bracket. These poles and brackets can be purchased in a U.S. flag home set or may be purchased separately in some stores that sell flags.

HOLIDAY HEARTSTRINGS

Cindy Trujillo
See picture on p. 27

Acrylic paints: white, Christmas red, Christmas green
Approx. 1 yd. red 3/16" picot-edge ribbon
Three wooden hearts cut of 1/2" wood

Draw hearts onto wood and cut out. Drill 3/16" holes where indicated. Paint both sides of hearts in white. Paint edge of hearts in green.

Float around face of heart with green. Print lettering and dots with green.

Paint comma strokes in red. Dot around edge in white. Paint holly leaves green. Dot holly berries in red.

Figure 1

drill hole

PEACE

ON

EARTH

drill holes in bottom
of 1st heart, top
and bottom of 2nd
heart and top of
3rd heart

String hearts with ribbon so that hearts hang one over the other. If desired, hearts may be placed side by side. (See Fig. 1.) If so, drill holes for ribbon accordingly.

SANTA AND REINDEER PLAQUE

Barbara Benson

See picture on p. 28

1"x2"x18" board
Three 1-3/8" length x 3/8" diameter
  mini shaker pegs
Picture wire and small tack nails
Stain or brown acrylic paint
Acrylic paints:
Ceramcoat by Delta: Medium flesh,
  black, ivory, antique gold
Accent Country Colors: Prairie green,
  Barn red, Roseberry

This plaque can be used for hanging stockings, candy canes, mittens, or whatever else you may think of.

Cut plaque from 1"x12" board. This pattern is set up for three pegs, although as many as eight or ten pegs will fit across the bottom. Use a 3/8" drill bit. To keep from drilling all the way through the board, affix masking tape on the drill bit 1/3" from the bottom for a guide. After drilling, sand edges, front and back of plaque.

Stain plaque and pegs with choice of wood stain or wash with a mixture of 80% water and 20% brown acrylic paint. Check for drips. Wipe off excess stain or paint. When dry, transfer pattern to board with tracing paper.

Paint Santa's fur trim, pompon, eyebrows, hair, mustache, beard and the reindeer's antlers with ivory paint. These areas may need two or three coats of paint.

Paint Santa's face, elf's face, and hand with medium flesh acrylic.

Paint Santa's hat, suit, elf's shirt and the reindeer's collar with barn red.

Paint the jingle bells with antique gold.

Paint elf's cap, pants and Santa's glove with prairie green.

With a medium to small stencil brush or stipple brush, dip in roseberry paint and tap out excess paint onto paper towel till only a very faint amount of paint is left in brush. With circular motion, blush reindeer's cheeks and inner ears.

WE BELIEVE

IN SANTA CLAUS!

Paint Santa's mouth roseberry.

Making sure flesh paint is dry on plaque, retrace face pattern onto elf and Santa. Blush cheeks and noses on the Santa and the elf. Retrace pattern of Santa's beard, hair and mustache.

With black paint, do Santa's boot, inner mouth, reindeer's hooves, nose, and all the eyes.

With thin liner brush, paint eyelashes. Start from inner eye, push brush down, then pull out and lift up at same time. You may want to practice a few brush strokes on a piece of paper first.

With ivory, highlight eyes with dot and comma stroke. Highlight reindeer's hooves and Santa's boot as indicated on pattern.

With a fine point (.35) permanent ink pen, ink in lines and dots using the pattern as a guide.

"We believe in Santa Claus!" lettering is done with ivory paint slightly thinned with water. With end of a paint brush or tip of a dull pencil, dot letters at their points.

To hang plaque, tack picture wire on back with two small nails, as you would with a picture.

Glue the pegs into the drilled holes with wood glue.

On bottom of the left antler, glue a green or red bow, a sprig of artificial greenery, half a miniature pinecone, and a couple of red berries.

STYROFOAM POKE WREATH

See picture on p. 98

12" or smaller styrofoam wreath
Tacky glue
Green and red tissue paper
> **or**

3 yds. (approx.) of scrap fabrics

Cut fabric or tissue in 2" squares. Pinking shears should be used for fabric and also provides an attractive edge on tissue paper.

Using a dull pencil, find the center of tissue or fabric square. Pull fabric around pointed end of pencil. Dip tip into glue and poke into styrofoam wreath.

Continue until wreath is as full as you desire.

Decorate finished wreath with a big bow, holly and berries, candy canes, etc.

RITZY RUDY

Carole Cole

See picture on p. 28

5/8 yd. beige fabric (head, body)
15"x17" piece of dark brown fabric (antlers, lining of ears)
1 yd. red and green plaid taffeta
2/3 yd. green taffeta (bow, headband)
9" Battenburg or eyelet lace (collar)
2/3 yd. red or green 1/4" wide ribbon (arms, legs)
16" piece of 1/4" wide elastic
8" square of batting
Polyester fiber filling
Two round 3/8" dia. black buttons (eyes)
Dark brown embroidery floss
1" red pompon (nose)
Sprig of silk or plastic holly w/berries
Hot-glue gun

GENERAL
Use 3/8" seam allowance throughout except where otherwise indicated. Backstitch at beginning and end of all seams. RSO = right side out; RST = right sides together.

HEAD AND EARS
Stay-stitch edges of head front by sewing 3/8" from raw edge. Clip to stay-stitching. Stay-stitch neck curve of head side. Clip to stitching. Pin each head side to head front, RST, matching notches. Stitch. Clip curves.

Baste batting to wrong side of each dark brown ear. Pin beige ear to dark brown ear, RST. Stitch, leaving lower edge open for turning. Cut corner diagonally. Clip curves.

Turn RSO. Press. Baste raw edges together. With dark brown side on inside, fold lower corner over about 1/2". (See Fig. 1.)

Figure 1

Baste ears to head side between squares, having folded edge near seams and dark brown side down. Stitch center back seam in head back from lower edge to circle at top. Pin head back to head front and sides, matching notches and circles. Stitch. Turn head RSO.

BODY
RST, stitch center back seam in body back, leaving an opening for turning and stuffing. Stitch center seam in body front. Stitch front to back at sides, RST, matching notches.

Stay-stitch neck and lower edge a scant 3/8" from raw edge. Clip to stay-stitching at neck and squares at lower edge.

Pin head to body, RST, matching center back seams and square to center front seam. Stitch.

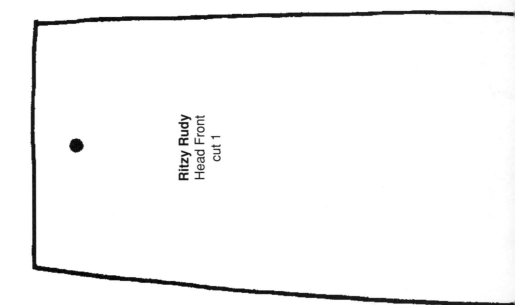

Ritzy Rudy
Head Front
cut 1

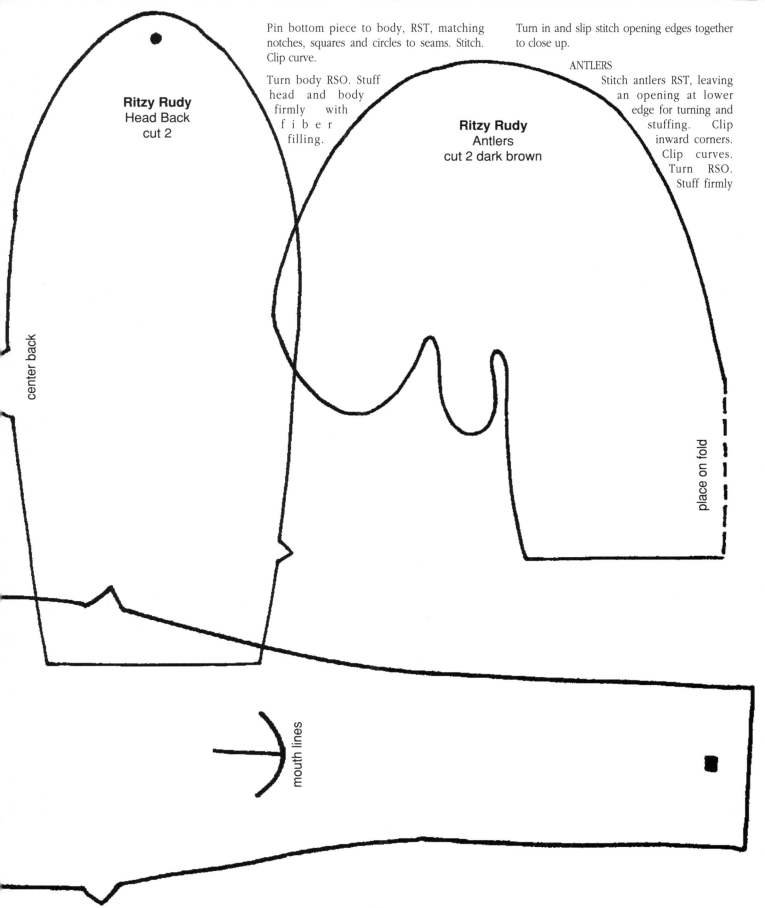

Ritzy Rudy
Head Back
cut 2

Pin bottom piece to body, RST, matching notches, squares and circles to seams. Stitch. Clip curve.

Turn body RSO. Stuff head and body firmly with f i b e r filling.

Ritzy Rudy
Antlers
cut 2 dark brown

Turn in and slip stitch opening edges together to close up.

ANTLERS
Stitch antlers RST, leaving an opening at lower edge for turning and stuffing. Clip inward corners. Clip curves. Turn RSO. Stuff firmly

center back

place on fold

mouth lines

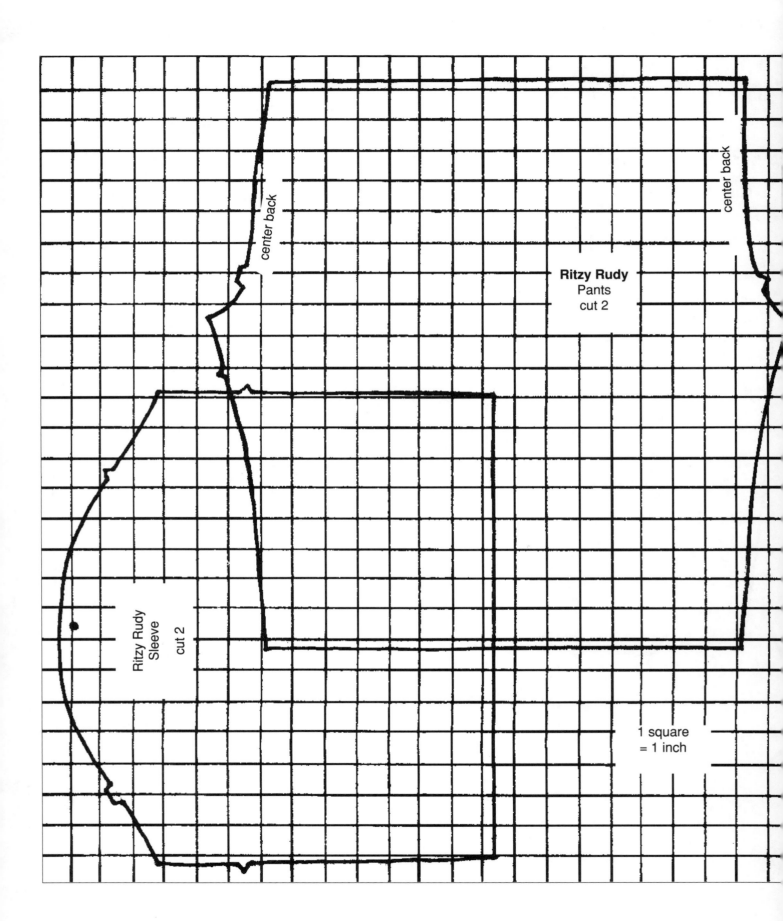

Ritzy Rudy
Pants
cut 2

center back

center back

Ritzy Rudy
Sleeve
cut 2

1 square
= 1 inch

24

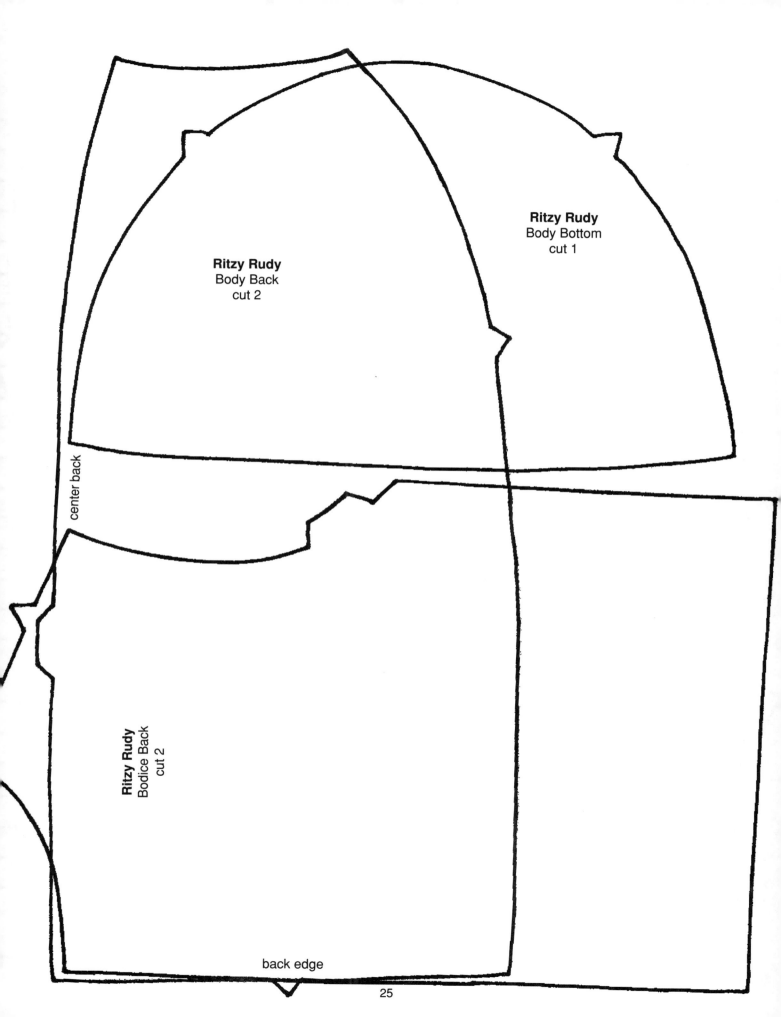

Ritzy Rudy
Body Bottom
cut 1

Ritzy Rudy
Body Back
cut 2

center back

Ritzy Rudy
Bodice Back
cut 2

back edge

25

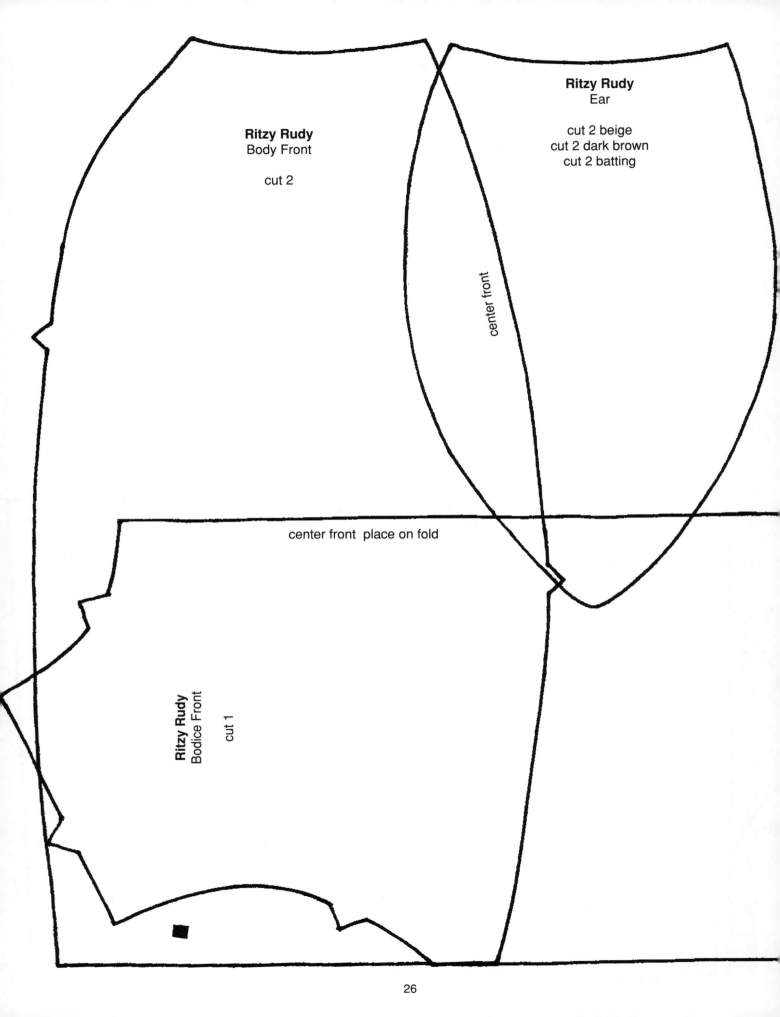

Ritzy Rudy
Body Front

cut 2

Ritzy Rudy
Ear

cut 2 beige
cut 2 dark brown
cut 2 batting

center front

center front place on fold

Ritzy Rudy
Bodice Front

cut 1

Clockwise, from top left: Christmas Flag, p. 17; Christmas Doll, p. 33; Holiday Heartstrings, p.18; Angel Banner, p. 10; Checkin' It Twice, p. 38; (on sewing machine) Christmas Trees Table or Piano Runner, p. 68; Santa's Helpers, p. 42; (on floor) Kate's Tutu, p. 94; Holly Berry Place Mat, p. 160; (on place mat) Reindeer Decoration, p. 33.

Clockwise from top: Santa and Reindeer Plaque, p. 19; Ritzy Rudy, p. 22; Tube and Bag Sachets (on floor near lantern), p. 132; Holly Leaf Place Mat (under candle holder), p. 160; Candle Holder, p. 126; Christmas Apron, p. 128.

with fiber filling. Turn under raw edges at bottom of antlers and blind stitch to head between ears.

FACE

Sew eyes (black buttons) to face as follows: thread long needle with carpet or button thread, knot one end, slip one button onto thread, push needle into spot marked for eye and bring through spot marked for other eye. Slip other button onto needle. Pull thread up until eyes are settled as deeply as desired on face. Stitch until eyes are secured firmly. Tie off and hide knot under one eye.

Thread three strands of brown embroidery floss into needle. Back-stitch mouth lines as marked on head front piece. Sew red pompon at top of mouth line.

PLAID SUIT

Sew front bodice to back bodice at shoulder seams, RST. Press seams open. Finish lower edge of each sleeve

piece with a 3/4" narrow hem. Sew a gathering seam (long, basting stitch) on each armhole along seam line.

With RST pin sleeve to armhole edge. Pull up bobbin threads and adjust gathers to fit. Pin, then stitch.

Pin underarm seam of bodice and sleeves, matching armhole seams. Stitch.

Cut the 1/4" wide ribbon in four equal lengths. Tie one piece of the ribbon tightly around the end of each sleeve. Secure with knot. Cut ends to desired length or tie in small bow. Stuff each sleeve with fiber filling up to the shoulders, making arms fat and puffy, but not rigid or hard.

Put bodice on reindeer body. Pin one edge of bodice back to reindeer body. Fold over other edge of bodice along center back and blind stitch through bodice and into body to

attach firmly to reindeer. (Be sure to remove all pins.)

Stitch center front seam of pants. Turn under 3/4" on upper edge of pants. Press. Turn under 1/4" on raw edge and stitch in place, creating a casing for elastic. Insert 16" piece of elastic through casing, having ends even. Stitch across ends, catching in elastic.

Finish lower edges of pants legs with a 3/4" narrow hem. Stitch center back seam of pants. Stitch inside leg seam, matching center seam.

With remaining 2 pieces of 1/4" ribbon, tie one piece tightly around the bottom of each pant leg. Secure with knot. Cut ends to desired length or tie in small bow. Stuff each pants leg with fiber filling up to waist of pants until fat and puffy.

Slip pants over bottom of body and lower edge of bodice. Blind stitch pants to bodice and through to body securely, all around waist at elastic casing line.

FINISHING

Finish cut edges of 9" piece of lace for collar. Place around neck and secure to back of plaid suit and reindeer body. Tack to plaid suit in 2 or 3 places so that collar lays flat.

sew ear here

sew eye here

Ritzy Rudy
Head Side

cut 2

Cut a green taffeta strip 11" wide across the 45" width of fabric. Cut another 11" wide strip that is 15" long. Sew these strips together with a 1/2" seam to make one piece 60" long. Sew with a 1/4" seam lengthwise. Press seam open. Turn RSO. Center seam in back of piece and press. Tie a large bow of this piece and attach it to plaid suit and body securely. Trim ends of bow as long as desired and finish them by tucking raw edges inside and blind stitching or zigzag machine stitching.

Cut piece of green taffeta 8" long and 1-1/4" wide. With RST, fold headband in half lengthwise and stitch a 1/4" seam. Turn RSO. Press so that seam is centered on back side of piece. Tuck in ends of piece and zigzag each end closed. Place around base of antlers and tops of ears. Sew to head securely at back of antlers.

Hot glue holly/berry sprig to headband at base of either right or left antler, as preferred. Prop Rudy in a chair or corner of sofa in time to enjoy the holiday with your family.

WOODEN FATHER CHRISTMAS

Pat Greenwood

See picture on p. 61

3/4" pine wood
Acrylic paints: White, Flesh, Green, Red, Black, Spice Brown, Adobe, Gold, Gray
Flat and liner brushes
1/4" dia. dowel
1/4 yd. burlap or Christmas fabric
1/2 yd. jute
Polyester fiber filling
Small artificial pine boughs
Baby's breath (optional)
Pinecones (optional)

RST = right sides together.

RSO = right side out.

Trace patterns onto 3/4" pine. Cut out. Sand all edges of wood with a fine-grade sandpaper. Trace details of pattern onto wood cut-out. Base paint white areas first (fur on hat, arms and coat; beard; and mustache.)

Paint flesh color on face. Paint green base on tree. Paint arms, coat, and base of figure with red paint.

Paint boots and eyes with black paint.

Float with spice brown around nose and mustache. Float with adobe flesh area above mustache. Blush cheeks.

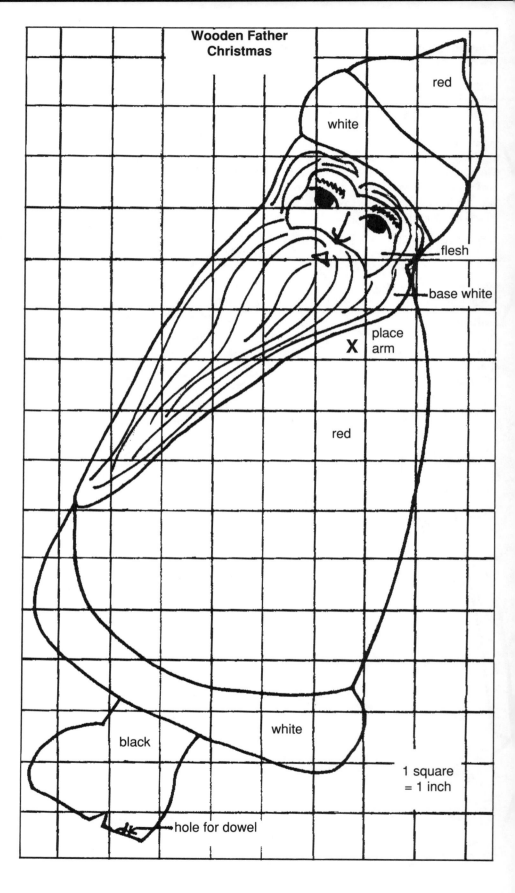

Wooden Father Christmas

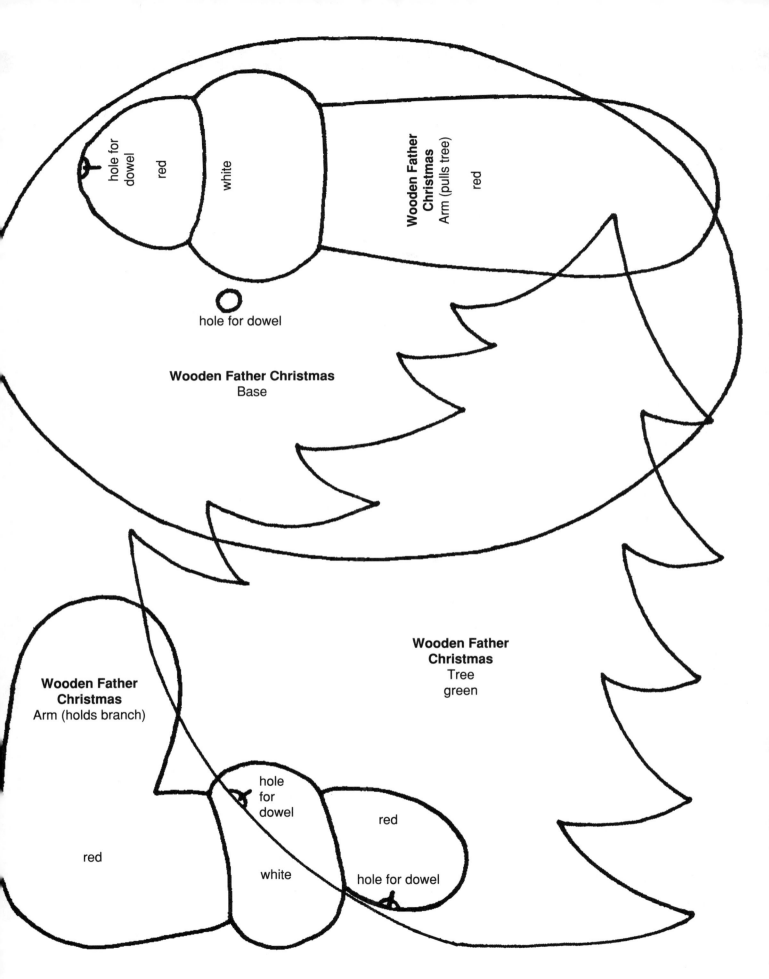

hole for
dowel

red

white

**Wooden Father
Christmas**
Arm (pulls tree)

red

hole for dowel

Wooden Father Christmas
Base

**Wooden Father
Christmas**
Tree
green

**Wooden Father
Christmas**
Arm (holds branch)

red

hole
for
dowel

red

white

hole for dowel

With liner brush, intermix lines through beard and mustache using gold, gray, black, and white. Do the same with eyebrows.

After paint has dried, sand edges to give an old look.

Drill holes where indicated. Using a small headless nail attach arms where indicated, straight arm on back and bent arm on front.

Using the 1/4" dowel for stability, attach body to base and tree to back arm. (The edge of the tree will rest on the base.)

Cut a bare branch to fit from front arm to base. Insert top of branch into hole and secure to the base with hot glue.

Cut a piece of fabric 14"x6". Fold in half, RST, to form a 7"x6" bag. Sew along both 7" sides. Turn RSO and fold over 1/2" on top to form casing. Stitch, leaving a small opening to insert jute. Thread jute through the casing leaving about 8" out.

Stuff bag with fiber filling and glue boughs to look as though they are hanging out of top of bag.

Add baby's breath and pine cones to embellish if desired. To fasten bag on body, run jute under front and back arms and hot glue ends to top of bag. Hot glue bag to the back of Santa.

BABY'S BREATH ANGEL

Shanon Allen

See picture on p. 62

1/4 yd. print fabric
1/8 yd. muslin

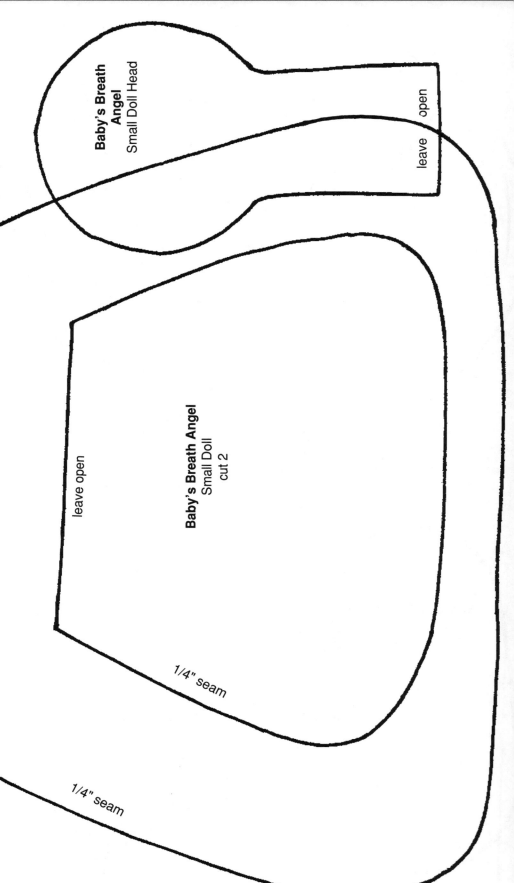

Baby's Breath Angel
Small Doll Head

leave open

Baby's Breath Angel
Large Doll
cut 2

leave open

Baby's Breath Angel
Small Doll
cut 2

leave open

1/4" seam

1/4" seam

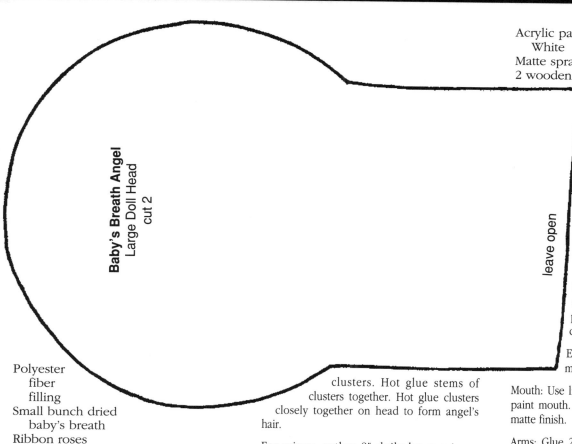

Baby's Breath Angel
Large Doll Head
cut 2

leave open

Polyester
fiber
filling
Small bunch dried
baby's breath
Ribbon roses
4" Battenburg doily (small collar)
6" Battenburg doily (large collar)
Blush for cheeks
Black pen to dot eyes
8" Battenburg doily (wings)
1-1/2 yds. of 1/4" wide satin ribbon
(bow)

Out of muslin, cut two doll heads. With right sides together, using 1/4" seam allowance, stitch head together leaving open where indicated. Out of print fabric, cut two body pieces. With right sides together, using 1/4" seam allowance, stitch body together leaving open where indicated.

Turn head and body pieces right side out. Stuff head up to neck with polyester fiber filling. Stuff body firmly. Insert head into body, turning body neck edges under. Slip stitch all around neck to close opening, gathering to fit.

For collar, cut to center of doily and make an opening large enough to go around neck. Hot glue or stitch bow to center front of collar.

Attach ribbon rose to bow.

For hair, pick off several bunches of baby's breath and form

clusters. Hot glue stems of clusters together. Hot glue clusters closely together on head to form angel's hair.

For wings, gather 8" doily by running a gathering stitch from one edge to the other through the center of doily. Pull tight and hot glue to center base of neck. Tie ribbon bow and glue to gathers.

CHRISTMAS DOLL

Marge Hazelgren
See picture on p. 27

3-1/2" wood
body cut
from 3/4"
pine
1" round
wood
head

arm   arm

Christmas Doll
Body

Christmas Doll
Head

Acrylic paint: Flesh, Red, Black,
White
Matte spray
2 wooden knobs or 1/4" to 3/8" beads
8" of 1-1/4" wide
gathered lace
7" of 1/4" wide ribbon
1 small ribbon rose
Spanish moss
Small package
Hot glue gun

Body: Paint red. Float scallops with white paint. Use pin head or stylus to make scalloped dots.

Head and hands: Paint in flesh tone.

Cheeks: Mix two drops Flesh and one drop of red. Use a small piece of sponge to dab on cheeks.

Eyes: Use pin head or stylus to make dots.

Mouth: Use liner brush or very fine marker to paint mouth. Glue head to body. Spray using matte finish.

Arms: Glue 2" piece of gathered lace around each hand, gathered edge against bead. (Continue until entire 2" length is used.) Glue other edge of lace to body where indicated, forming arm.

Glue 4" lace piece around neck overlapping in back. Glue rose to center front of lace.

Hair: Glue moss to head to form hair. Make a small bow and glue in hair. Glue small package to both hands (beads) in front of body.

REINDEER DECORATION

Sharon Murano, Reneé Condie
See picture on p. 27

1/2 yd. fur (preferably long
hair)
Polyester fiber filling
Two felt squares (in colors
to match fur)
Six 12", 12mm (extra
large) pipe cleaners
(to match color of
fur)
Two 9mm pony
beads (eyes)
Black embroidery
floss

Four empty toilet paper rolls
Hot-glue gun and 4-5 glue sticks
Extra heavy-duty thread
One 3/8" red pompon
One yd. of 3/4" wide ribbon
One large bell

Cut an 18" circle of fur. Knot a double or triple piece of thread at the end and hand stitch in large basting stitches around the edge of the fur circle, about 3/4" from edge. Pull

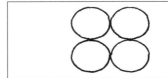

Figure 1

thread to slightly gather. Fill with polyester fiber filling until quite firm. Pull thread as tight as possible, bringing edges of fur together in the center. Tie off with a knot.

Figure 2

Place pieces for "face top" and "face bottom" right sides together and stitch by machine 1/4" around edges indicated. Turn right side out.

Embroider face as shown on pattern (See Fig. 1), then stitch through pony beads with floss and secure. Stuff face with polyester fiber filling. Hot glue nose in place.

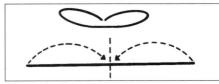

Figure 3

Cut four toilet paper rolls to 3-1/2" lengths. Cover the outside with a 3-1/2" strip of felt, gluing in place at seam. Glue all four legs together with glue gun. See Fig. 2 for top view.

Figure 4

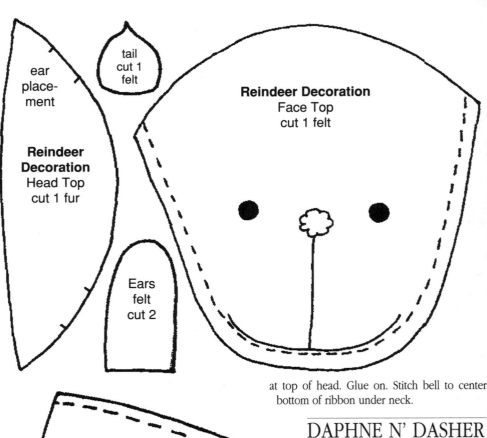

ear placement

tail cut 1 felt

Reindeer Decoration Head Top cut 1 fur

Reindeer Decoration Face Top cut 1 felt

Ears felt cut 2

Reindeer Decoration Face Bottom cut 1 felt

at top of head. Glue on. Stitch bell to center bottom of ribbon under neck.

Glue body to legs, centering body on legs. Attach ears to back of small fur pieces as indicated on pattern. Glue straight edge of small fur piece to top back of felt head. Glue head to front center of body.

Make antlers out of pipe cleaners as shown in Figs. 3 and 4. Glue to head behind ears. Tie 3/4" wide ribbon around neck and tie a bow

DAPHNE N' DASHER

Patti Funk

See picture on p. 98

1/4 yd. solid cotton (body)
1/4 yd. wool or fleece (head and hands)
1/6 yd. cotton knit (antlers)
1/8 yd. print cotton (ear centers)
3/4 yd. white cotton (nightgown and nightcap)
2-1/8 yds. ruffled lace trim, 3/4" wide
1/3 yd. red/white stripe (nightshirt)
1 yd. 1/4" wide ribbon (bridle)
Four 1/4" bells (bridle)
Four 1/4" black ball buttons (eyes)
Two 1/4" red pompons (nose)
Scrap of white cotton (yoke)
9"x12" piece of red felt (slippers— these are optional)
Red knit stocking (other nightcap)
Pompon (purchased or made from red and green yarn) (other nightcap)
Rice or bird seed
Polyester fiber filling
Carpet thread, Black and Camel
Embroidery floss, Red
Blush

Please read all instructions before beginning. Use 1/4" allowance on all seams unless otherwise indicated. Cut out all pattern pieces as directed. Transfer all markings to fabric. Stitch carefully and accurately to insure proper shape of finished item.

Abbreviations: RST = right sides together; RSO = right sides out

ANTLERS
RST stitch antlers. Turn RSO and stuff firmly. Set aside.

HEAD
RST stitch ears (one wool and one print). Turn RSO and fold sides to center and baste across bottom. Place ears (calico side next to face front) in the slits at top of head. Stitch slits RST, ears between, as you would a dart. Stitch darts at lower face. RST stitch all around head. Turn RSO and stuff firmly.

Using heavy thread, sew eyes in place where indicated. Pull in slightly to indent. Secure stitching. Wrap two strands of black

Figure 1

buttonhole thread around eye (for Daphne only), tie tightly and trim to form eyelashes. Stitch mouth area by entering side of face where indicated and coming out other side. Bring thread around to form mouth and go through dot where you began. Repeat and then come through at center seam and go up about 1" and into head again. Use a tiny back stitch to secure. (See Fig. 1.)

Glue a 1/4" red pompon on face for nose. Glue 1/4" Christmas print ribbon or trim around nose and up sides of face and around back of head for halter (see photograph). Glue tiny bells at sides of halter.

BODY
RST stitch body side seams. Stitch body base to body. Turn RSO and put about 2" of rice or bird seed in body. Stuff the remainder of body firmly with fiber filling. Gather top edge by hand and pull gathers to fit bottom edge of head. Again, using strong thread, stitch head to body, making sure head is centered.

Now let's dress our little "deers" . . .

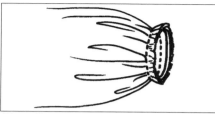

Figure 2

Cut the following pieces for clothes:
5"x30" (cut 1) for nightgown skirt
3"x44" (cut 2) for ruffle
5-1/2"x8-1/2" (cut 2 for each garment) sleeve for nightgown and nightshirt
1-1/2"x 8" (cut 1) neckband for nightshirt
1-1/2"x4-1/4" (cut 2) sleeve band for nightshirt

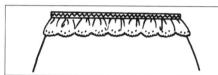

Figure 3

DAPHNE'S NIGHTGOWN
Make a pleat in the front of the nightgown bodice by folding on fold line and bringing to dotted line. Place ruffled lace trim under each pleat and stitch down. Make three red French knots (buttons) down front. Stitch darts where marked. Set aside. Gather one long edge (8-1/2" side) of sleeve to fit hand. RST, place sleeve, lace trim, and hand, raw edges even, together and stitch across width. (See Fig. 2.)

RST, stitch around hand and under seam. Turn RSO and stuff hand firmly and sleeve loosely up to 1" from raw edge. Gather top edge of sleeve to about 1" width. RST, stitch sleeves into bodice front and back at side seams. RST, and using zigzag stitch, stitch lace trim to neck edge of bodice. (See Fig. 3.) Turn lace up and edge stitch in place. (See Fig. 4.)

Figure 4

RST, stitch back seam of skirt up to about 2" from top edge. RST, join ruffle pieces. Narrowly hem one long edge of ruffle and gather the other to fit the bottom of skirt. RST, stitch ruffle to bottom of skirt. Gather the top edge of skirt to fit bodice waist. RST, stitch bodice and skirt. Place dress on deer and hand-stitch back seam closed.

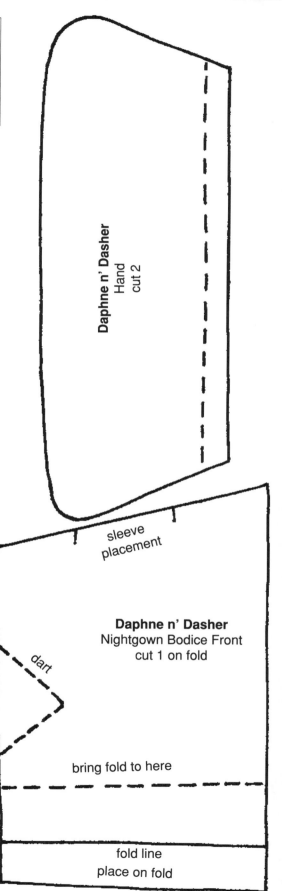

Daphne n' Dasher
Hand
cut 2

sleeve placement

dart

Daphne n' Dasher
Nightgown Bodice Front
cut 1 on fold

bring fold to here

fold line
place on fold

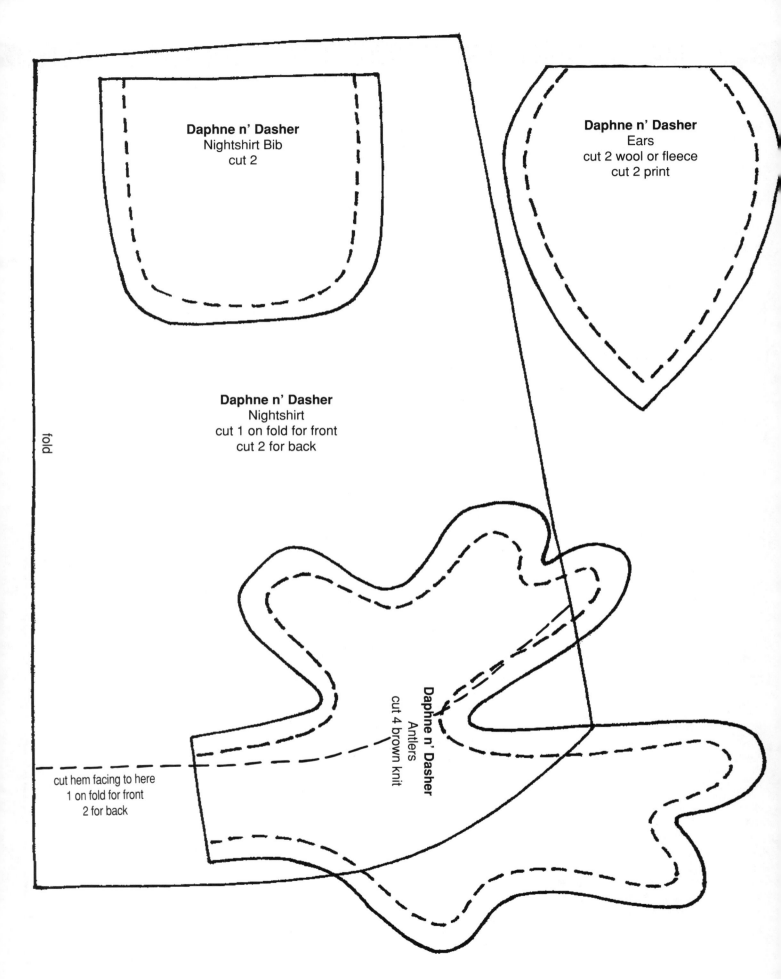

Daphne n' Dasher
Nightshirt Bib
cut 2

Daphne n' Dasher
Ears
cut 2 wool or fleece
cut 2 print

Daphne n' Dasher
Nightshirt
cut 1 on fold for front
cut 2 for back

fold

cut hem facing to here
1 on fold for front
2 for back

Daphne n' Dasher
Antlers
cut 4 brown knit

36

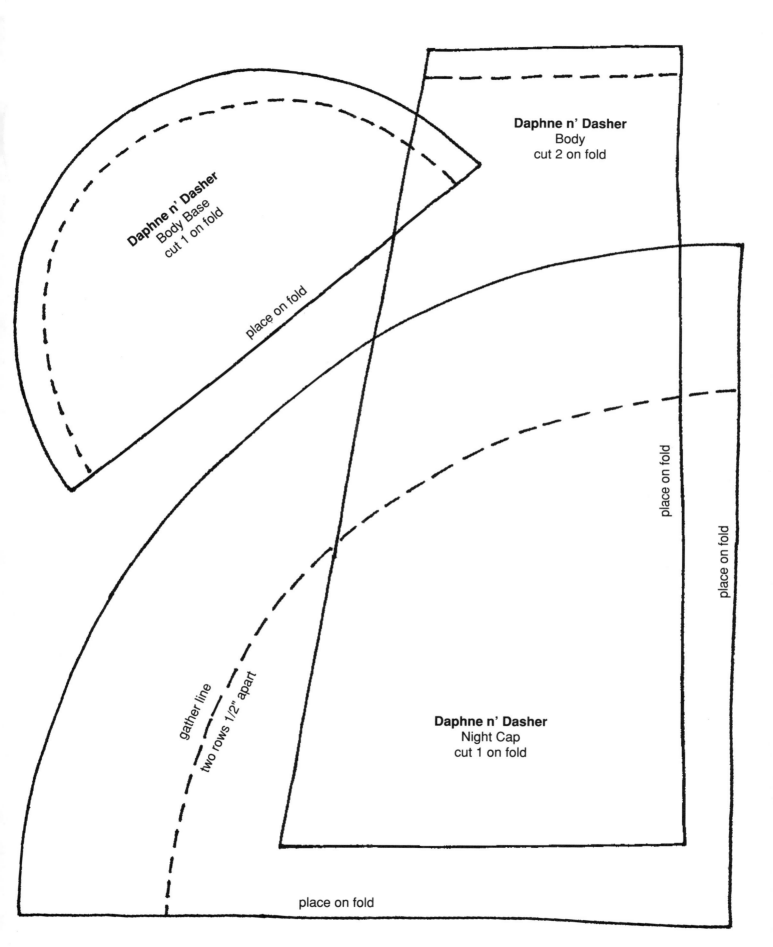

Daphne n' Dasher
Body Base
cut 1 on fold

Daphne n' Dasher
Body
cut 2 on fold

place on fold

place on fold

place on fold

gather line
two rows 1/2" apart

Daphne n' Dasher
Night Cap
cut 1 on fold

place on fold

Daphne n' Dasher
Head
cut 2

slash here for dart

slash here for dart

*

Daphne n' Dasher
Slipper Sole
cut 2

Slipper Toe
cut 2 to dotted line

at center front of nightshirt. Stitch French knot buttons (as on Daphne's).

Stitch arms to side seams just as you did Daphne's. Gather neck edge to fit folded and pressed (as sleevebands) neckband. Apply neckband to neck edge just as you did sleevebands. RST, stitch back seam of facing. RST, stitch facing to bottom edge of nightshirt. Turn and press. Turn under raw edge and hand-hem to nightshirt.

NIGHTCAP
Using a purchased red knit stocking, cut off foot. Put remaining portion cuff side down on head and mark the ear positions. Make a tiny slit. Pull ears thru slits. Put a little glue here and there to secure. Glue or stitch a pompon on end (you will need to gather cut edge of sock in tightly).

SLIPPERS (OPTIONAL)
Stitch slipper sole to slipper top. Turn RSO and stuff the toe part. Glue to bottom of deer's body so that raw edge is under deer and toe is just peeking out under nightshirt.

Glue a little Christmas sock in Dasher's hand with a note to Santa tucked inside. Or he can hold a little candlestick or wreath.

CHECKIN' IT TWICE

Patti Funk

See picture on p. 27

1/4 yd. Osnaburg or homespun (head, hands)
1/3 yd. plaid cotton (body)
1/3 yd. corduroy or wool (pants)
1/6 yd. black solid cotton (boots)
15" of 3/8" wide elastic
1/4 yd. burlap or wool (toy bag)
Raw wool or wool roving
Feather quill
Glasses
Two 3/8" buttons (eyes)
Two 5/8" buttons (suspenders)
Polyester fiber filling
Mini toys, packages, etc. for bag
Glue or hot-glue gun

Please read all instructions before beginning. Use 1/4" allowance on all seams unless otherwise indicated. Cut out all pattern pieces as directed. Transfer all markings to fabric. Stitch carefully and accurately to insure proper shape of finished item.

NIGHTCAP
RST, stitch lace trim to edge of cap, as you did neck edge. Gather on line indicated. Pull up to fit the deer's head. Put a handful of fiber filling in crown of cap. Glue in place on Daphne's head, arranging ruffles nicely around her ears. Glue in place. Now glue antlers securely on top of cap. See photograph, p. 27. Place a ribbon bow at front of cap. Glue a tiny teddy or quilt in her hands and blush her cheeks a bit.

DASHER'S NIGHTSHIRT
RST, stitch back seam of nightshirt up to about 2" from top. Stitch arms just as you did Daphne's, except use sleevebands instead of lace. Fold the sleevebands in half lengthwise and press, apply just as you did lace.

RST, stitch bib, leaving open at top straight edge. Turn RSO and press. Top-stitch in place

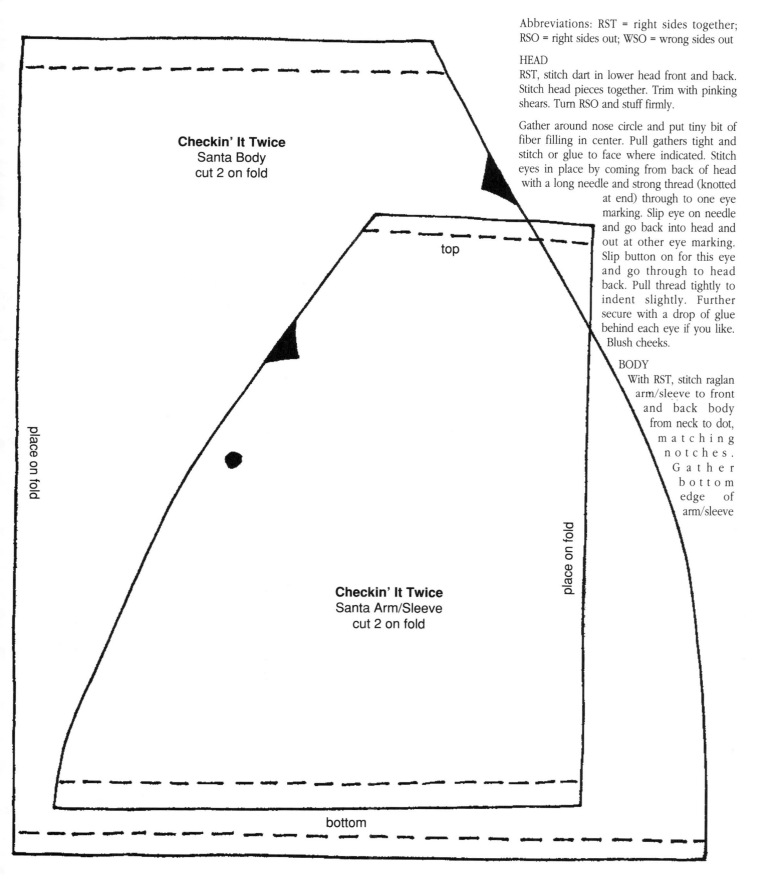

Checkin' It Twice
Santa Body
cut 2 on fold

place on fold

top

Checkin' It Twice
Santa Arm/Sleeve
cut 2 on fold

place on fold

bottom

Abbreviations: RST = right sides together; RSO = right sides out; WSO = wrong sides out

HEAD
RST, stitch dart in lower head front and back. Stitch head pieces together. Trim with pinking shears. Turn RSO and stuff firmly.

Gather around nose circle and put tiny bit of fiber filling in center. Pull gathers tight and stitch or glue to face where indicated. Stitch eyes in place by coming from back of head with a long needle and strong thread (knotted at end) through to one eye marking. Slip eye on needle and go back into head and out at other eye marking. Slip button on for this eye and go through to head back. Pull thread tightly to indent slightly. Further secure with a drop of glue behind each eye if you like. Blush cheeks.

BODY
With RST, stitch raglan arm/sleeve to front and back body from neck to dot, matching notches. Gather bottom edge of arm/sleeve

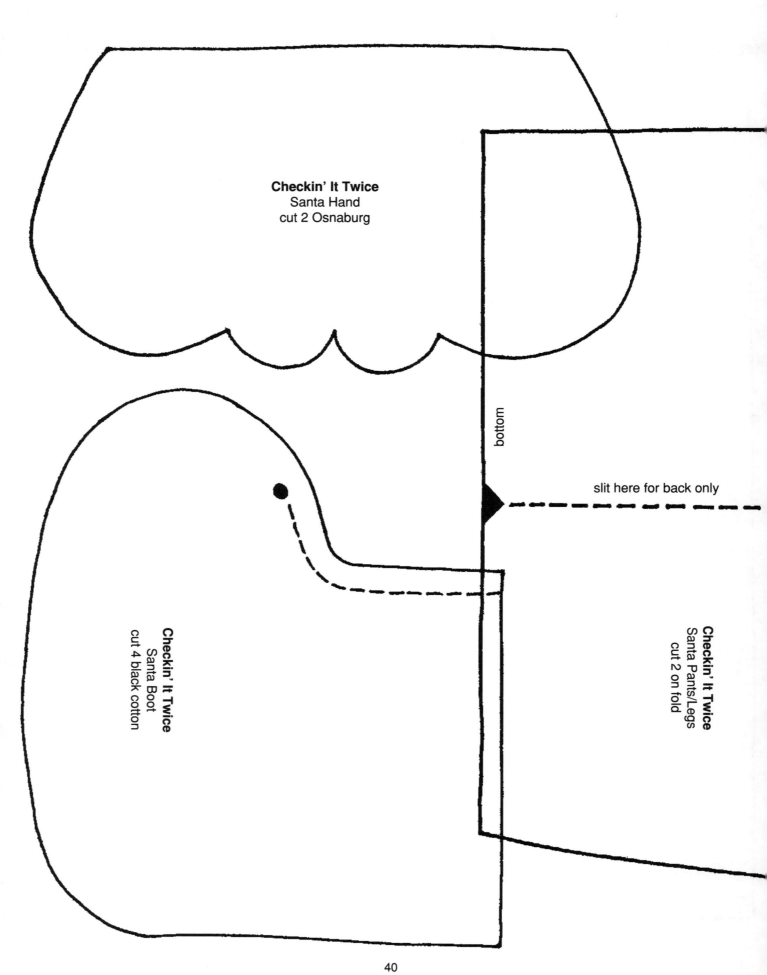

Checkin' It Twice
Santa Hand
cut 2 Osnaburg

bottom

slit here for back only

Checkin' It Twice
Santa Boot
cut 4 black cotton

Checkin' It Twice
Santa Pants/Legs
cut 2 on fold

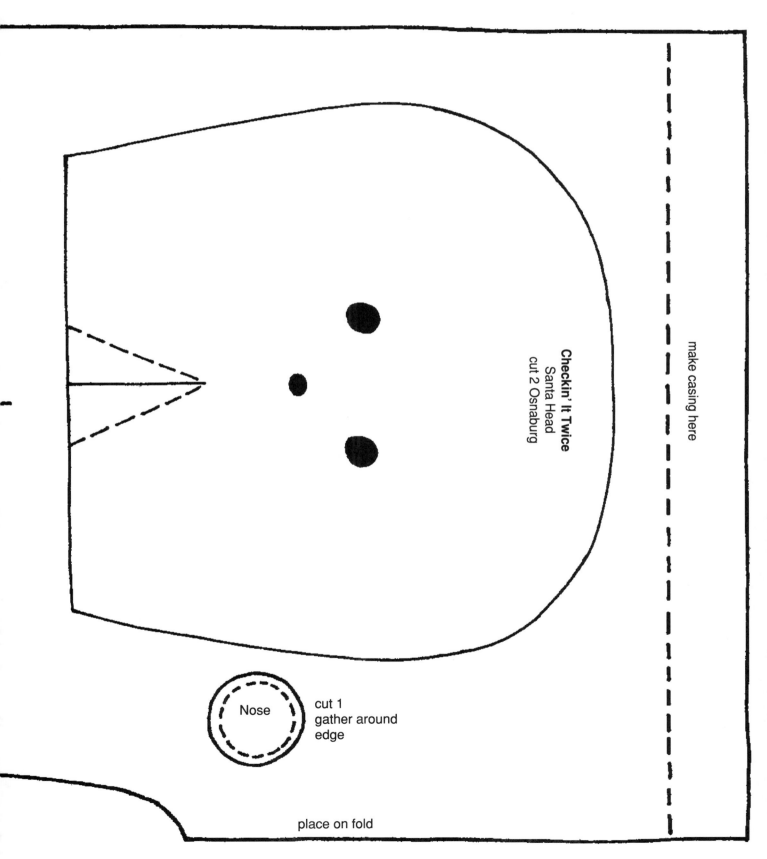

Checkin' It Twice
Santa Head
cut 2 Osnaburg

make casing here

Nose

cut 1
gather around
edge

place on fold

to fit top straight edge of hand. RST, pin and stitch. RST, pin and stitch around hands, underarm seam, and down body side seams. Don't turn RSO yet.

Bring side seams together and run a gathering stitch across the bottom raw edge. Pull up gathers to measure about 4". Stitch across gathered edge again to secure. Now turn RSO and stuff firmly. Run a gathering stitch around the neck edge. Pull up snugly to fit neck edge of head. Handstitch the head in place, using strong carpet thread.

Pull raw wool or wool roving into pieces and glue around back of head (covering threads attaching eyes). Cover sides and front of face to give him a long beard. Glue eyeglasses to his head at back and sides.

LEGS/PANTS/BOOTS

RST, stitch front seam of boots to dot. RST, stitch side seams of pants. Make a slit in the back lower legs of pants (as indicated on pattern). Stitch crotch seam of pants. Gather lower edge of pants to fit top straight edge of boots. RST, pin and stitch the gathered lower edge of pants to top edge of boots. Raw back edges of boots should be even with raw edges of slit in pants legs.

With RST, stitch slit and around the boot to dot where previous stitching stopped. Make a casing in top of pants by turning under 1/4" then again 1/2". Stitch, leaving a small opening at one side seam for insertion of elastic. Run a 15" length of 3/8" wide elastic through casing. After inserting elastic in pants casing, stuff only the boots, not the legs. Stitch ends of elastic together and enclose in casing. Stitch casing closed. Make suspenders by folding a 2"x11" strip of fabric in half lengthwise, RST. Stitch down long side and across one short end. Turn RSO and press. Stitch crossed ends of suspenders at back of Santa's pants and bring over shoulders to front. Secure in front with two 3/4" buttons.

TOY BAG

With RST, stitch side seams of bag. Turn RSO and stuff with fiber filling. Glue tiny toys, gifts, etc. to top of bag. Tie 1-1/2 to 2" down from top with jute twine. Glue a feather quill in one hand and a wish list from good boys and girls to the other hand.

Sit Santa in a chair or just lean him against his toy bag while he's "Checkin' It Twice"!

SANTA'S HELPERS

Camille Jackson

See picture on p. 27

Wood cutouts (see instructions below)
Fabric:
18"x22" piece (fat quarter) for shirt
1/4 yd. for pants or overalls (this will make 2 pair of pants)
6"x8" piece for apron
10"x11" piece for hat
Paints: (all paints are Delta unless specified otherwise)
 Medium flesh
 Adobe
 White
 Black
 Christmas green or green to match fabric
 Tomato red or red to match fabric
 Deep forest (Country Colors)
 Maroon
Paint brushes - flats and liner
Scraps of yarn for hair
Embroidery floss or 1/16" wide ribbon
Tiny jingle bell for hat
Tiny buttons for overalls and suspender pants
1 yd. 1/8" elastic
Hot-glue gun and glue sticks
Tacky glue
Jute twine
(Amounts given are for one elf. When making more than one elf, adjust amounts accordingly.)

WOOD

All pieces are cut from 3/4" wood. Drill small holes on body and legs where indicated on pattern. Drill a 3/8" hole for nose. Use a 3/8" wood plug or button for nose. Glue wood plug in hole. Sand all pieces before painting .

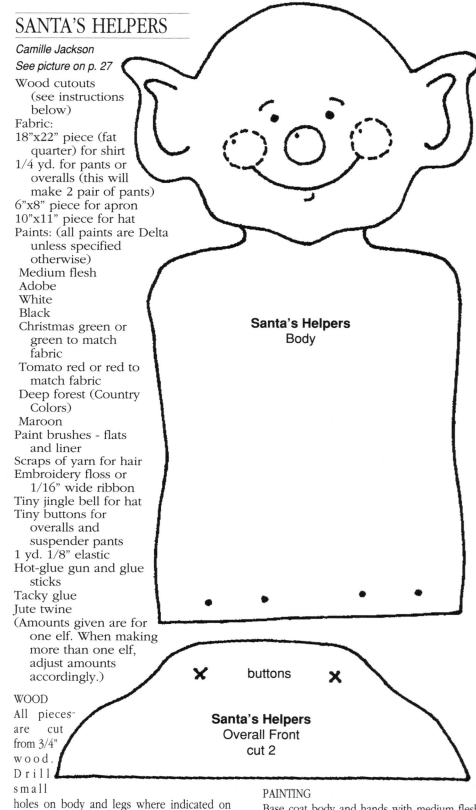

Santa's Helpers
Body

Santa's Helpers
Overall Front
cut 2

buttons

PAINTING

Base coat body and hands with medium flesh color. Base coat legs white, red or green. Base coat shoes red or green. Transfer pattern to wood using graphite paper.

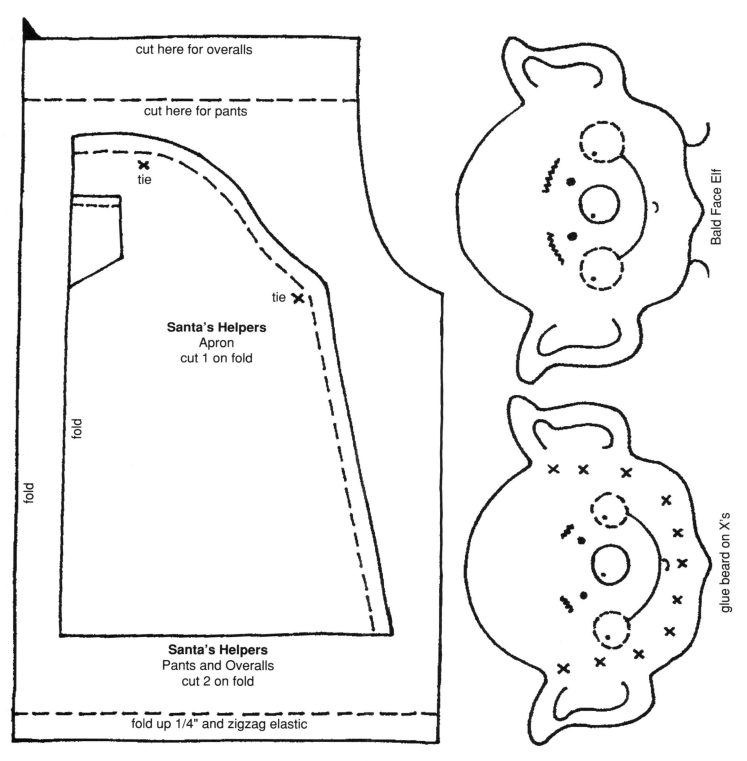

suspenders

overalls

fold line

Santa's Helpers
Overall Strap or Suspenders
cut 2

fold line

cut here for overalls

cut here for pants

✗ tie

tie ✗

Santa's Helpers
Apron
cut 1 on fold

fold

fold

fold

Santa's Helpers
Pants and Overalls
cut 2 on fold

fold up 1/4" and zigzag elastic

Bald Face Elf

glue beard on X's

43

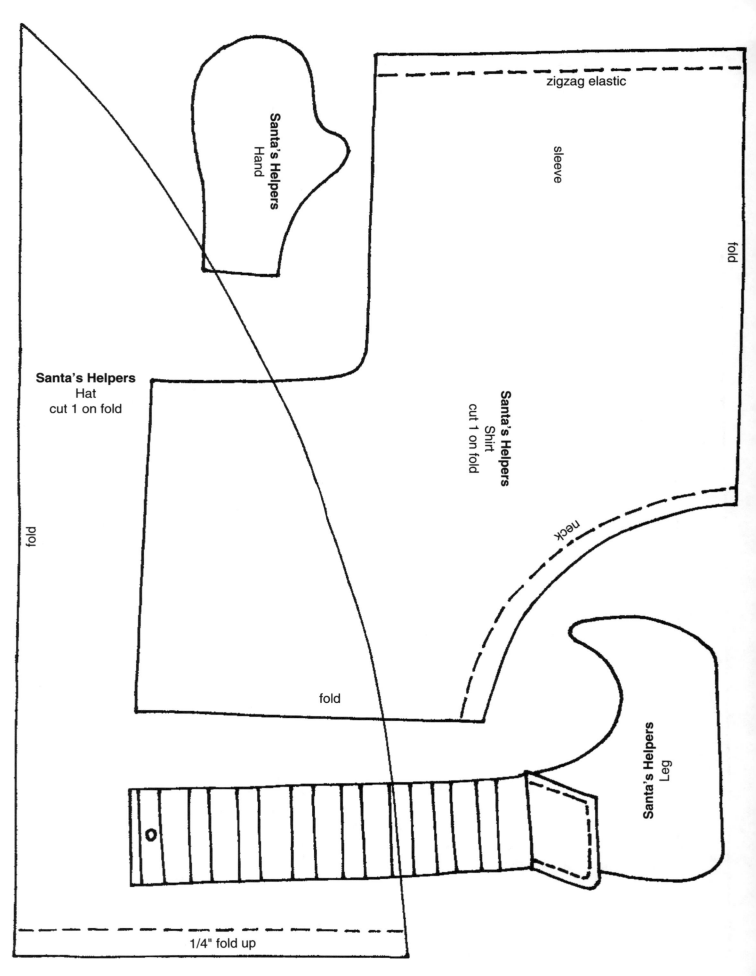

Santa's Helpers
Hand

zigzag elastic

sleeve

fold

Santa's Helpers
Hat
cut 1 on fold

fold

Santa's Helpers
Shirt
cut 1 on fold

neck

fold

Santa's Helpers
Leg

1/4" fold up

44

Using adobe color, float all around edge of head. Float inside of ears, top half of nose and under mouth. Dry brush cheeks.

Using black, line mouth and eyebrows. Using handle of liner brush, dot eyes.

With white, dot highlights on cheeks and nose.

Paint red, green, or white stripes on legs. Float under flap on shoe with maroon or deep forest. Paint stitching lines on flap of shoe with white.

Tie a bow with floss, ribbon or twine and glue to front of shoe.

CLOTHING
Shirt: Fold bottom of sleeve up 1/4" and zig-zag a 4" piece of elastic to sleeve close to folded edge. Stitch side seams.

Pants: Stitch front seam. Turn top edge down 1/4". Zigzag an 8" piece of elastic close to folded edge. Turn bottom edge of pant leg up 1/4". Zigzag a 4" piece of elastic close to folded edge. Stitch back seam. Stitch inside legs together matching crotch seams. For suspender pants, fold sides in on straps where indicated on pattern and press. Stitch buttons on front of pants at waist.

Overalls: Stitch overall bib front and back together. Stitch front seam on pants. Gather between notches. With right sides together, stitch bib to pants front between notches, matching notches to sides of bib. Stitch back seam. Fold waist edge under 1/4". Zigzag a 4" piece of elastic across back of pants close to folded edge between notches. Fold bottom edge of leg up 1/4" and zigzag a 4" piece of elastic to leg close to folded edge. Stitch inside legs together matching crotch seam. Fold straps and press. Stitch buttons on bib front.

Hat: Fold bottom edge of hat up 1/4" and stitch. Stitch side seam. Attach a jingle bell to hat using a 6" piece of ribbon or floss threaded through a needle. Tie into a bow.

Apron: Fold all edges under 1/4" and zigzag. Using black paint and a liner brush, paint pocket. Dry brush some splotches of paint on apron. For ties on apron, thread an 8" piece of floss or ribbon through a needle. Tie a big knot in one end. Put needle through apron where indicated on pattern. Knot should be on the right side of apron.

FINISHING
Cut two pieces of jute twine 12" long. Thread twine through hole in back of body, through leg and back through front of body. Leave legs loose enough so elf can sit or stand. Tie twine in square knot. Put a dot of Tacky glue on each knot to secure.

Put shirt on elf. Cut an 18" piece of floss or ribbon and thread through needle leaving only about a 4" tail and a 14" tail. Beginning at center front, turn neck edge under 1/4" and gather. Adjust gathers. With ends of floss or ribbon even, tie a bow at neck. Put hands in sleeves and hot glue. Put pants on elf and tuck shirt into pants.

ELF IN OVERALLS
Hot glue straps on at front and back. Cut a piece of cardboard 3-1/2" wide and 5" long. Wrap a 3-yd. piece of yarn around cardboard loosely. Carefully remove yarn from cardboard keeping loops in place. Hot glue yarn to edge of head from ear to ear leaving about an inch in front for bangs. Glue yarn to back of head about 1" up from bottom. Glue hat on with seam in center back.

PAINTER ELF
Tie apron on elf. Glue hair on in same manner as Elf in Overalls. For beard, cut a piece of yarn about 45" long. Wrap loosely around finger and slide off carefully keeping loops in place. Beginning at one ear, glue beard in place. Trim any excess. Glue hat on with seam in center back.

BALD ELF
Hot glue suspender straps at front and back. For hair, wrap a piece of yarn four or five times around two fingers. Make five bunches. Tie each bunch in the middle to secure. Glue one bunch on top of each ear. Glue the rest across the back of head to cover.

24" SANTA

Bonnie S. Olaveson

See picture on p. 100

1/3 yd. muslin (body, legs)
2/3 yd. 60" wide red fleece
1/8 yd. 45" wide black broadcloth (arms)
1/4 yd. 45" wide calico fabric (bag)
1/4 yd. 60" wide lamb's wool
6 inches 45" wide black vinyl (boots, belt)
1" buckle
Matching thread
1 ft. crepe wool (hair)
12 oz. polyester fiber filling
1/2" wood plug (nose)
Brown floss (eyes)
2/3 yd. twine (bag handle)
Crochet thread
5-1/2" horn (optional)

3" stuffed bear (optional)
Cinnamon stick (optional)
Hot-glue gun, glue sticks
Powder blush

Please read all instructions before beginning. Use 1/4" allowance on all seams. RST = right sides together. Fuzzy side of fleece is right side.

Cut body, arms, boots, hat, ball, and coat as pattern pieces indicate.

Measure and cut the following which do not have a pattern piece:
Legs: four 3-1/4"x10" muslin
Pants: two 18"x14" fleece
Bag: two 9"x9" calico
Fur on coat: two 2-1/2"x60" strips of lamb's wool
Belt: 1"x15" vinyl

BODY
With RST, stitch legs to boots. Stitch around legs, arms, and body. Leave open as pattern indicates.

Clip curved areas of arms, legs, and body. Turn right sides out. Stuff body. Stuff arms to stitching line. Stuff legs to 6" from top. Stitch across arms and legs and continue stuffing to within 1" of opening.

Turn raw edges of openings of arms, legs, and body inside 1/4". Pin and zigzag closed. Hand or machine stitch arms and legs to body as pattern indicates.

PANTS
Cut a 10" line up center of both pieces as Fig. 1 shows. Stitch around line using a 1/4" seam. Stitch down sides.

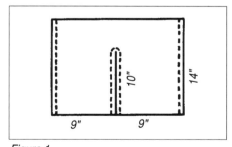

Figure 1

Hand gather around waist 1/4" from edge. Place on Santa, pull thread tight and knot. Hand gather around each leg. Pull tight and knot. (Do not fold raw edges under—they will be covered.)

COAT
Cut up the center of the coat and across neck as Fig. 2 shows. With RST, stitch from bottom

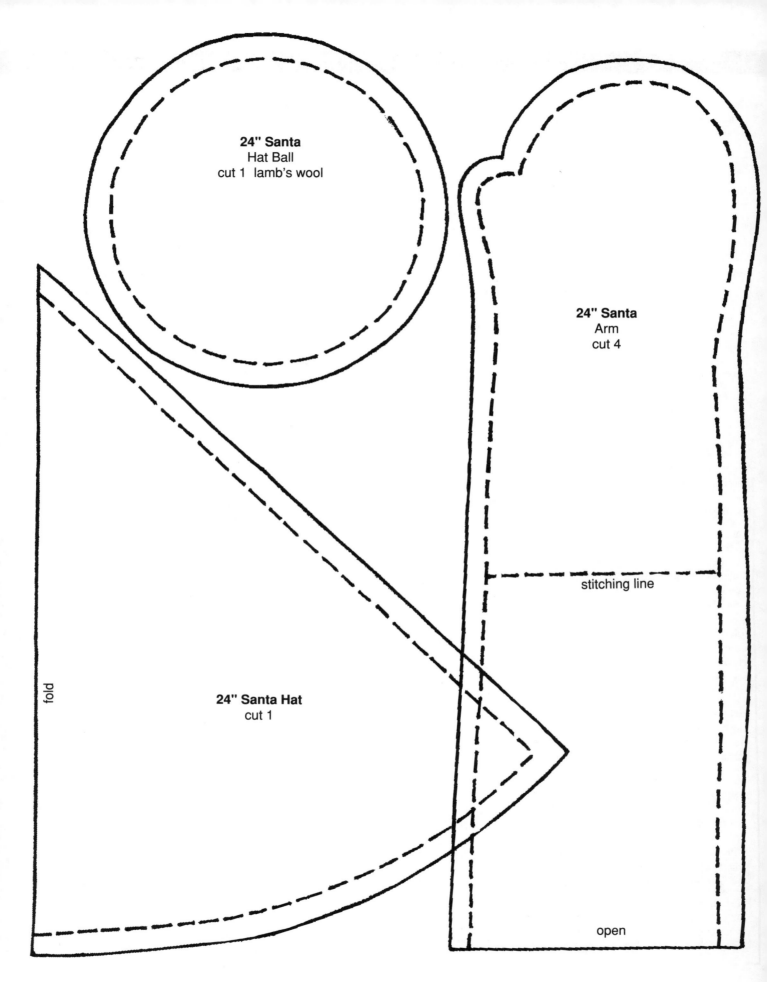

24" Santa
Hat Ball
cut 1 lamb's wool

24" Santa
Arm
cut 4

stitching line

fold

24" Santa Hat
cut 1

open

46

of sleeve to bottom of bodice. Clip under sleeve and turn right side out.

Place on Santa. Overlap front of coat 1/2" and, using glue gun, glue shut. Hand gather around each arm as with legs.

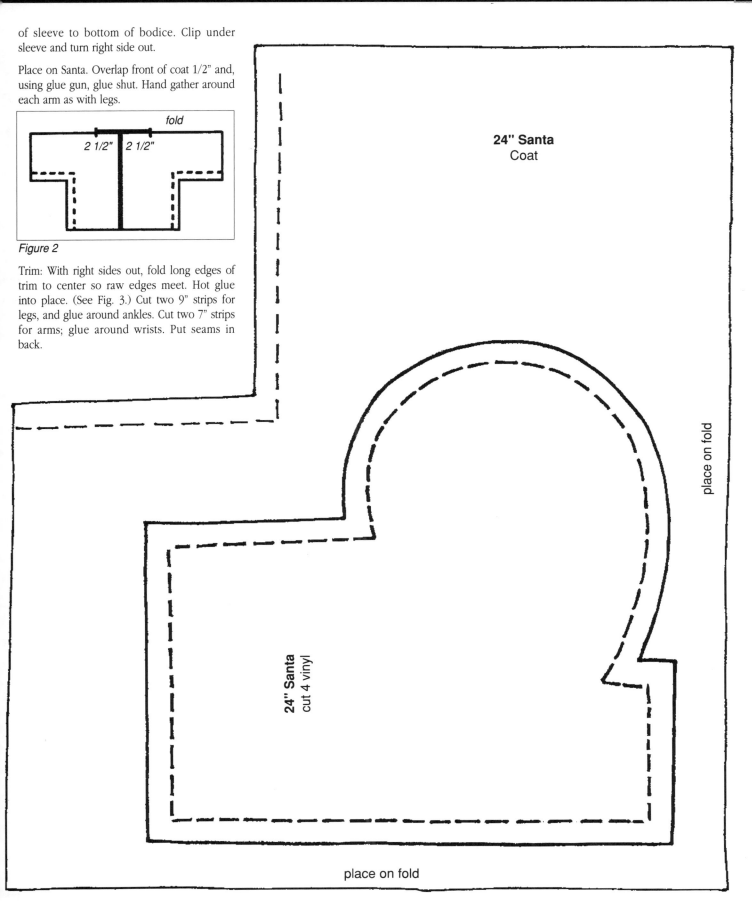

24" Santa
Coat

fold

2 1/2"   2 1/2"

Figure 2

Trim: With right sides out, fold long edges of trim to center so raw edges meet. Hot glue into place. (See Fig. 3.) Cut two 9" strips for legs, and glue around ankles. Cut two 7" strips for arms; glue around wrists. Put seams in back.

24" Santa
cut 4 vinyl

place on fold

place on fold

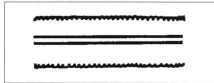

Figure 3

Cut a 21" strip and glue around bottom of coat. Cut an 11" strip and glue around neck. Put seams at center front.

Cut a 10" strip and glue down center front of coat. Start at top of neck and go down to bottom of coat. Turn extra under and glue to finish the edge. Glue one end of belt around buckle. Cut the other end to a point. Put around Santa's waist.

FACE
To make eyes, thread a darning needle with six strands of embroidery floss. Double floss, knot at end. Mark eye placement with

a pin. Tie a French knot for each eye as follows: from back of head, pull thread through to front of one eye. Wrap around needle four times. Push needle through head very near the hole it first came through. Knot. Repeat for other eye.

Take a stitch for nose as pattern indicates, knotting at back of head. Pull to slightly indent. Blush wood plug. Powder blush and a cotton swab work well. Start out with a small amount. It is easier to put more on than to get it off. Hot glue plug over stitch.

Blush a small circle for mouth as pattern indicates.

Unravel hair. Cut four 4-1/2" strips. Hot glue around chin as pattern

indicates. Pull and fluff. Cut a 5" strip for mustache. Pinch together in the middle. Hot glue under nose. Separate a piece for each eyebrow. Hot glue above each eye.

Blush Santa's cheeks. You may also want to put a little blush under each eyebrow.

HAT
With RST, stitch up center back. Turn right side out. Hot glue trim around bottom of hat. Stuff lightly. Hot glue to head. Hand gather circle of fur. Stuff lightly. Pull tight. Knot. Hot glue tip of hat down, glue ball over tip.

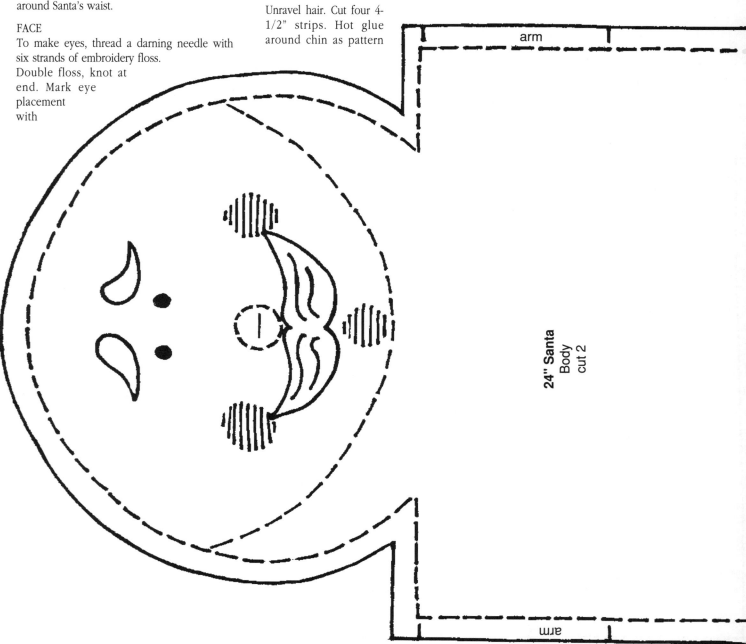

arm

24" Santa
Body
cut 2

arm

BAG

Stitch around three sides of bag leaving fourth side open. This will be the top. While bag is wrong side out, tie a string around each corner 1" up from point. (See Fig. 4.) Turn right side out. The corners will look gathered. Fold raw edge under 1" and hand gather around top of bag. Stuff bag lightly almost to the top. Pull strings until top of bag measures 4". Knot thread. Tie a knot in each end of the twine 1-1/2" from end. Fray ends. Hot glue to each side of bag. Hot glue horn, bear, and cinnamon stick (or whatever you desire) in bag.

Figure 4

DRESDEN PLATE PILLOW

Doris Peterson

See picture on p. 97

1/4 yd. each of six Christmas fabrics
1/2 yd. of plain fabric
1/2 yd. of red velvet or plain fabric for back
2 yds. gathered lace
2-1/4 yds. of 1/2" wide flat cotton lace
5/8 yd. of one Christmas fabric for ruffle
16" pillow form
or
Polyester fiber filling

Cut two of each of the Christmas fabrics from template A. Cut two from circle template B for center. Cut one piece 14-1/2" square from the background fabric. Cut two strips 1-1/2" for four borders around pillow. Cut three 7" widths for ruffle out of Christmas fabric of your choice.

Sew white edging on right side of template A on each piece, then join each piece together. Cut a piece of fabric for the back of plate, place right sides together. Sew 1/8" seam all the way around. Clip and turn right side out through the center opening. Work edges until they are rounded, turn the plate face up and press seams toward center.

Sew center circle right sides together with 1/8" seam. Clip a hole or small X in one layer only. Turn the center circle right side out through the hole. Press thoroughly.

Find center of background material. Place plate face up and pin. Appliqué the plate all of the way around and then appliqué the center piece in place.

Sew the white edging on each side of background material. Sew on borders of red velvet or your choice of color, then sew on gathered lace.

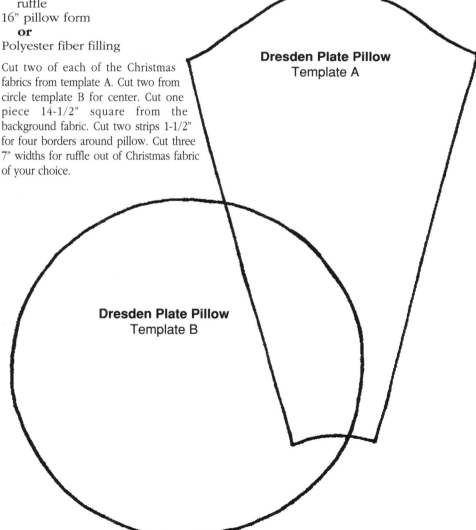

Dresden Plate Pillow
Template A

Dresden Plate Pillow
Template B

leg

open

leg

Sew the three widths of 7" pieces together to make one long piece. Press seams open. Fold in half lengthwise and gather ruffle to the size of square front. Sew to ends of top of pillow. Be careful not to catch the lace ruffle in at corners. Trim corners.

Sew on back velvet piece, right sides together. Fold in ruffle on corners, avoiding catching them when sewing. Sew around three sides.

Stuff finished piece with 16" pillow form or use polyester fiber filling. Slip stitch the opening closed.

BASKET PILLOW

Doris Peterson

See picture on p. 97

1/4 yd. each of Christmas and plain fabric for basket
1/2 yd. red velvet for border and back
5/8 yd. of dark green (same color as basket) for ruffle
2 yds. of 2-1/2" wide gathered lace
1 spool gold thread
1/4 yd. of trim for top of basket (optional)
18" pillow form or polyester fiber filling

SEWING INSTRUCTIONS
Use 1/4" seam allowance. Sew triangles into squares as shown in Fig. 1. Starred (*) pieces are Christmas fabric.

Berry add 1/4"

Basket Pillow
Leaf

add 1/4" seam allowance to turn under for appliqué

Sew handle squares (D) into strips as shown in Fig.1. Sew first handle and second handle on basket.

Sew the two foot pieces (D) on the ends of rectangles (B). Sew onto basket sides and then sew on bottom (C).

Cut the first border 1-3/4"; cut the second border 2-1/2". Sew on borders. Use gold thread and embroider around the basket and diagonal squares using crazy quilt stitches from the Glossary.

Using holly template, cut two pieces of holly out of desired fabric. Cut two holly berries using a dime as a template. Appliqué holly and berries onto piece. Hand sew trim to top of basket.

Ruffle: Sew three 7" strips together lengthwise and then gather it. Sew on gathered lace and then the material ruffle. Sew on back on three sides.

Fill pillow piece with 18" pillow form or polyester fiber filling. Slip stitch opening closed.

YO-YO DOORKNOB WREATH

See picture on p. 61

Scraps of different colors of green fabric
Soft batting
12" of 1/8" or 1/4" wide ribbon
24" of cotton crochet thread
Red beads (optional)

Cut 17 circles (using largest circle template on p. 7) from green fabrics. Using a running stitch, sew 1/8" away from edge on all circles. Pull gently to gather; place a small puff of batting in the center of each circle and pull thread tight. Tie off thread.

Using a needle and cotton crochet thread, run needle and thread through center of each yo-yo, selecting circles randomly.

Form a circle of the threaded yo-yos and tie tightly into place. Finish by tying a bow and attach it to front center of wreath. Add red bead accents, if desired.

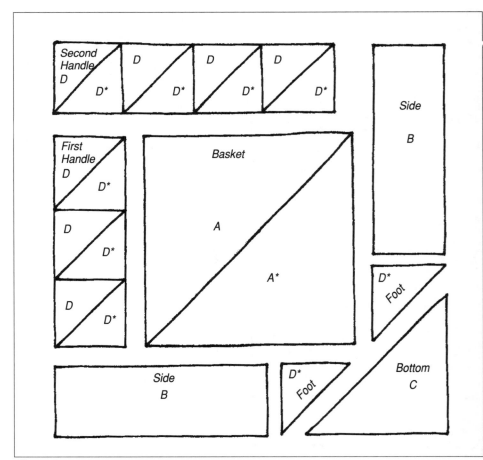

Figure 1

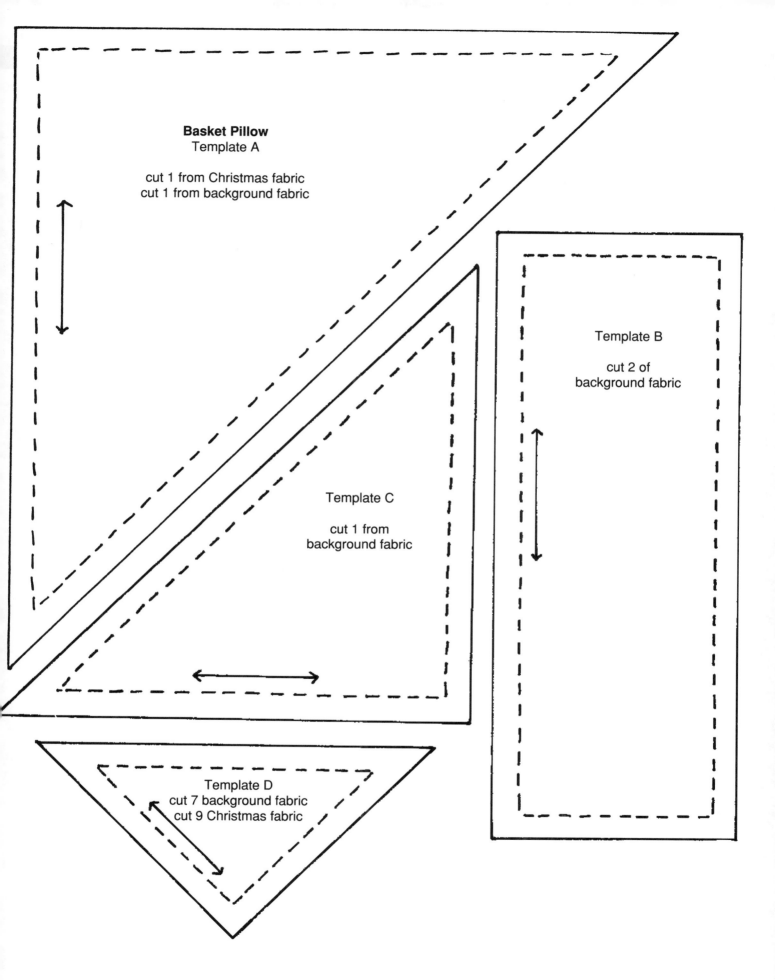

Basket Pillow
Template A

cut 1 from Christmas fabric
cut 1 from background fabric

Template B

cut 2 of
background fabric

Template C

cut 1 from
background fabric

Template D
cut 7 background fabric
cut 9 Christmas fabric

51

GIFTS

KEEPSAKES

TO MAKE FOR CHILDREN

QUICK AND EASY

CHRISTUS CROSS-STITCH PICTURE

Designed by Kae Strong
Model stitched by Carol Briggs
See picture on p. 100

DMC EMBROIDERY FLOSS:
415 Med. dark grey
X 414 Dark grey
   413 Charcoal grey (outline stitch)
= 762 Very light grey
O 800 Very light blue
/ 739 Light tan
\ 738 Very light tan
< 809 Light blue
+ 318 Light grey
» 433 Brown
Σ 898 Dark brown
| 820 Dark blue
— 796 Med. dark blue
   798 Blue (between mountains and clouds)
π 550 Dark purple
2 552 Med. dark purple
3 553 Purple
4 554 Light purple
◊ 211 Very light purple
√ 924 Dark green-blue
ø 926 Green-blue
Δ 3371 Black-brown
• Ecru
V White
14"x17" piece of 14 ct. black Aida cloth,
   or
11"x14" piece of 18 ct. black Aida cloth,
   or
14"x17" piece of 25 ct. black Lugana cloth
#24 tapestry needle (with 14 ct. Aida)
#26 tapestry needle (with 18 ct. Aida or
   25 ct. Lugana)
5" hoop (optional)

Model is stitched on 14 ct. black Aida cloth. If
25 ct. Lugana cloth is used, stitch over 2
stitches and use a #26 tapestry needle.

Design area is 110x160 stitches.

Three options for lettering are illustrated on
pp. 54-55. Lettering is done in 762 very light
grey. Slanted lines on the ends of the letters
(/ \) are sewn as such, not a whole cross.

Nose: two spaces on nose, use white under
backstitch.

Upper lip: Use 762 very light grey under
backstitch.

All squares between lover clouds and upper
sky and world are filled in with 798 blue.

Outline stitch is done in 1 strand of 413
charcoal grey.

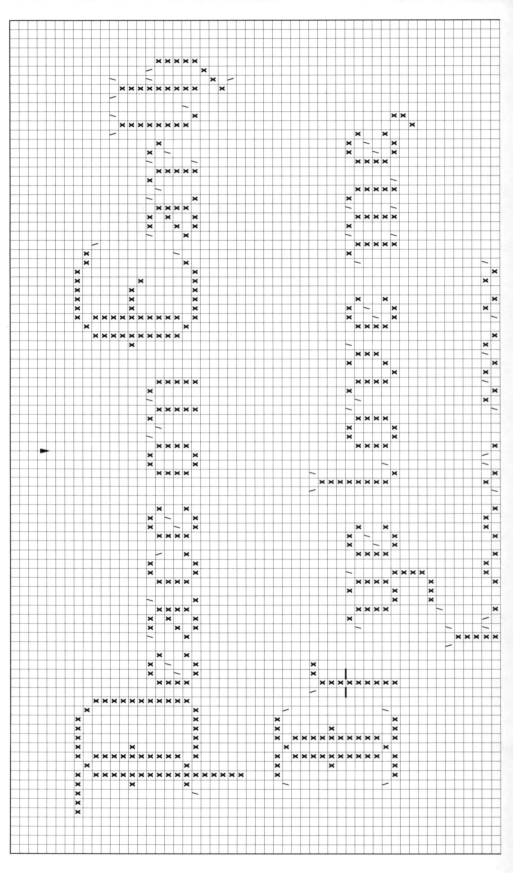

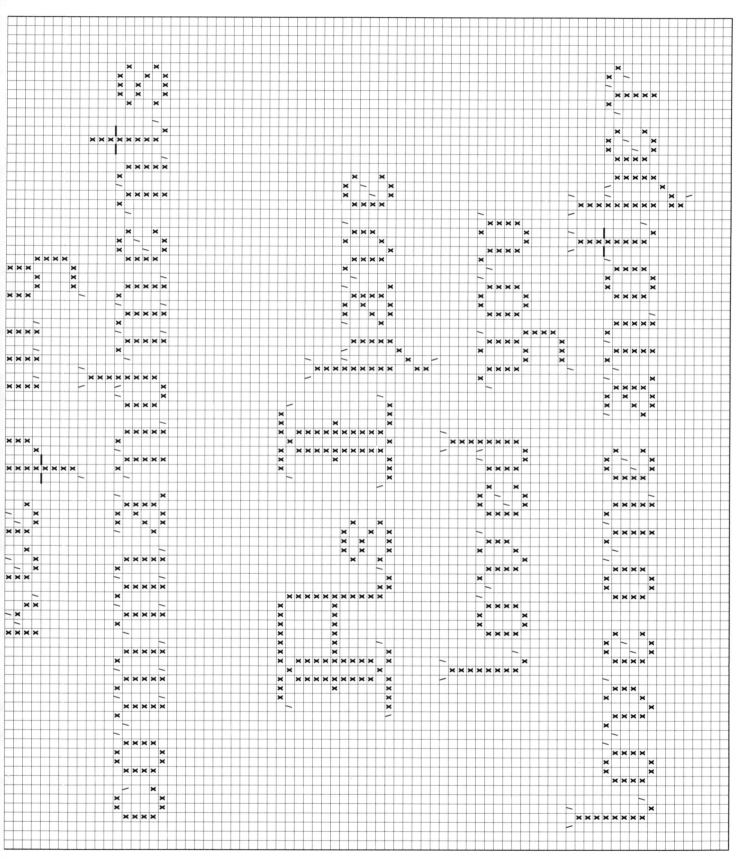

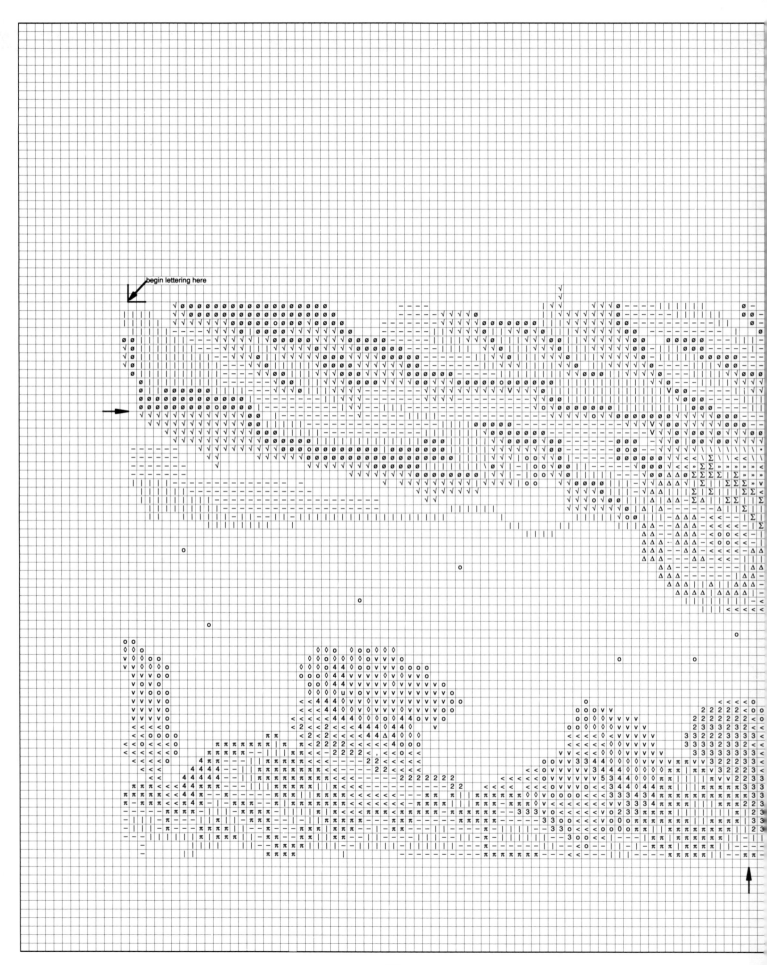

begin lettering here

PUFF WREATH
AND STOCKING

Ann Danzig

See picture on p. 64

1/4 yd. each of six different coordinating
　　Christmas prints
1 yd. of Christmas print for backing of
　　stocking and wreath
1/8 yd. cream satin
2 ft. of cream colored lace
1 pkg. tiny jingle bells
Polyester fiber filling
3 yds. muslin
1/2 yd. "Wonder Under"

Use 1/4" seam allowance unless otherwise
indicated. Stockings require 70 puffs, wreaths
144 puffs (36 puffs of each color of fabric).

Cut 214 two-inch squares of muslin. Cut 36
two-and-one-half-inch squares from each of
the six pieces of printed fabric. Sew muslin
and print squares together on three sides.
Pleat print fabric in center of each side in
order to fit. (See Fig. 1.) Stuff finished squares
lightly with batting and sew closed, pleating
print fabric in center of seam.

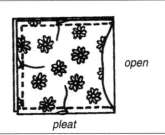

Figure 1

Sew puffs together in rows arranging the
colors in random order. For wreath sew puffs
to form a 18" square. For stocking sew in rows
so that you can cut the stocking pattern out.
Cut wreath and stocking pieces out of puff
pieces.

For wreath trace an 18" circle with 5-1/2" circle
in the center. Sew around 18" and 5-1/2"
circles before cutting. Use two thicknesses of
muslin fused together with Wonder Under or
muslin fused to one of the Christmas prints for
the back piece of the wreath. This will
reinforce the wreath.

Pin two circles together RST, and sew around
outside edge using a 1/4" seam allowance.
Turn right side out. To sew center circle turn
two edges under 1/4" and slip stitch closed.
Leave a 6" area open. Stuff wreath and slip

stitch opening closed. Embellish with a big
French ribbon bow or any other treatment you
like. To finish stocking, cut toe piece. If you
want piping across the top of the toe piece,
you can purchase piping or make your own.
To make your own piping, cut 1-1/2" bias strip
of fabric. Use cording or heavy string and

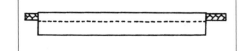

Figure 2

cover with bias fabric right side out and stitch
close to cording. (See Fig. 2.)

Attach piping to straight edge of toe, raw

edges together. Topstitch lace on toe of
stocking close to piping. Sew to puff portion
of stocking. (See p. 168.)

Cut two muslin stockings and a print stocking
for back. (HINT: Remember the back must be
the opposite of the front.)

You are now ready to sew the stocking
together. You will have four layers. Pin all
layers together in the following manner: first, a
muslin stocking, then the back of stocking
right side up, then the front of stocking right
side down, and then the other muslin
stocking. The muslin will form the inner lining
of the stocking. Sew through all layers using
1/4" seam allowance.

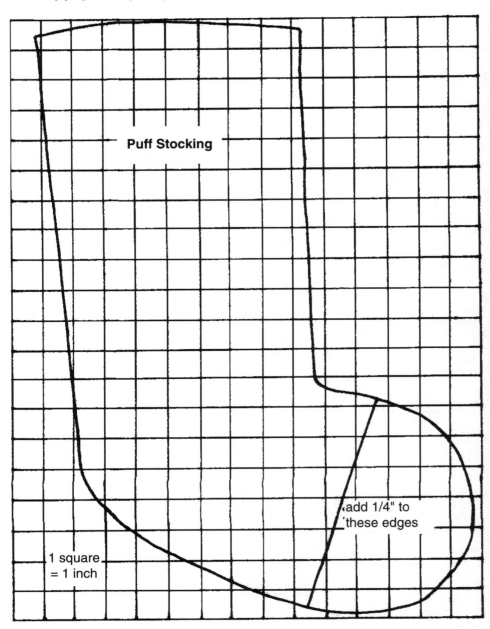

Puff Stocking

add 1/4" to
these edges

1 square
= 1 inch

Clip curves and turn right side out. Cut a 14-1/2"x8" piece of satin. Fold in half lengthwise, wrong sides together. Press. Attach lace to bottom folded edge.

Gather or pleat ends of satin. (See p. 168.) cuff in half, right sides together and sew pleated edges together.

Sew cuff to top of stocking, right side of cuff to inside lining of stocking.

Turn cuff out (the seam will be hidden when you turn the cuff). Add bells and bow.

CHRISTMAS PHOTO ALBUM

Lori D. Sorensen and Julie Simmons
See picture on p. 98

1 photo album or loose-leaf binder
3/4 yd. Christmas fabric
3/4 yd. coordinating fabric
1/2 yard Pellon fleece
Embroidery floss in desired colors
2 pieces of cardboard large enough to fit
    inside covers
1 Manila file folder (or cardboard)
1 yd. each of two colors of 1/8" wide
    ribbon
4 yds. of lace
Hot-glue gun and glue sticks

Open binder and lay flat on top of Pellon fleece. Cut fleece to size of binder.

Hot glue the Pellon fleece to the photo album, front, spine, and back of album.

Lay Christmas fabric right side down. Cut fabric about 1" bigger than open binder all the way around.

Pull edge of fabric to inside of album and glue, overlapping fabric to inside edge of cover. Do not pull so tight that binder will not close. Glue in following order: one side, other side, top, bottom.

(HINT: where the middle of the binder meets, clip the material on both sides of it about one inch. This will allow you to push the fabric under the metal clip.)

Once the Christmas fabric is glued, it's time to do the inside cover. Cover cardboard pieces with contrasting fabric. Be sure to leave extra fabric on the side running vertical to binding clip, this will allow you to tuck it under the binding clip.

Next, hot glue these covered cardboard pieces to the inside covers. Remember to put the extra fabric side next to binding clip. Then put a dab of hot glue alongside of the binding clip and with a butter knife gently push extra material under it.

The front cover decoration allows much room for creativity. A cross-stitch pattern of a Christmas horn was used on the model. The front could also be used as a frame for a photograph.

Draw a 4-1/2" diameter inner circle on the Manila file folder. Draw a second circle two inches larger all around the first circle. Cut out the inside circle. Cut through one side of circle.

To make the material ruffle cut out 4-1/2" strips from the contrasting fabric making them 72" to 90" long. Sew these strips right sides together, making a 2-1/4" wide tube. Turn right side out.

Next, work the strips onto the circle (made out of the Manila file folder) and gather tightly. Then wrap ribbon around the circle. Lay the decorated Christmas piece on top of the front of the album and place the ruffle on top of it. Hot glue both pieces down. Make a bow and place at top of decorated circle.

CRAZY QUILT PILLOW

Karla Gerome
See picture on p. 100

12" pillow form or polyester fiber filling
1/8 yd. each of 10 different fabrics
    (satins, velvets, etc., preferably dark
    colors that coordinate)
Pearl cotton, size 8: Black, Gold, Red
1/2 yd. black cotton fabric for backing
Old buttons
Lace
1/2 yd. fabric for ruffle
Braid, Black and Gold
12-1/2"x12-1/2" piece of muslin for base

Select a dark piece of fabric of the ten collected for project. Cut five angles on it for your center piece and pin to center of muslin base piece. Cut the second piece and lay against the first angle, right sides together. Sew 1/4" seam allowance, flip over to right side, then press flat.

Cut the third piece and lay it along the next angle, working clockwise. Be sure the shape extends beyond the previous piece and sew. Trim excess fabric from seam.

Continue around center piece until all angles are stitched.

Continue working clockwise until muslin base is covered with pillow top fabrics. Keep fabrics consistent in color.

After completing the base, add decorative stitches using pearl cotton. (See stitching guide in Glossary.)

Decorate with lace, buttons, braid—to your liking. Go a little crazy! You're entitled around Christmas!

The pillow in the picture has a ruffle. If you want to make a ruffle for the pillow, follow the instructions in the Glossary to determine how much fabric is needed.

Cut fabric to desired ruffle width. Sew pieces together to form a continuous strip. Hem outer edge of ruffle strip or fold in half to make a double ruffle. Gather raw edge. Pin to four edges of right side of pillow top, distributing gathers evenly and stitch to pillow top.

To finish pillow, cut backing fabric to size of finished crazy quilt piece. With right sides together, place back on ruffle and stitch around three sides, leaving fourth side open. Turn pillow right side out. Stuff with pillow form or polyester fiber filling. Slip stitch opening closed.

MILE-A-MINUTE AFGHAN

Afton B. Ricks
See picture on p. 63

16 four-ounce skeins of 4-ply washable
    yarn
Crochet hook size F or G

TERMS AND SYMBOLS
Ch Chain
SC Single crochet
DC Double crochet
St Stitch
Sl St Slip stitch

To begin: Ch 6, join to make a circle by using a Sl St. Ch 3. Do 2 DC in the circle. Ch 3. Do 3 DC in the same circle. Ch. 3 Turn your work over. Make 3 DC into the opening you've made. Ch 3 and make 3 DC in the same opening. Join your work by going into the top of your last DC and do 1 DC. Ch 3. Turn your work over and begin making 3DC, Ch 3, 3DC. Now make a DC into the last Ch stitch.

Make 90 of these holes for an average-sized afghan.

Optional: At this point change color of yarn. Join by tying a square knot.

Ch 3 in the first hole and add 2 DC to it. Work down the whole length by putting 3 DC in each hole. At the end, make one Ch St. Now make 15 DC in the end circle or hole. Make one Ch St. Work down the other side making 3 DC in each opening and put 15 DC in the end hole. Do a Ch St before and after each of these 15 DC. This completes one strip.

Make 13 of these strips for an average-sized afghan.

To join strips: Place the wrong sides of two strips together. Make sure the shells are going the same way. Tie your other color of yarn onto the piece of yarn you left after finishing your strip. Go through the first hole of both strips to tie, making a square knot.

Now do a SC in the inside part of the second DC on the strip next to you. Do the same in the next DC. Now go to the second inside DC on the other strip and make a SC in each of the next 2 stitches.

Go back to the strip next to you and do the same in the next 2 stitches. Go back to the other strip and do the same. Do not skip any stitches. Continue until all strips are joined.

After all 13 strips are joined together, go around the whole afghan with a SC in each stitch. To finish afghan, work around entire piece with a DC in each stitch.

To make scallops lay smooth, you will need to add a stitch or two at the top of the scallop, and omit a stitch or two at the bottom of each scallop. This is especially necessary on the row of DC.

HAND-PIECED CENTER SQUARE QUILT

The Four of Us (Carol Bitner, Carol Morgan, Beth Ann Neville, Joy Knowlton)
See picture on p. 97

This 19th century Pennsylvania quilt top is a striking reminder of the beauty of a simple design. While lovely worked in only three fabrics, it is stunning worked in a variety of red and light print fabrics, using a single green fabric to unify the design.
Finished quilt: 64-1/2" x 64-1/2"
Finished wall quilt: 56" x 56"

3/4 yd. (total) of Fabric A, red calicos
1 yd. (total) of Fabric B, light calico prints
3-1/4 yds. of Fabric C, dark green calico print

4 yds. red or green calico print for backing. (A large paisley or floral print is wonderful.)
Cotton batting

TEMPLATES
Cut from a file folder a 2-1/2" square and a 2-1/2"x6" rectangle.

Draw a 6" square marked at middle point on all sides, then connect middle points to form a square. Cut corners off. These are the triangle templates. Square that is left is the center square template. (See Figs. 1a, 1b, and 1c.)

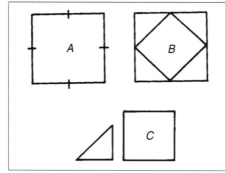

Figure 1

Please read General Instructions carefully. Note instructions for cutting triangles. Trace around templates on wrong side of fabrics. Add 1/4" seam allowance on all sides. Cut out the following pieces:

Fabric A: 36 lg. squares (25 for wall quilt) 25 2-1/2" squares (16 for wall quilt)

Fabric B: 144 triangles (100 for wall quilt)

Fabric C: 60 2-1/2"x6" rectangles (40 for wall quilt)

*2 8"x48-1/2" strips (8"x40" for wall quilt). Add seam allowances.

*2 8"x64-1/2" strips (8"x56" for wall quilt). Add seam allowances.

*Note: Measure completed quilt top before cutting strips and make length adjustment, if necessary.

GENERAL INSTRUCTIONS
Prewash and iron all fabrics. All fabrics must be 100% cotton. Cut off selvages. Pieces should be cut from the selvage edge down, on the lengthwise grain.

Cut large pieces first. Never tear fabric as this will stretch and distort it. Trace accurately around all sides of templates with sharp pencils. This is the stitching line. Before cutting from fabric, add 1/4" seam allowance on all sides.

Squares, rectangles, and strips should be cut on the lengthwise grain of fabric. Triangles should be cut at right angles to the selvage.

Pin corner points together first, then the marked lines between, checking to be sure seam lines are lined up exactly. Stitch on pencil line from fabric edge to fabric edge.

When starting to stitch by hand, take one stitch, leaving 1/2" tail of thread; backstitch, pulling thread tightly; backstitch again, leaving a loop; put needle through loop, then pull thread tightly. Proceed with small running stitches, then end stitching as started, leaving 1/2" tail when cutting thread.

Always sew on traced pencil line with smallest stitches possible. Finger press unopened seam toward darker fabric.

GENERAL FINISHING INSTRUCTIONS
Back: Seam two lengths of backing fabric, selvages removed, 68" in length to form a back that is 68" square. Cut backing fabric four inches larger than finished quilt top. Seam if necessary.

Cut cotton batting four inches larger than finished quilt top. Place backing fabric right side down, cotton batting on top of backing fabric, centering neatly and with finished top right side up, making a "fabric sandwich."

Baste from the center out in large stitches every few inches.

Starting at center, quilt inside each piece 1/4" from each seam with additional quilting as desired.

BINDING
The binding may be cut on the bias or on the lengthwise (straight) grain and it may be pieced.

Cut 4 strips 1-1/8" wide and 66" long. This includes 1/4" seam allowance on either side of strip. With right sides together, pin binding to top edges of quilt and bottom edges of quilt. Stitch to quilt top 1/4" from edge, then fold over to back side of quilt. Fold edge under 1/4" and stitch in place using a blind stitch or a running top stitch.

Before adding side binding, turn under ends of binding 1/4", then attach binding to sides of quilt and stitch in manner described above.

CONSTRUCTION
Stitch triangles to large squares to form block. (See Figs. 2a, 2b, and 2c.)

Clockwise, from top left corner: Bunny Stocking, p. 5; Country Bells, p. 16; Yule Log Tree Wall Hanging, p. 67; Wooden Father Christmas, p. 30; Yo-yo Tree Ornament (on box to left of violin), p. 7; Yo-yo Doorknob Wreath, p. 50; Bread Cloths (on trunk and in basket), p. 129; Tree Place Mat and Napkin Rings, p. 161; Noel Banner, p. 11.

Beginning at top of trunk: Gathered Fabric Heart, p. 122; (right, on trunk) Closet Sachet, p. 120; (on back and on suitcase) Bows and More Bows, p. 80; (left, in front of suitcase) Cloth Basket with Dried Flowers, p. 123; (in front of white collar) Bow Napkin Ring, p. 161; (over back of and laying on suitcase) Lace Collars from Linens, p. 132; Potpourrii Doll, p.122; Baby's Breath Angel, p. 32.

Clockwise from top left: Camille, p. 106; Grandchildren Cross-stitch Sampler, p. 65; Mile-a-Minute Afghan, p. 59; Mopsy Locks, p.111; Alexandra's Bonnet, p. 87; (on floor) Strip-quilted Bag, p. 130; Grandma's Paddle, p. 130; Persistence, p. 76; Christmas Ball with Doily, p. 4.

*Starting at center of picture with Puff Stocking and (top right) Puff Wreath, p. 58, clockwise: Joy Wall Hanging, p. 16;
Fabric Bags, p 128; Christmas Present Place Mat, p. 161; Yule Log, p. 154; (far left) Victorian Candle Ornament, p. 7;
Mimi's Rabbit, p. 94.*

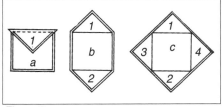

Figure 2

Stitch rectangles to blocks to form strip. (See Fig. 3.)

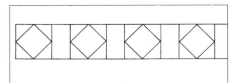

Figure 3

Stitch small squares to rectangles to form strip. (See Fig. 4.)

Stitch strip containing blocks to narrow strips alternately until all have been joined.

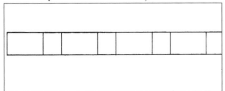

Figure 4

Stitch border strips to top and bottom of pieced top, then add side border strips.

GRANDCHILDREN CROSS-STITCH SAMPLER

Shanon Allen

See picture on p. 63

15"x18" piece of ivory 14-count Aida cloth

14"x18" frame

11"x14" mat

DMC Embroidery floss as follows:

♥ 223 Dark mauve

● 930 Dark antique blue

◆ 224 Mauve

✿ 754 Light peach

❙ 758 Dark peach

▲ 501 Green

✳ 931 Medium blue

☆ 930 Dark antique blue

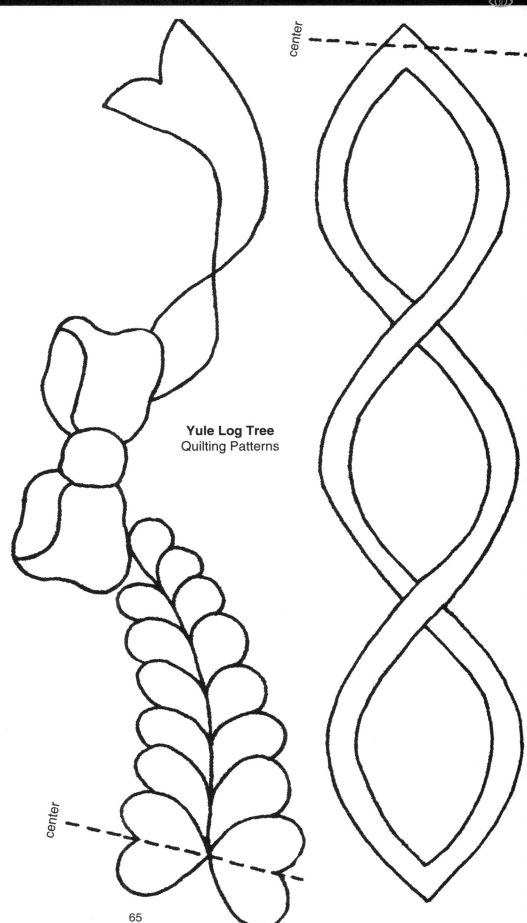

Yule Log Tree
Quilting Patterns

center

Center

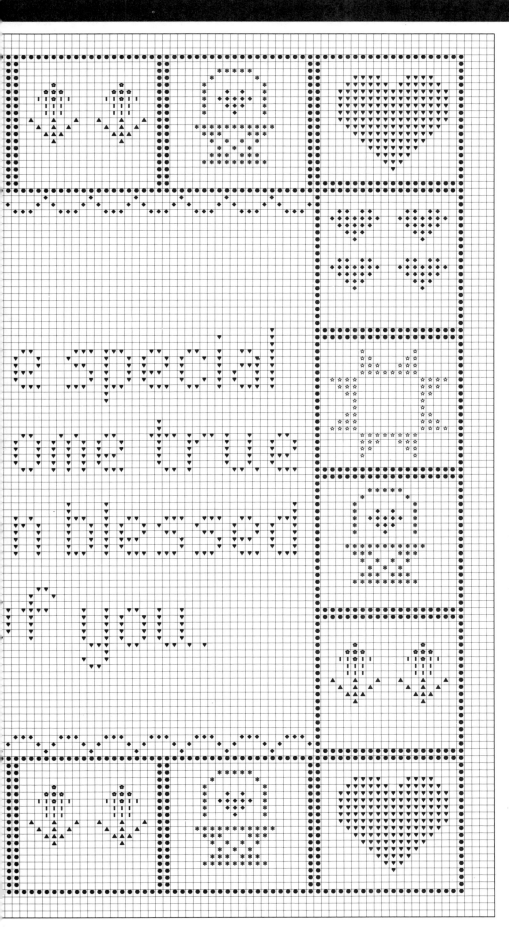

YULE LOG TREE

Jodi G. Warner

See picture on p. 61

Finished size: 24" square

1 yd. light print fabric for background
   (includes enough for backing)
1/4 yd. for red border
1/8 yd. each of three to five different
   fabrics for tree logs
3/8 yd. of additional green fabric (for
   binding, corner, and one log)
2-3/4 yds. of 1/8" poly cord for piping
28" square of batting

GENERAL

The tree is machine-pieced of rotary-cut strips in the traditional "log cabin" method. Background "logs" and vertical tree (green) logs are formed with narrow strips; horizontal tree logs are formed by wider strips. Two mirror-image blocks are constructed, with an extra background strip on the bottom. Then the two blocks are joined with the trunk strip. Background strips (3-1/4") are added at the top and bottom horizontal edges to complete the center panel.

Cutting measurements include 1/4" seam allowances. Cut the strips along the crosswise straight grain of fabrics. Stitch seams with right sides together, then press together toward the darker fabric.

CUTTING

Determine the arrangement of selected dark green fabrics for the "logs" of the tree, then cut strips of the following widths and lengths:

1-3/8" strips: A - 4"; B - 9"; C - 14"; D - 18"; E (trunk) - 13"

1-7/8" strips: B - 5"; C - 10"; D - 13"; E (trunk) - 17"

From background fabric, first cut and set aside for quilt backing a 26" square, then cut two strips 3-3/4"x18-1/2". For log cabin piecing background, cut 1-3/8" strips approx. equaling 2-5/8 yds. Cut one strip 1-7/8"x20".

CONSTRUCTION

Construct the center two-log unit. Seam together the A tree strip and a background strip, press seams toward green fabric, then cut into two 1-7/8" sections, taking care that corners are square and cut edges perpendicular. As block construction progresses from this point, a RIGHT and a LEFT block should be made. (Instructions will

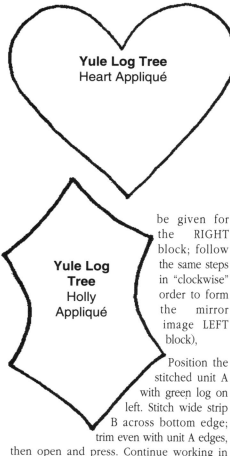

Yule Log Tree
Heart Appliqué

Yule Log Tree
Holly Appliqué

be given for the RIGHT block; follow the same steps in "clockwise" order to form the mirror image LEFT block),

Position the stitched unit A with green log on left. Stitch wide strip B across bottom edge; trim even with unit A edges, then open and press. Continue working in counter-clockwise order around block, stitching, trimming and pressing two background strips to block edges, then narrow strip B. This completes one ring of logs continue adding logs in similar manner, beginning with wide green strip, then two background strips, finally the narrow green strip for C and D rings. Add wide strip E and two background strips.

Stitch the 1-7/8" wide background strip to bottom edge of E strip and trim ends even. Press toward tree. Join left and right blocks with narrow E strip between. Stitch a 3-3/4" wide background strip to top and bottom edges of center panel.

Cut four strips 3-3/8"x18-3/4" from red border fabric. Cut four corner squares 3-3/8"x3-3/8" from dark green fabric. Stitch two border strips to top and bottom of center panel. Stitch corner squares on ends of remaining border strips, then stitch strips with corners on side edges of center panel, aligning intersecting seams.

Duplicate template patterns for heart and holly leaf onto cardboard or plastic. On the right sides of appropriate fabrics, trace around the template allowing space for 1/4" seam allowances; cut out. Carefully fold seam allowance back along traced lines and hand baste close to folded edge all around. Position hearts at top of trunk and in corner squares and appliqué in place by hand using matching thread with a tiny whipstitch. Position two holly leaves on each side of center heart, overlapping inner points slightly and appliqué in place by hand with matching thread.

Transfer quilting design lines to red borders using the template given, overlapping ends as indicated. Transfer feather and ribbon swag under tree, and ribbon ends only extending downward from holly leaves parallel to tree log corners. Mark a 3/4" diagonal grid in remaining background areas. Layer with backing fabric and thin batting, then quilt on marked lines, next to border, corner and appliqué seams, and in-the-ditch around tree logs.

Prepare and stitch piping from remaining corner square fabric; stitch to outer edge of quilt and batting prior to quilting the corner square appliqués and seams (keeping backing fabric free). Turn raw edges toward back of quilt, fold backing seam allowance under and invisibly stitch folded edge over piping stitching. Add one final row of quilting through top layers of quilt near piping seam. Sign and date quilt.

CHRISTMAS TREES TABLE OR PIANO RUNNER

Jodi G. Warner

See picture on p. 27

45"-wide, 100% cotton:
1/2 yd. muslin print for block background and backing
1/8 yd. dark green solid for narrow block borders
1/2 yd. red solid for border triangles, strips, end points, and binding
Small amounts of 3 coordinated green prints for tree, brown solid for trunk, black solid or print for bucket
Five purchased yellow star appliqués, approx. 1" tall

Christmas Tree Runner

Small Triangle Template and Quilting Pattern

12"x56" piece of thin batt for fine hand quilting
Matching sewing threads
Contrast quilting thread, green recommended
Freezer paper

Tree blocks are constructed using the freezer paper method. Duplicate the block line diagram onto freezer paper, transferring letter labels, grainlines, and center marks for alignment. Carefully cut apart along lines, then with medium warm iron press paper pattern pieces with waxy side down onto WRONG sides of appropriate fabrics, allowing space for 1/4" seam allowances all around. Cut around paper pieces adding seam allowances. Assemble the horizontal sections of block by placing edges of pieces to be joined RIGHT sides together, checking alignment of paper corners and edges by pushing pins through both fabric layers, making adjustments as necessary.

Machine stitch from cut edge to cut edge, then press both seam allowances together toward tree parts, trunk or bucket. Next, stitch horizontal strip units in sequence, matching centers and checking paper pattern corner and edge alignment before stitching. Press bucket-to-trunk seams down, all other seams toward top of block. Turn block to WRONG side,

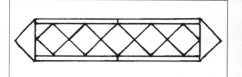

Figure 1

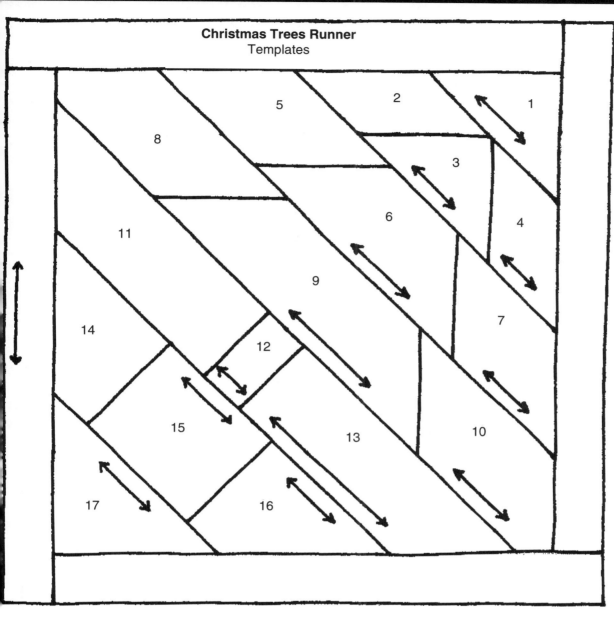

Christmas Trees Runner
Templates

runner unit; press seams toward narrow strips

Stitch end triangles in place and press seam allowances toward ends.

With matching thread attach purchased appliqué stars to tree tops with small machine straight stitches. Transfer quilting design lines to border and end triangles.

Cut and seam 12" strips of backing fabric to form a 59" length. Layer backing, batting and runner top, and baste together. Quilt, using contrast thread on marked quilt design lines, in-the-ditch around narrow green borders, and tree outline. (If center square is an unpieced block, duplicate the tree outline with quilting stitches.)

Binding: From remaining red fabric, cut 1-3/8" bias strips and seam together to form a 130" length. Using a 3/4" strip of folder cardboard as a template, press edges over cardboard along entire strip length to form 3/4" finished width tape. Press fold edges together over raw edges to form double-fold bias binding. Working from the RIGHT side of the quilted runner, open binding and lay one outer fold line over the 1/4" seam line of runner. (Trim excess batting and backing even with quilt top edges.) Blunt cut the beginning end of binding and fold back 1/2", then stitch along the binding fold line through all three layers of the quilt. Miter the binding at all corners. Apply binding around entire quilt edge and trim 1/2" past beginning fold edge of binding. Fold binding around runner raw edges to back side and pin outer fold edge over previous stitching. Invisibly whipstitch fold edge in place. Sign and date the quilt.

center a 6" square cardboard template over block and mark around edge, then trim away excess. Complete five blocks. (If center block will be covered during runner use, a red square can be substituted for pieced block.)

Cut 1" strips across width of green fabric. Stitch strips around each tree block in the Log Cabin style: begin stitching the first strip 1" in from upper block edge, then stitch remaining edge of block to strip. Trim upper "free" end 1" longer than block, opposite end even to match block. Press seams toward borders. Continue adding strips around block, stitching from previous border edge to opposite edge of block. When fourth strip is in place and pressed open, replace free end of first border

strip over it and complete the stitching of first seam. Trim excess even and press.

Cut 8 larger border triangles and 8 small end triangles from red fabric. Arrange blocks and triangles on flat surface in correct positions. (Tree blocks can be turned with tops pointing inward from points toward center section for table runner, or placed with top-bottom axis reaching across narrow width for piano runner.) Assemble blocks and triangles in "diagonal" rows; press seams toward borders. Next sew diagonal units together, aligning crossing seams, and adding remaining end triangles. (See Fig. 1.) Press seams toward borders.

Cut 1-1/4" red strips and seam ends, then cut into two 46" lengths. Stitch to long edges of

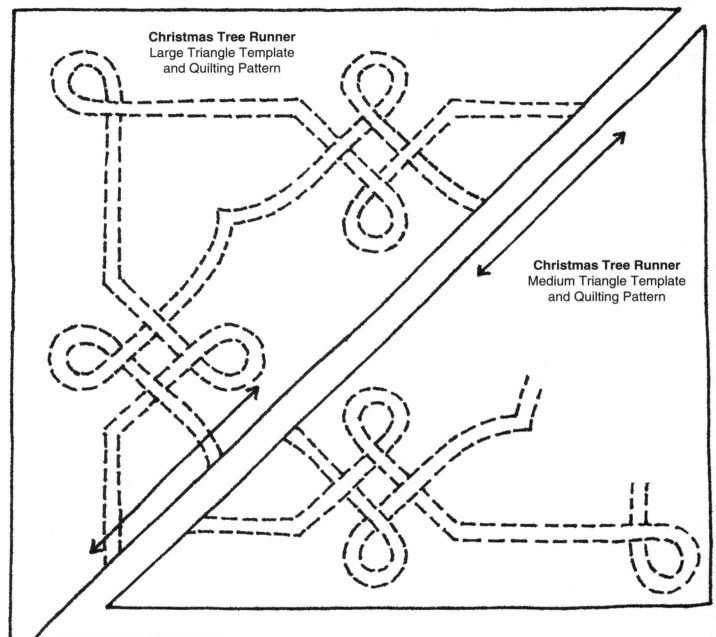

Christmas Tree Runner
Large Triangle Template
and Quilting Pattern

Christmas Tree Runner
Medium Triangle Template
and Quilting Pattern

CHRISTMAS TREE WALL HANGING

Sandra Bair

See picture on p. 100

If done in various greens (23 or 24 pieces used alternately are shown in photograph), 13 different prints are needed. Fat quarters will do.

If done in one color of green, 1 yd. is needed.

1/2 yd. for background

1 fat quarter of dark fabric (maroon) for tree stand

12" square of red fabric for candles

10-12" square of yellow fabric for star and flame

BLOCKS NEEDED

4 background blocks

2 trunk blocks—1/2 of background, 1/2 of maroon (center square maroon)

6 completely green blocks with red candle strip (3 with strip on right, 3 with strip on left)

8 blocks—1/2 of green, 1/2 of background, with green center square (4 with red strip on left, 4 with red strip on right)

Wall hanging may be machine- or hand-pieced. It is important to watch piecing pattern for different sides. Sew 1/4" seams throughout.

When piecing remember that X is the center square. It is green except for corners and stand.

Cut greens and background into 1-1/2" strips. Cut red into 1-1/2" strips.

Sew blocks following general log cabin instructions on page 17 if using one color of green.

If using multiple pieces of green, sew one block at a time to vary placement of the different greens. The candle strip is always the

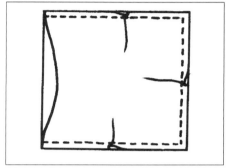

Christmas Tree Wall Hanging
Star Template

**Christmas Tree
Wall Hanging
Flame Template**

third strip sewn on but must be placed on the right half the time and on the left the other half. This means that half the time blocks will be sewn in a clockwise position, and half the time in a counter-clockwise position. Sew blocks together. Sew on borders. Appliqué flames and star. Quilt.

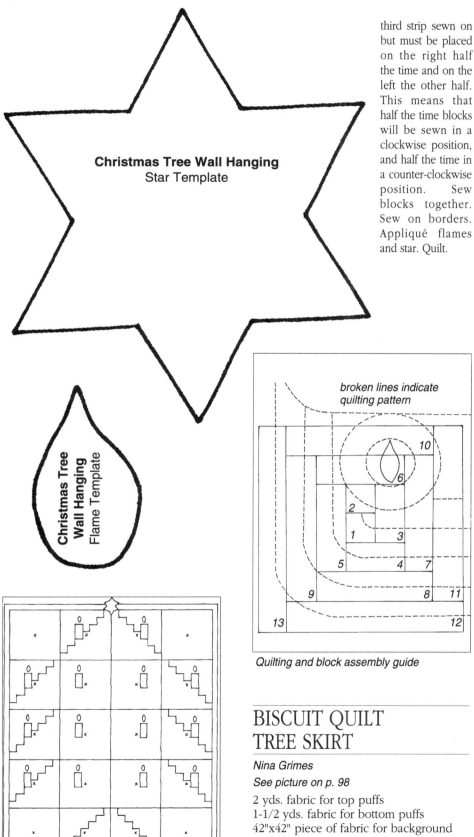

*broken lines indicate
quilting pattern*

Quilting and block assembly guide

Block placement guide

BISCUIT QUILT TREE SKIRT

Nina Grimes

See picture on p. 98

2 yds. fabric for top puffs
1-1/2 yds. fabric for bottom puffs
42"x42" piece of fabric for background

Biscuit quilting is done with machine piecing and the "biscuits" are made with two pieces of fabric. The top piece should be cut 1/2" larger than the bottom piece. The bottom piece should be made of lightweight material, such as muslin. The bottom piece does not show. The top piece may be made of whatever fabric you choose—cotton prints, silks, or materials of comparable weight. Squares may be cut separately with scissors or in several layers using a rotary cutter, a faster method.

Figure 1

SEWING DIRECTIONS FOR ONE BISCUIT
Place wrong sides of squares together. Using a 1/8" seam and starting at one corner, pleat the top (larger) square to fit bottom square. (See Fig. 1.)

Stitch to next corner. Turn and stitch next side.

Continue pleating and stitching until three sides are completed. Then stuff lightly with polyester fiber filling and pleat and stitch fourth and final side.

Join biscuits by placing right sides together and stitching.

DIRECTIONS FOR TREE SKIRT
Biscuit pieces are 4-1/2" square for top, 4" square for bottom.

Using basic biscuit piecing method (see above), make a 12-biscuit by 12-biscuit square. Turn finished square wrong side up. Using a pencil and string, draw a circle on the back.

With long stitch, machine stitch around circle on back side. Cut away excess material outside machine stitching. Cut out a 4" circle in center. From center cut-out, cut a straight line to outside of circle.

Sew lining to back of skirt. Outside edge may be lace- or ruffle-trimmed. Using bias strips, bind inner circle, straight edges, and outer edge.

JEREMIAH BEAR

Kathy Pace

See picture on p. 97

Jeremiah is made from a gorgeous distressed mohair fabric that makes him look like the antique bears so popular in the early 1900s. It would be very difficult to make him out of thick, fake fur with a stiff backing. If you use synthetic fur, look for a thin fur with a soft, woven backing.

1/4 yd. distressed mohair with a woven
    backing
Matching thread
5 sets of 1-1/2" disc/cotter pins or doll
    joints
1 tan 3"x6" piece of wool felt
2 safety eyes, 10 mm
Carpet or button thread or embroidery
    floss
1/2 lb. or 1-1/2 c. weighted plastic pellets
    (optional)
1 yd. wired ribbon for neck (optional)
Polyester fiber filling
Dental floss

A 1/4" seam allowance is included in pattern pieces. Use 1/4" seam allowance throughout.

Cutting: Fold fur in half the long way with fur side in. Cut out pieces from fur and felt as directed on pattern pieces. (See Fig. 1.) Arrows showing fur direction are just a suggestion. Choose a regular head or a head looking up. Mark joint holes in arms and legs. Mark eye dot and dots E and D for ear dart.

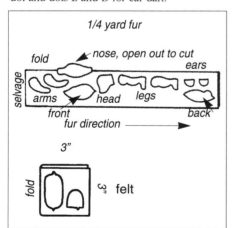

Figure 1

If you use synthetic fur with a back of knitted fabric, be aware that it stretches. You might be happier with the finished product if you cut medium-weight interfacing and sew it to the wrong side of the fabric to stabilize it. Stretchy fur is not recommended. For best results, use 100% wool or mohair pile as used in antique bears.

Joints: Cotter pin/disc joints are easiest to use and fit tightest. Plastic joints tend to loosen up as the fur in the joint area wears down, but they are quicker to use. Both joints are illustrated. (See Figs. 2 and 3.)

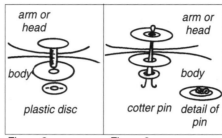

Figure 2   Figure 3

Directions apply to any form of the joint as the term shank is used to describe the part of the joint that goes from arm, leg or head into the body. If using plastic joints, be aware that you may need help to snap the locking disc in place.

RST = Right sides together
RSO = Right side out

CONSTRUCTION

Sew two heads together from A to B, RST. (See Fig. 4.)

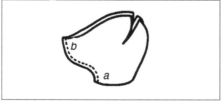

Figure 4

Carefully pin nose to heads, RST, matching notch B (nose) to dot B (head). Ear slits and lower edge should match. Sew where pinned. (See Fig. 5.) Backstitch at ear slits.

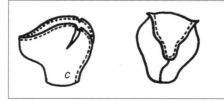

Figure 5

Sew two ears RST from D around to E. Turn right side out and fold as shown, making two tiny tucks. (See Fig. 6.) Baste across lower edge of ear. Repeat for other ear.

Figure 6

Slip ear into head with front of ear facing nose. (Ear will cup forward because of the pleats.) Pin ear into slit. Let 1/4" of raw edges of ear extend past raw edges of head. Sew ear dart from D to E. (See Fig. 7.) Repeat for other

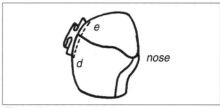

Figure 7

ear. Fasten in safety eyes at dots. Stuff head firmly except for last 1/2" of neck.

Baste around lower edge of head 3/8" from raw edge with two strands of dental floss. Begin with a 10" tail and take long stitches (3/8"). Leave a tail 10" long. Place plastic snap in joint or disc with washer and cotter pin, inside head. (Pin or shank sticks out.) (See Fig. 8a.) Draw up basting thread so raw edges of fabric just touch shank. Tie off thread by tying two ends together, knot firmly. Sew back and forth several times across opening to hold raw

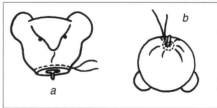

Figure 8

edges together around shank. Then knot ends of thread, backstitch and trim off ends. (See Fig. 8b.)

Use a brush or needle to pull fur out of the seam in the head. Or, optionally, clip off fur 1/4" away from seams at nose. Using a single

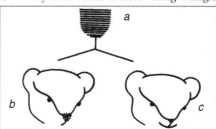

Figure 9

strand of carpet or button thread, stitch nose and mouth, starting with a backstitch. (See Figs. 9a and 9b.) Stitch just over nose seam. Bury a backstitch in nose to end off. (Fig. 9c shows finished nose and mouth.)

Sew two fronts together from G to H, RST. (See Fig. 10a.) Sew two backs together RST from I to J and K to L. Clip to stitching near tail. (See Fig. 10b.)

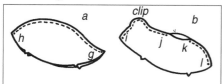

Figure 10

Sew fronts to backs RST, all the way around. Match dots L and G at top, notches for arms and legs, and seam at I and H. Clip tiny holes in fronts just in front of seam at notches and top of body just to the right of center front seam for head (these are joint holes). (See Fig. 11.) Turn right side out.

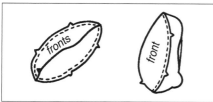

Figure 11

Sew two legs RST from A to B, and from C around leg to D. (See Fig. 12.)

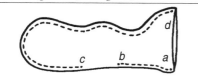

Figure 12

Sew felt foot in opening. Match dots A and D. Clip to stitching on upper leg. (See Fig. 13.)

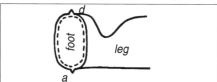

Figure 13

With finished legs laying opposite each other, make joint holes in one layer of leg. Turn leg right side out. Place joint inside leg with shank sticking out through hole. Set aside. (See Fig. 14.)

Figure 14

Make a hole in short arm at joint dot. Sew one felt paw to a short arm RST. Match notch F on arm to notch on paw. (See Fig. 15a.) Sew short arm to regular arm, RST. Backstitch at A and B. Clip to stitching at inner arm. (See Fig. 15b.) Turn right side out, put joint into arm with shank sticking out the hole. Put arm and leg and head shanks into body at correct holes, and fasten, one at a time.

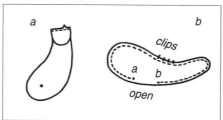

Figure 15

Make sure tail is down, arms face front, paws on inside, legs toward front, toes up. Place a large disc inside body over an arm shank, place washer over shank, next to disc. Gently, but firmly roll up ends of cotter pin to tighten joint. Repeat for other arm, legs and head. See notes on joints.

Stuff legs and arms and hand stitch openings closed. Pour weighted pellets into body, if desired. Stuff upper body gently with enough stuffing to hold the head up nicely and fill out the chest and tummy—not rock hard. Whip-stitch opening closed. If desired, stitch claws on arms and legs. Use a tiny backstitch to secure thread at beginning and end. Make three stitches on paws and feet about 1/4" long, just to seam. Finishing details are shown in Fig. 16.

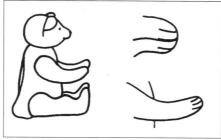

Figure 16

Use a large needle or little brush to lift fur out of seams.

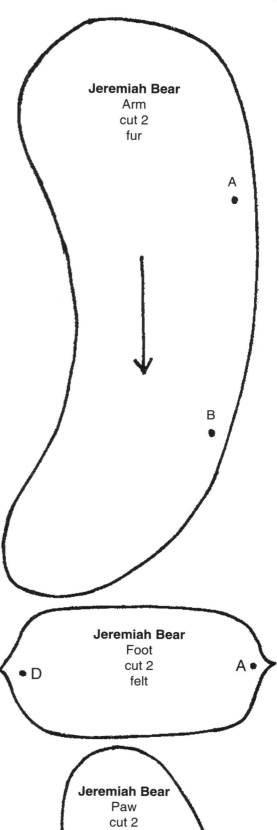

Jeremiah Bear
Arm
cut 2
fur

A

B

Jeremiah Bear
Foot
cut 2
felt

D   A

Jeremiah Bear
Paw
cut 2
felt

F

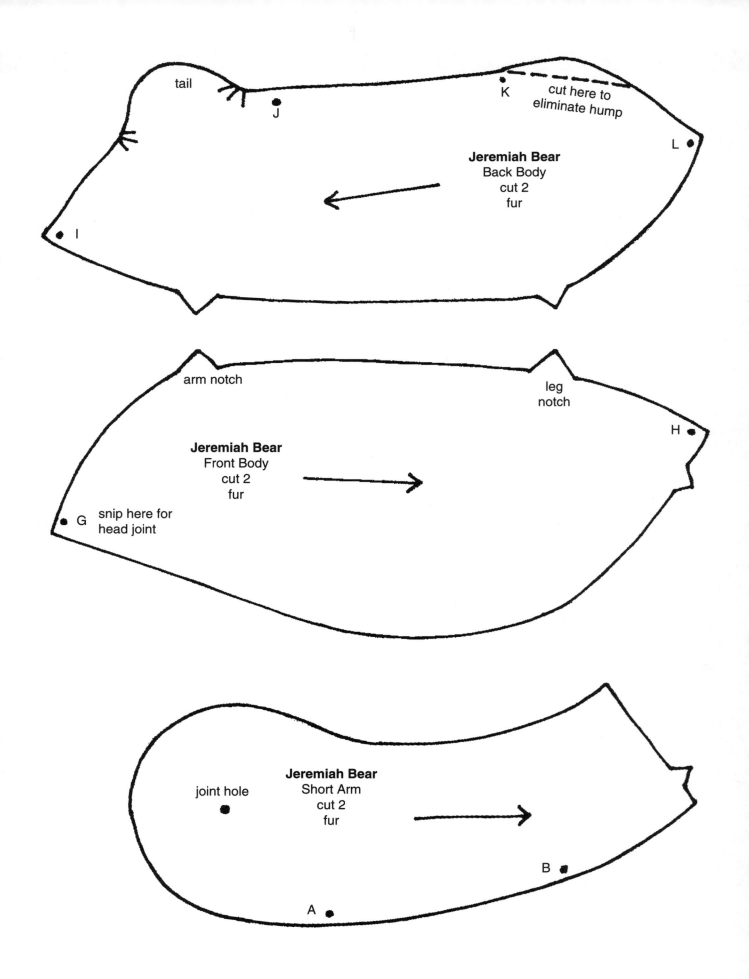

tail

K

cut here to
eliminate hump

J

L

Jeremiah Bear
Back Body
cut 2
fur

I

arm notch

leg
notch

H

Jeremiah Bear
Front Body
cut 2
fur

G snip here for
head joint

joint hole

Jeremiah Bear
Short Arm
cut 2
fur

B

A

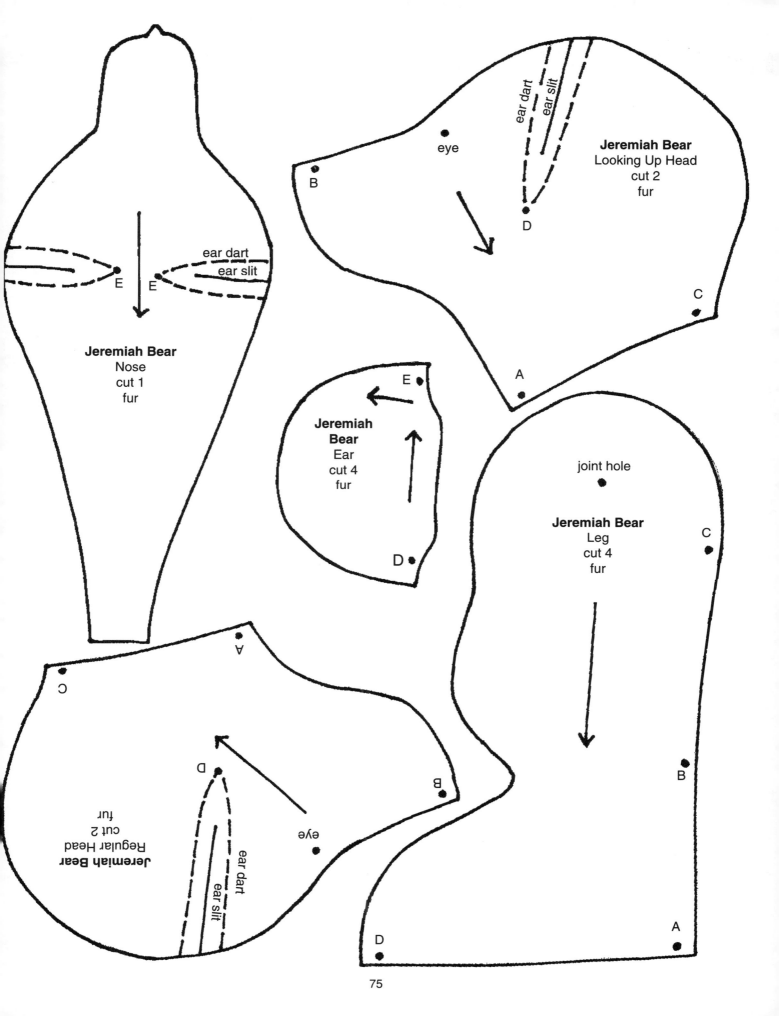

Jeremiah Bear
Nose
cut 1
fur

ear dart
ear slit

Jeremiah Bear
Looking Up Head
cut 2
fur

eye

ear dart
ear slit

B

D

C

A

Jeremiah Bear
Ear
cut 4
fur

E

D

joint hole

Jeremiah Bear
Leg
cut 4
fur

C

B

A

Jeremiah Bear
Regular Head
cut 2
fur

ear dart
ear slit

eye

A

C

D

B

D

75

PERSISTENCE

Marilyn Anderson

See picture on p. 63

13"x14" piece of 14-count Aida cloth
DMC embroidery floss (1 skein each
  color):

x 930 Dark country blue
+ 931 Medium country blue
O 932 Light country blue
  or
x 839 Dark brown
+ 840 Medium brown
O 841 Light brown

Use two strands of floss throughout. Finished
design size is 7"x8" and allows for three inches
of matting on each side.

FAMILIES ARE FOREVER

Rose Anderson

See picture on back cover

15" square of white 14-count Aida cloth
DMC embroidery floss (1 skein each
  color):
316 Mauve
930 Dark country blue

Stitch count is 168 wide x 173 high. See center
markings on pattern to determine starting
point.

Use two strands of floss to stitch words and
outside border and line (mauve).

Use single strand of floss to stitch inside
border (diamonds and window panes) in dark
country blue.

Finished design measures 11-1/2" x12-1/2".
Sampler in picture is framed in 13"x14" silver
frame.

BOWS AND
MORE BOWS

Cathy Crowther

See picture on p. 62

BASIC BOW
Cut 1 yd. of 1-1/2" wide satin ribbon.

Angle cut ends. Lay ribbon on table and loop
toward you twice. Loops are approx 5-6" long.

Pinch and gather up center of bow. Wrap with
1/4" ribbon.

TIP: Always secure bow with narrow ribbon to
obtain a more secure and tighter bow, then

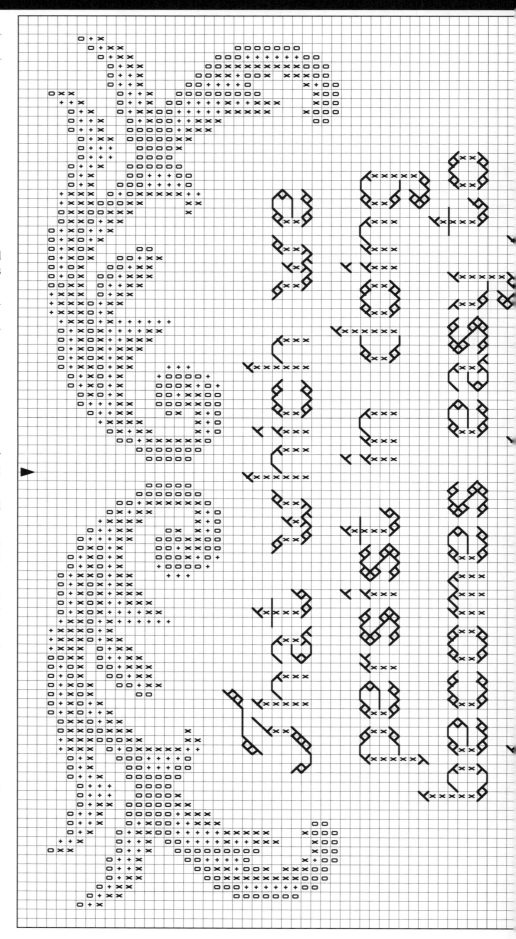

78

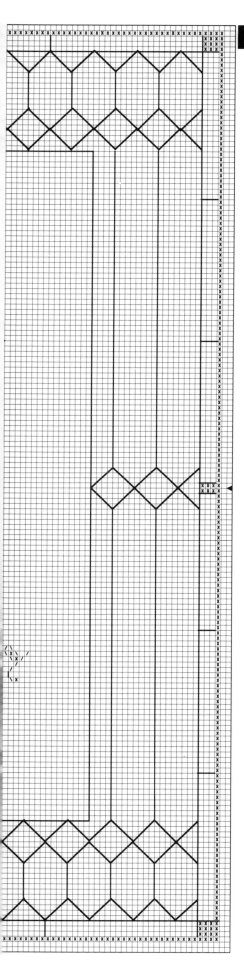

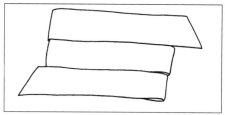

Basic Bow—step one

finish off with a knot and flower of 1/2" ribbon in center.

Finish off edges with Dritz Fray Check.

Basic Bow

VARIATIONS: Use 1" or 2-1/2" wide satin ribbon, or lay 1-1/2" wide lace over ribbon and treat it as one piece.

Place smaller bow on top of larger bow. Vary colors. Place lace, a satin rose, or gathered Battenburg lace in center.

Glue on clip and wrap 1/4" ribbon around center of bow.

Glue knot in back, then wrap around front and secure again in back. It can be loose or tight.

For a French knot center, use 1" or 5/8" ribbon for knot. Tie loose knot.

Basic Bow—wrapping with French knot

BASIC BOW WITH TAILS

See instructions for Basic Bow but use longer lead strips and end with longer strips—38" to 40" satin or grosgrain ribbon.

When gathering up center, take top tail and wrap it around back.

VARIATIONS: Single loop: Also add smaller bow on center of same fold.

Double loop: When finished, fan out loops with fingers. Stretch upper loops up and bottom loops down.

REVERSED BASIC BOW

See Basic Bow instructions. Fold away from you. It gives a different shape.

Reversed Basic Bow—step one

VARIATIONS: It's fun to put a smaller bow of a different color or printed ribbon in center.

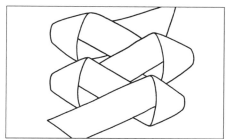

Reversed Basic Bow

EYELET BOW

Use 2" wide gathered eyelet. Cut two 10" strips. Zigzag finished seams right sides up and flat. This results in finished edges on both sides.

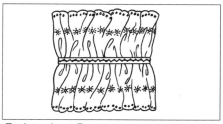

Eyelet or Lace Bow—step one

VARIATIONS: Place a small basic satin bow on top. Place smaller eyelet loop on top of larger bow.

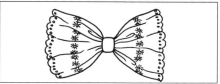

Eyelet or Lace Bow

LACE BOWS

Create beautiful bows by stitching two 10" strips of lace together and making loops and gathering on clips. These bows can be layered by adding different widths of lace. Loop, glue and gather lace. Secure on clip. The best width to secure all bows is 1/4". Then add wide ribbon to finish bow.

LAYERED FABRIC BOW

These are fun because you can make bow to match any outfit. They are also great for formal dances.

Suggested fabrics: Velvet, satin, gold metallics, denim, bandanna prints, taffeta and cotton florals. Use two or three layers.

Cut two of each kind of material. With right sides together, sew 1/4" seam. Leave 1" opening at bottom. Turn right side out. There is no need to finish small opening. There are many ways to decorate center of bow. Be creative!

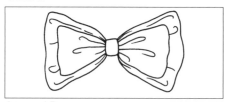

Layered Bow

When you layer, place all openings face down. Gather up the center.

Lay fabrics on top of each other in center. Gather with hands up to middle. Secure with 1/4" ribbon. Glue on clip.

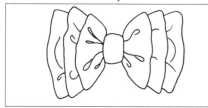

Layered Bow—variation

LAYERED SATIN OR GROSGRAIN BOWS

Cut 2" wide ribbon into three lengths: 14", 12" and 10".

Loop and glue each strip. Then center loops.

Gather loops with 1/4" ribbon. Secure on clip.

Combinations of colors and prints such as polka dots and stripes are fun to experiment with.

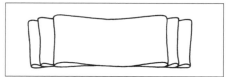

Layered Ribbon Bow—loops

STRIP BOW

Cut four 14" strips of satin or grosgrain ribbon.

Sew the strips together using 1/8" overlap seams. Vary bow by how you pattern the strips together.

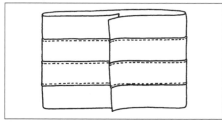

Strip Bow—sewing strips together

Loop the finished product and secure with hot glue. Secure clip with 1/4" ribbon, then place 5/8" ribbon around center to finish off.

Sew a button or French knot in center.

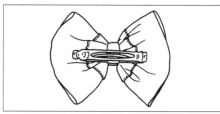

Strip Bow—back view

Vary colors: red, white, red, white or white, white, red, red. Gather with fingers up to the middle, then wrap with 1/4" ribbon. It's fun to do school colors combinations for your children.

VARIATION: Layer with smaller bow.

BASIC HEADBAND

Large Headband: Cut 36" length of 1" wide satin ribbon.

Place 1/4" wide elastic at top of strip in the center. Fold half the ribbon over elastic. Secure elastic with several zigzag stitches at top.

Basic Headband

Stitch down right side. At the end of the ribbon, push ribbon upward and pull elastic down.

Finished product should measure 17-1/2".

Secure bottom same as top with zigzag stitches.

TIPS: Iron ribbon in half to avoid uneven fold. Do not cut elastic. Use large piece and then cut at the end of stitching.

Satin works better than grosgrain. It is softer to wear and easier to fold.

Avoid twisted band by connecting the two ends, matching seam sides before finishing off the band.

Small Headband: Cut 30" strip of satin. Finished product will be 16-1/2" long. Proceed as for large headband.

VARIATIONS: Make fabric headbands using 2" wide ribbon in 36" length.

Use 1-1/2" wide satin for an extra wide headband.

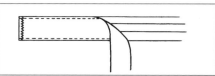

Headband—using two ribbons

Rather than fold over one piece, use two pieces and stitch on both sides. You can even use two colors.

Top headbands with satin bows, silk flowers, gathered lace bows, or gathered pull-string ribbon.

CHIFFON CREPE LACE SCARF

8" strips cut from 45" width fabric

Finish off with pearl edge on serger. Use on ponytail or tied around head with bow or tied on top.

BRIDE'S DRESS FOR BARBIE

Emma Mosser

See picture on p. 99

10"x33" polyester taffeta
10"x33" lace yardage
9"x14" tulle or net veiling
1/2"x1" Velcro fastener
Ten 3/4" silk flowers
30" 1/4" wide polyester ribbon
24" of 3/8" wide polyester ribbon
4-1/2 yds. 3/4" wide pregathered lace
7"x9" "Wonder Under" (optional)

OPTIONS: A taffeta-only gown may be made by omitting lace. If so, omit Wonder Under and apply fusible interfacing to back side of the 7"x9" rectangle of taffeta.

Raw edges may be sealed with "Fray Check" rather than zigzagged.

GENERAL DIRECTIONS

This pattern was designed for a perfect fit for Barbie. Size of side seams, folds and darts will vary the proper fit. Be very accurate! Different weights of fabric will cause the pattern to fit differently, so adjustments may be needed.

RST=right sides together.

One stitch coming loose on these tiny fashions will cause big problems. Back tack beginning and ends of all seams. Starting a seam is easier if you sew onto a scrap of material, and then to the next step.

Trace pattern pieces onto lightweight Pellon or tissue paper to keep pattern pieces intact. This also helps to cut the fabric accurately.

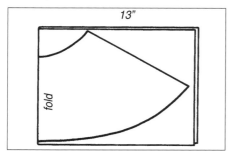

Figure 1

Following layout guide (Fig.1) cut skirt. Before cutting hat and bodice (Fig.2), and following directions for Wonder Under in Glossary, bond 7"x9" rectangle of taffeta and lace yardage together. If preferred, omit Wonder Under and cut hat and bodice out at the same time and baste around edges.

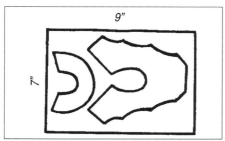

Figure 2

BODICE

Zigzag neck and sleeve edges. Place pregathered lace right side down. With right side of fabric down, align the zigzag edge, overlapping the binding of the lace. Stitch in place. (See Fig. 3.) Turn to right side. Spacing evenly, sew on two rows of lace on indicated

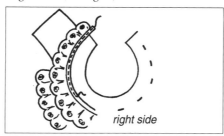

Figure 3

lines. Always keep right side of lace to outside of garment. (See Fig. 4.)

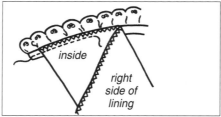

Figure 4

Working from the inside, turn lace toward bodice. Align the edge of the lace binding. Stitch in place. (See Fig. 5.)

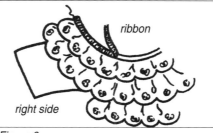

Figure 5

Stitch 1/4" satin ribbon on top of lace binding. (See Fig. 6.)

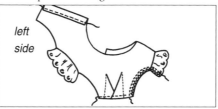

Figure 6

Zigzag center back edges keeping lace straight. Trim. Press left side over 1/4" and baste in place. (See Fig. 7.)

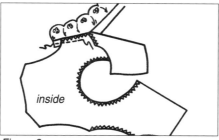

Figure 7

To make darts, fold on line and stitch on dotted lines. Press darts to center front. Baste darts in place at waist. Being careful not to catch lace in seam, with RST, sew seam with regular stitch and again with zigzag stitch. (See Fig. 7.) Trim.

Trial fit bodice on doll and make necessary adjustments. The right back will later be folded over. The waistline needs to be a little big to allow fullness of skirt.

SKIRT

Zigzag bottom edge of taffeta skirt. Sew lace to the hemline same as sleeve edge. (See Fig. 5.) Sew lace trim to hemline of lace skirt same as above. On right side of lace skirt, sew on two rows of lace trim, aligning over lower lace binding. (See Fig. 8a.)

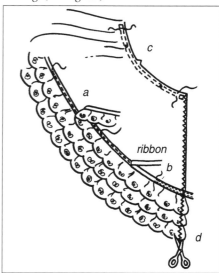

Figure 8

Stitch 3/8" ribbon over bound edge of top row of lace trimming. (See Fig. 8b.) With right sides up, pin lace skirt to taffeta lining, matching center front and having back edges even. Baste waist seam and back edges. (See Fig. 8c.)

Zigzag back edges keeping lace trim straight. Trim excess lace. (See Fig. 8d.) To gather waist, machine baste 1/4" and 1/8" from top edge between squares. Pull top threads to gather. Do not gather 3/8" from ends. (See Fig. 8c.)

Pin skirt to bodice, RST, matching center front notch, circles at side seams and squares at back. Folded left side should be even with edge of skirt. Pull top threads, adjusting gathers to fit. Hand baste. (See Fig. 9.)

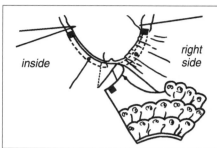

Figure 9

Stitch skirt to bodice. Pull out bottom row of gathering stitches. (See Fig. 9.) Trim even and zigzag seam allowance. Turn seam toward bodice.

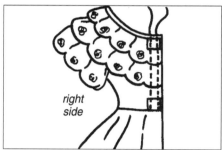

Figure 10

Cut Velcro into 1/4"x1/4" pieces. Sew sticky side on outside of left front, one piece at top and one on top of waist seam. (See Fig. 10.) Fold back edge of right side of bodice over 1/4". Baste. Stitch fuzzy side of Velcro on inside of bodice corresponding left side. Stitch center back seam from lower lace edge to circle and across seam allowance. (See Fig. 11.)

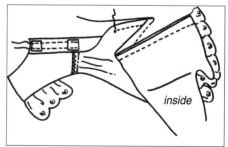

Figure 11

Make bows with 1/4" ribbon. Position a silk flower in center of bow and sew onto skirt ribbon, spacing evenly. See photograph on p. 99. A bow and flower are also centered on bodice neckline ribbon.

HAT

Zigzag curved edges of hat. Sew lace on bottom edge, same as sleeve edge. (See Fig. 12.) Center one row of lace on right side of fabric and stitch in place. (See Fig. 13.) Sew

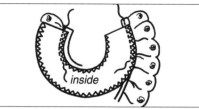

Figure 12

lace and 1/4" ribbon on inside curve same as neckline. (See Fig. 13.)

Figure 13

Zigzag and trim back edges. Fold RST and stitch back seams. (See Fig. 14.)

VEIL

Following Fig. 15, cut tulle or net. To gather, machine baste 1/4" and 1/8" from top edge. (See Fig. 16.) Pull up gathering stitches to 1-1/4". Fasten threads. Center gathered edge on inside of hat at bottom of base. Sew in place being careful to keep lace even on the right side of hat. (See Fig. 17.)

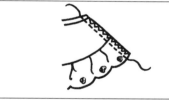

Figure 14

Make a bow with 1/2 yd. of ribbon. Tack on top of stitching with flower on top of bow.

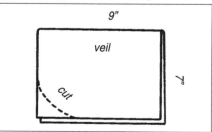

Figure 15

VARIATIONS

The same techniques used to make the bridal gown may be used to design dresses and

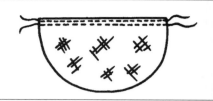

Figure 16

formals for Barbie. For a dress, the materials needed are:

9"x36" of calico blend fabric. Cut skirt
    3-1/2"x14" and a ruffle 2"x28"
7" square of "Wonder Under"
2-1/2 yds. 5/8" wide
    pregathered lace
2-1/4 yds. of
    rickrack
    trim

1/2"x1"
Velcro
fastener

For a formal, materials needed are same as for dress above, except the skirt should be

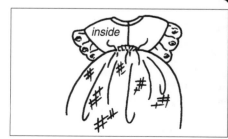

Figure 17

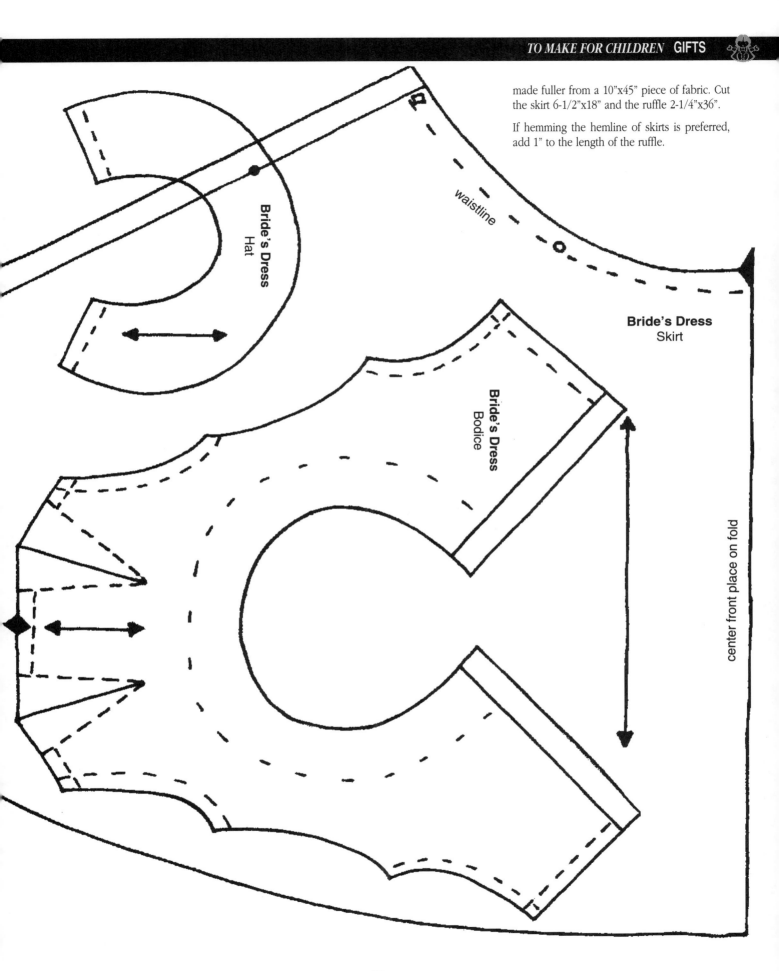

made fuller from a 10"x45" piece of fabric. Cut the skirt 6-1/2"x18" and the ruffle 2-1/4"x36".

If hemming the hemline of skirts is preferred, add 1" to the length of the ruffle.

Bride's Dress
Hat

waistline

Bride's Dress
Skirt

Bride's Dress
Bodice

center front place on fold

CHILD'S CHRISTMAS SWEATSHIRT

Deanna Hartvigsen
See picture on p. 99

1/4 yd. Christmas fabric
Tacky glue
Scribbles paints in assorted colors
Craft plastic
Sweatshirt
1/4 yd. "Wonder Under"

Purchase ready-made sweatshirt, or buy a white sweatshirt and dye with Rit dye according to directions.

Fuse tree to shirt following Wonder Under instructions in Glossary.

Cut out desired number of ornaments from craft plastic and glue the edges only to the tree using Tacky glue. Cut out star for tree top from craft plastic, and adhere edges only to the top of tree with Tacky glue.

Place piece of cardboard inside sweatshirt. Using Scribbles paints, seal edges of tree, ornaments and star. Use a fine, thin line of paint. Thick lines will chip off when dry.

Let sweatshirt dry for 48 hours before wearing. Launder inside out.

STOCKING DOLL

Ruby Henderson
See picture on p. 99

Ladies' cotton
  stocking, size 11 or
  11-1/2 or
Ladies' stocking,
  size 9-11,
  75% cotton
  and 25%
  nylon

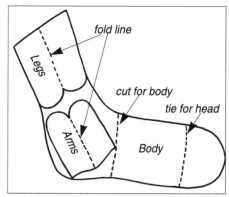

Figure 1

DMC embroidery floss,
  Light blue and Pink
1/2 yd. fabric for dress
20" of 1/4" wide elastic
2-1/2 yds. of 1/2"
  wide lace
Bias tape
Needle
String
Polyester
  fiber
  filling
Yarn (for
  hair)

**Child's Christmas
Sweatshirt
Tree**

Ornament

Star

Cut doll parts from stocking according to diagram in Fig. 1.

Stuff body with polyester fiber filling. Tie string on line (see Fig. 1) after body has been stuffed.

Sew 1/4" seam to finish arm and leg pieces. Turn and stuff. (See Fig. 2.)

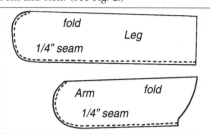

Figure 2

Sew arm and legs to body. (See Fig. 3.)

Figure 3

Cut cardboard 7" x 14". Wind yarn lengthwise around the cardboard 70 times.

Carefully remove yarn strands for hair from cardboard and sew down center of yarn. (See Fig. 4.)

Cut a piece of heavy paper 4"x1". Wind yarn around paper 60 times for bangs. Sew across top of paper. (See Fig. 5.) Tear paper out of yarn.

Embroider eyes using a satin stitch in light blue, nose and mouth in pink. (See Fig. 3.)

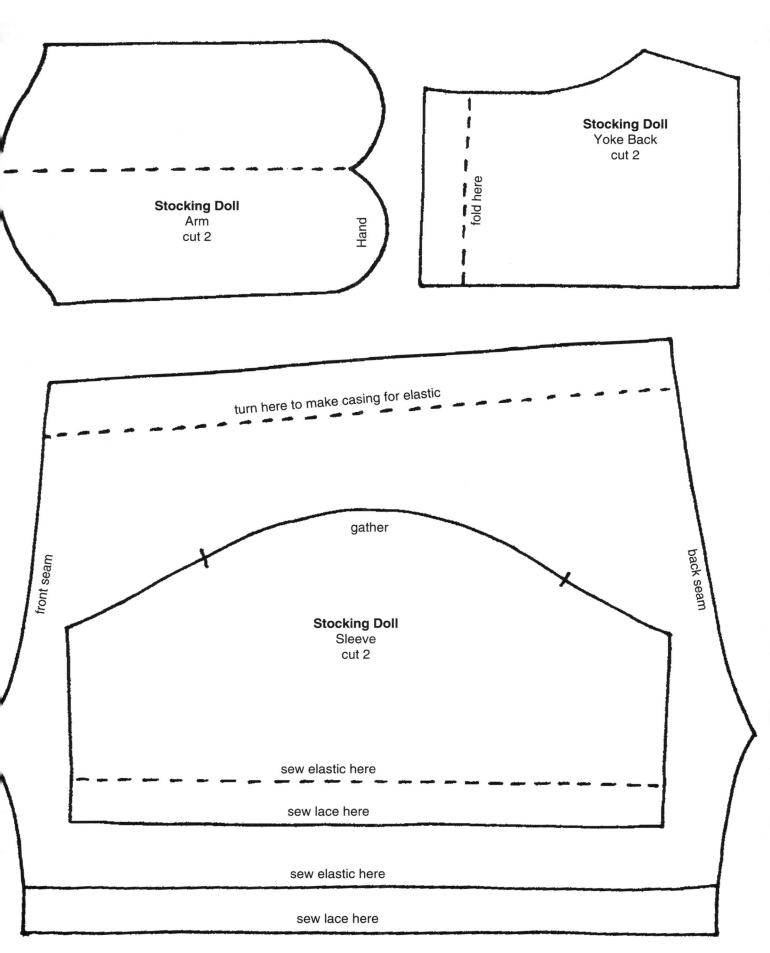

Stocking Doll
Arm
cut 2

Hand

Stocking Doll
Yoke Back
cut 2

fold here

turn here to make casing for elastic

gather

front seam

back seam

Stocking Doll
Sleeve
cut 2

sew elastic here

sew lace here

sew elastic here

sew lace here

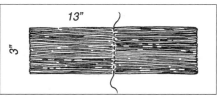

Figure 4

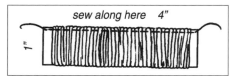

Figure 5

Sew hair and bangs to head. Tie yarn to form ponytails.

DOLL DRESS
Cut out dress according to pattern. Use 5/8" seams where indicated on pattern. Cut a 2" slit in top center back of skirt piece.

Figure 6

Gather where indicated on pattern.

Cut a piece of material 1-1/2"x45" for ruffle on bottom of gown. Gather and sew ruffle to bottom of gown.

Sew gathered lace around neck and bind with bias binding. Sew lace to bottom of sleeve. Sew lace to bottom of panty.

Sew elastic on markings on sleeve and panty.

Turn top of panty piece under 1/2" to make casing for elastic. Sew 8" piece of elastic to marked line on edge of sleeve piece.

Turn under facing on back yoke pieces and stitch in place. Sew yoke to gown. Use snaps or buttons to close. Sew sleeves to gown. Sew seams.

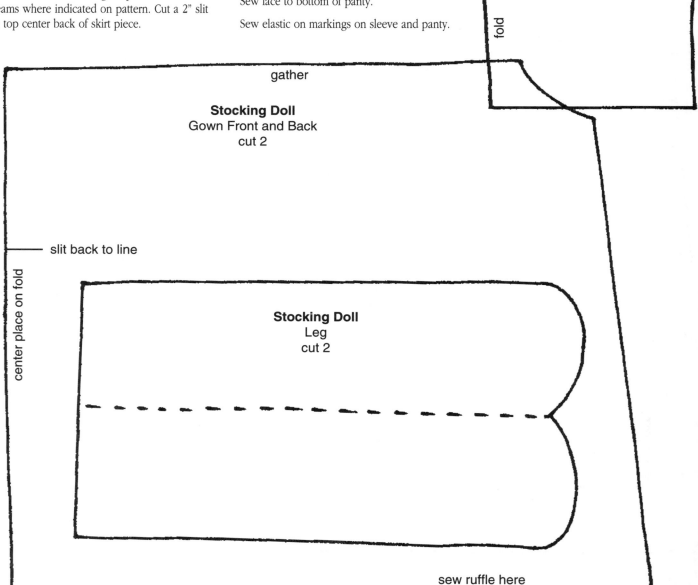

ALEXANDRA'S BONNET

Vanisha Griggs

See picture on p. 63

Directions are for newborn size

20"x7" Swiss batiste
20"x 1-1/2" Swiss batiste
Two 10"x1/2" pieces Swiss embroidery
One 10"x1/2" piece French lace
20" French edging (fine 1/2" wide lace)
Two 12" French edging
1/2 yd. of 1/4" wide ribbon
1 yd. of 1" wide ribbon

Make fancy band. (See Fig. 1.)Sew one piece of Swiss embroidery (embroidered batiste tape insertion) to French lace by trimming off excess batiste and zigzag (2.0 width, 1.0 length) into the holes of the lace insertion piece and into the heading of the French lace.

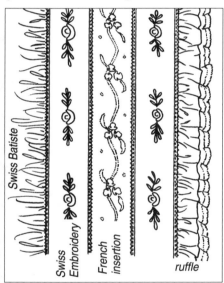

Figure 1

Apply second piece of Swiss embroidery on opposite side of French insertion.

Gather 20"x7" of Swiss batiste and sew to Swiss embroidery.

Apply lace edging to 20"x1-1/2" piece of fabric. Gather and apply to front for the ruffle batiste edge to Swiss embroidery edge.

Apply lace edging on both sides of bonnet. Miter corners where the 2 laces meet at front of bonnet. Make a 1/4" casing in back of bonnet. Run an 18" piece of 1/4" ribbon through back casing. Tie into a bow.

Sew 36" piece of 1" ribbon to side of bonnet. Secure with bullion roses.

WOODEN DOLL

Sharlene Wayment

See picture on p. 99

Doll cut from 1" pine wood
Apron cut from 1/2" pine wood
Heart cut from 1/2" pine wood
Acrylic paints: Flesh tone, Ivory, and color desired for dress
7 pieces of twine 1-1/2" long (hair)
7 bows of 1/8" wide ribbon for hair
7 ribbon pieces 9" long for bow
2 ribbon roses for apron

RIBBON COLORS

White

Red or Burgundy

Purple or Mauve

Blue or Country Blue

Orange or Peach

Yellow

Green or Mint Green

Paint face, hands, and legs in flesh tone.

Paint dress on doll any color desired. Paint apron ivory.

Paint heart base color to match dress.

Paint or draw face on—apply blush to cheeks and knees.

Glue heart (feet) to legs with tip of heart to t h e back.

Glue wooden apron to front of doll. Tie a knot in the end of each piece of twine. Glue knots to head,

spacing equally. Glue the 7 small bows to each knot of hair.

With 9" pieces of ribbon held together, tie a bow. Glue to front of apron. Embellish with ribbon roses.

Wooden Doll
Heart

Wooden Doll

Wooden Doll
Apron

CLOTHESPIN DOLL

Linda Wilcock

See picture on p. 100

4 round clothespins
One 38mm x 12mm hole natural bead
6" copper wire cut into 3" pieces
Acrylic paints: White, Black, and Flesh
Fixative spray
Stylus (optional)
10" of fleece or roving for hair
3" straw hat
12"x5" piece of calico print fabric
Scrap of fabric for apron
Muslin for pantaloons
2 5-1/2" pieces of bias tape
1 yd. of 1/2" wide lace
Ribbon
Carpet thread
Pastel chalk to blush cheeks
Hot-glue gun

PREPARING PINS
Cut one pin in half down center lengthwise to make 2 arms. Cut 1/2" off other 2 whole pins inside only (see Fig. 1) to make legs.

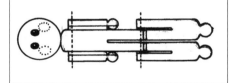

Figure 1

Sand down ball on fourth pin to fit hole in bead. Glue on bead to form head. Drill small hole through tops of body pin 1/4" from bottom of head. Also drill small holes 1/4" from bottom of body pin.

Drill holes in arms and legs 1/4" from bottom. (See Fig. 1.)

FACE
Paint face with the flesh color paint. Let dry. Using stylus, dip large end into black paint and dot the eyes. Dip stylus back in to paint for each eye to keep even. Let eye dry and highlight with white dots made with small end of stylus.

Using small makeup brush or soft bristle brush blush cheeks with pastel chalk. Spray with fixative spray and allow to dry.

HAIR
Cut 1" off the fleece and sew to scrap of lace lengthwise so lace does not show. Glue to head for bangs. Find center of remaining piece of fleece and sew lace to it forming center part. Glue lace to head. After glue has dried

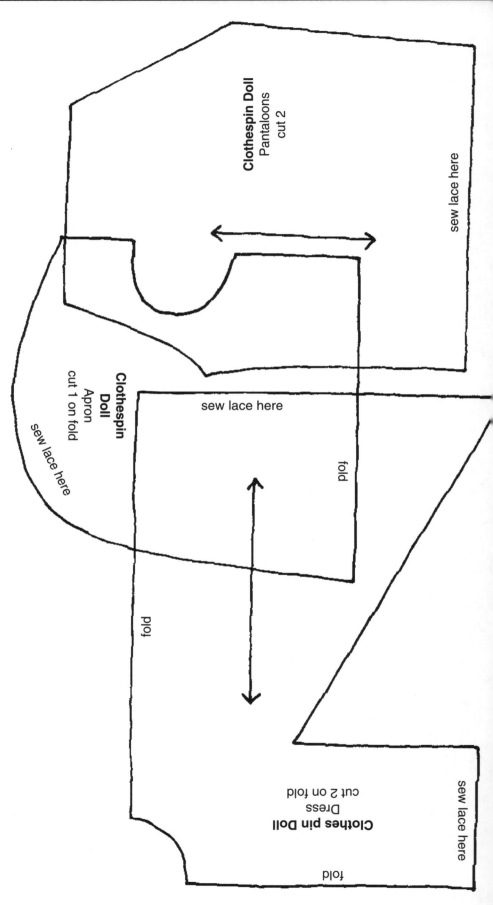

braid each side of hair and tie off braid with string or thin wire. Trim.

Tie a ribbon bow around the string to finish hair. Place hat on head and glue in place.

PANTALOONS
Cut two pieces (see pattern).

Fold under 1/4" and sew lace on bottom of leg edge. With right sides together sew up leg seams using 1/4" seam allowance. Put right sides together matching inseam. Sew 1/4" seam allowance. Turn right side out.

Run gathering stitch around top of pantaloons and put on doll body. Draw tight. Tie knot to secure.

DRESS
Sew lace to edge of sleeves. With right sides together sew from sleeve to bottom of dress on each side. Sew finished edge of lace over raw edge of fabric at bottom of dress.

Run a gathering stitch around neck and sleeves. Put dress on doll and turn under neck Pull tight and tie.

APRON
Fold under 1/4" edge on front top of apron. Use bias tape around arm and leave 1-1/2" above top of apron to form strap.

Sew lace around bottom of apron. Gather front yoke to 1/2" in width.

Place apron on doll with straps over shoulder. Stitch straps and back of apron together to close.

DOLL BLANKET

See picture on p. 99

3/4 yd. print baby fabric
3/4 yd. Pellon fleece (two pieces, each 27"x23")

Cut print fabric in half. Put right sides together. Cut Pellon fleece the same size as the halved print fabric. Place the Pellon on top of print fabric and pin all three layers together. Sew together using a 1/4" seam allowance on all sides, leaving a 6" opening. Turn right side out and slip stitch the opening closed. Tie with baby yarn in desired colors.

BUG CONDO

Jeff Clark
See picture on p. 99

1/4" pine wood
14"x7-1/2" piece of screen

Wood glue
Screw to hold door in place
Paint or stain
Rope to use for handle
1/8" dowel cut to hang out 1" on each side of box
Duct tape
Small finishing nails

Drill hole for dowel in the two short sides where indicated. Place dowel in holes and glue in place.

Put wood glue on the top of side A. Place side C on top of glue and let dry. Turn over and nail into place using small finishing nails. Do the same thing to sides B and D.

Attach door with screw in wood side D. Find the middle edge of screen (lengthwise) and staple it to the top center of sides C and D.

Continue stapling down the sides, keeping it very tight. Turn over and pull screen tight, staple the screen on the bottom of base for better support.

To finish, stain or paint the wood. Decorate by painting pictures of your child's favorite bugs. The bugs you catch will feel right at home.

PILLOWCASE

See picture on p. 98

1 yd. Christmas fabric
1/4 yd. contrasting fabric

Fold 1/4 yd. of contrasting fabric in half lengthwise, wrong sides together. Pin folded piece to raw edge of 1-yd. piece, right sides together, match cut edges and sew with 1/4" seam allowance. (See Fig. 1.)

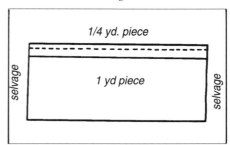

Figure 1

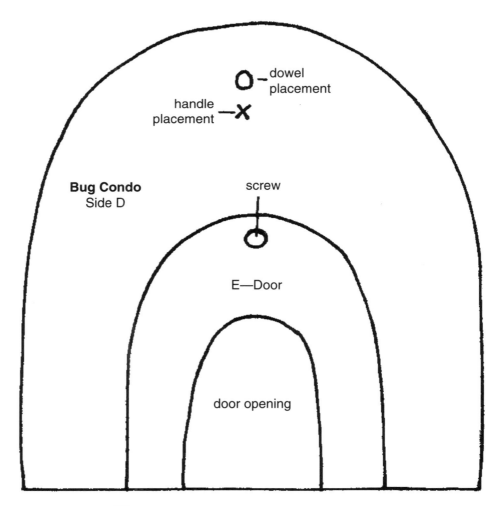

Press seam away from the 1/4 yd. of fabric. With right sides together fold fabric in half matching selvage edges. Stitch across cut end and down the side using 1/4" seam. (See Fig. 2.)

Turn pillowcase right side out.

If you have a zigzag machine or a serger, it is nice to finish the seams. This makes a large pillowcase. To make it standard size, shorten

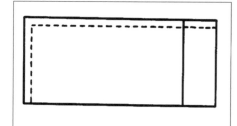

Figure 2

about 10". When giving as a gift, the following poem could be included.

PILLOWCASE POEM

December the first starts a magical time,
With all sorts of colors, ribbons, and
*   rhyme. . .*
Sugar plum fairies will dance in your
*   head . . .*
If you put this special pillowcase on your bed.

The reason it's special, as you will soon see
Is that it's been dusted with Christmas
*   Fancy!!*
Visions of candy canes, Santa and treasures
Will fill each dream with sweetness and
*   pleasures.*
When the time comes for it to be washed
Do it quickly so no magic is lost.

JOINTED BUNNY

Brenda Bench

See picture on p. 99

Scroll saw to cut wood pieces
1/2" pine wood
Two 12" pieces of twine
Drill with small bit
Small 1" sponge brush
Paint brush (small)
Acrylic paints: Antique white, Stoneware
    blue, Rose and Black
Inexpensive black fine-tipped art pen
Old toothbrush for flecking

Cut out pattern pieces and sand edges. Using sponge brush paint all pieces, front and back, with antique white. Let dry.

Using pattern as example, paint middle of ears blue with small brush. Paint nose, tail, and large part of paw with rose. Using end of paint brush, make three dots for paw.

To make eyes and mouth use rounded end of paint brush. Dip in black paint and dot for eyes first, then mouth. Let dry.

To fleck, put blue paint on the end of toothbrush as you would toothpaste. With bristles down, run finger nail along the bristles until you get the amount of flecks desired on the bunny.

Drill holes all the way through wood pieces as indicated on pattern.

Knot one end of twine. Thread free end through the hole and knot, making sure twine is tight. NOTE: For help in working with twine, put wood glue on free end and let dry 10 minutes. Then thread through.

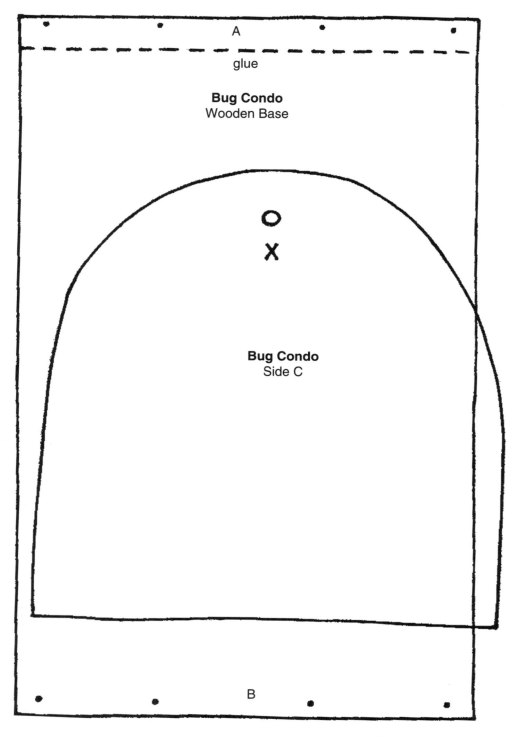

A

glue

Bug Condo
Wooden Base

O
X

Bug Condo
Side C

B

Jointed Bunny
cut 1
1/2" pine

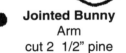

Jointed Bunny
Arm
cut 2 1/2" pine

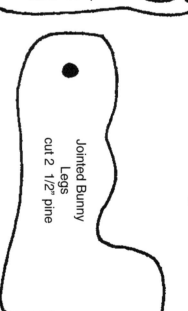

Jointed Bunny
Legs
cut 2 1/2" pine

Make sure paws are painted on insides of wood pieces and threaded that way.

Cut off excess twine.

HORSE JUMP ROPE

Nola J. Stever
See picture on p. 99

1/4 yd. fabric (makes two)
Small piece of coordinating felt
16" coordinating 1/4" wide ribbon
4 small black beads (eyes)
16 yds. of coordinating yarn
72" piece of plastic clothesline
Polyester fiber filling
Button and carpet thread
Hot-glue gun

Wrap yarn around 3" piece of cardboard, or use hairpin lace maker, to make about 7" of mane. Sew down middle. Cut into two 3-1/2" pieces, and set aside.

Cut two horse heads from fabric; cut four ears from felt; cut 8" piece of ribbon into two 4" pieces.

Fold one piece of mane in half and place on inside of horse head. Fold over and stitch, leaving bottom open for stuffing. Clip curves and turn. (See Fig. 1.)

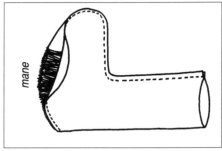

Figure 1

Stuff firmly. Sew on eyes, and trim mane. Put a dot of glue on nose to secure bridle, and glue under chin.

Make about a 3/4" indentation in fiber filling and put in a dab of hot glue. Put one end of clothesline in. The glue secures it while you turn under a 1/4" hem and sew a gathering stitch around the bottom. Pull tight and knot. Put needle through clothesline three or four times, and knot. (See Fig. 2.)

Repeat for other end of line, and you are done!

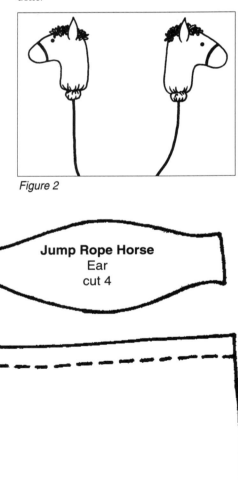

Figure 2

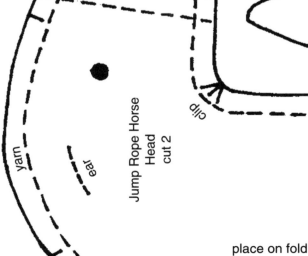

Jump Rope Horse
Ear
cut 4

yarn

ear

clip

Jump Rope Horse
Head
cut 2

place on fold

BARRETTE HOLDER DOLL

Cathy Finnegan
See picture on p. 99

6-1/2" circle cut out of 1/2" pine
1 skein of yarn (any color)
Acrylic paints: Fleshtone, Light green,
    Dark green, White, Black, Adobe
8-1/2" straw hat
Ribbon, 1/2" wide, to tie two bows

FACE

Start with the fleshtone and paint the front and sides of circle. Trace with a stylus or pencil the eyes, nose, mouth, cheeks, and hearts. Paint the eyes with white. Paint the iris light green.

Float the nose, mouth, and hearts with adobe. Float bottom of iris with dark green.

Blush cheeks with stencil brush and blusher. With black, fill pupil and line eyes, eyelashes, nose, and mouth. Highlight when dry with white. Dot eyes. (See pattern for detail.)

HAIR

Cut a heavy piece of cardboard 24" square. Wrap yarn around until desired thickness.

Cut through yarn at one end and open up. Tie one end with yarn and have someone hold on to it while you braid the rest. Tie other end and cut both ends even.

Take another 2" piece of cardboard and wrap the yarn around it about 10 times. Slip off and tie in the middle to make a little bundle. Make 15 bundles.

Glue bundles to head starting at the top center and continuing to center side of head. Do the same on other side. (See pattern for hair placement.) Glue braid over head and along sides, making sure it is centered.

Place hat on hair and glue in place. Make a slight cut in back of hat to hang.

HOLLY SUE AND KITTY PAPER DOLLS

Sue Higley
See picture on p. 99

Copy paper doll and glue to heavy paper for added strength. Copy clothes to paper and color with crayons. Cut out and enjoy.

Be creative and make new clothes to fit Holly Sue.

VARIATION

Cut doll out of 1/4" wood and paint. Cut clothes out of pellon or felt and attach to doll using small Velcro pieces.

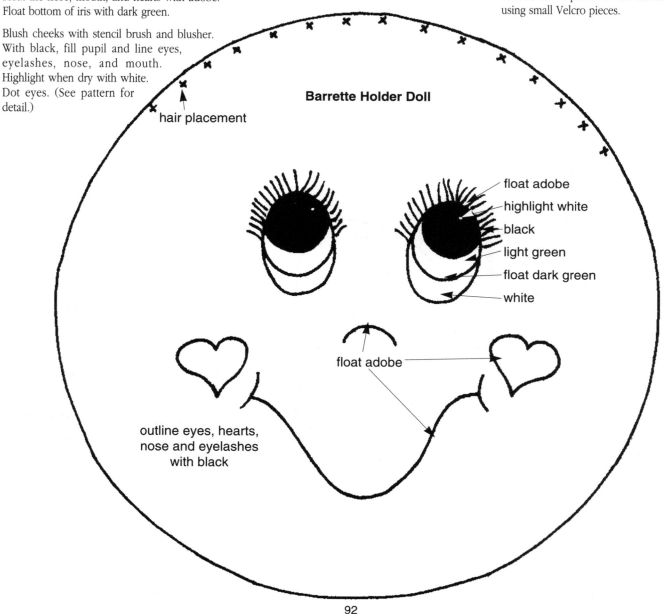

Barrette Holder Doll

hair placement

float adobe
highlight white
black
light green
float dark green
white

float adobe

outline eyes, hearts, nose and eyelashes with black

Kitty

Holly & Sue

93

KATE'S TUTU

Vanisha Griggs
See picture on p. 27

1/2 yd. fine netting
1-3/4 yd.1" wide ribbon
2-1/4 yds.1/4" wide ribbon
3 large ribbon roses
6 small ribbon roses

Cut 1 piece of netting 10"x45" and another 8"x45". Gather both pieces on one side of netting (long side).

Cut 1 piece of 1" wide ribbon 48" long and center both pieces of netting 9" from center. (See Fig.1.) Sew.

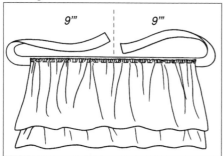

Figure 1

Cut 1 piece 1" wide ribbon 18" long and make a sandwich of netting between the two pieces of ribbon. Sew all four sides. (See Fig. 2.)

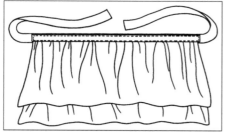

Figure 2

Cut three pieces of 1/4" ribbon 24" long. Tie into bows. Sew in center and 4-1/2" out on both sides. (See Fig. 3.)

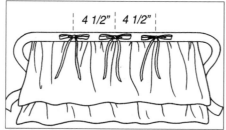

Figure 3

Embellish tutu with ribbon roses and your little ones will be the most beautiful ballerinas around.

MIMI'S RABBIT

Ann Nelson
See picture on p. 64

1/2 yd. fabric for body
1 yd. fabric for dress and bonnet
Matching thread
1 yd. fabric for apron and bloomers
Matching thread
Interfacing for ears and bonnet brim
1 yd. lace (optional)
4 yds. thin elastic
1-1/4 yds. 3/8" wide ribbon
Embroidery thread, Dark brown
Polyester fiber filling

Finished rabbit is 15" high (not including ears)

HEAD
Sew notched fronts of head together. Clip. (See Fig. 1.)

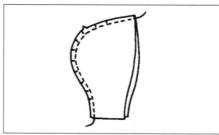

Figure 1

Sew darts in ears. Iron or stitch interfacing to wrong side. Sew right sides of ears together, leaving straight edge open. Then clip. (See Fig. 2.)

Figure 2

Turn ears right side out, press. Place ears on right side of head front. Sew in place.

Sew notched backs of head together. (See Fig. 3.) With right sides together, sew front of head to back, leaving straight edge open. Clip. Turn right side out. Stuff head with fiber filling

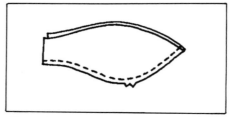

Figure 3

firmly. (See Fig. 4.) Then sew straight edge closed.

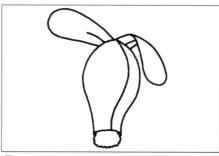

Figure 4

ARMS
With right sides together sew arms, leaving ends open. Turn right side out. Stuff with fiber filling. Sew end closed. (See Fig. 5.)

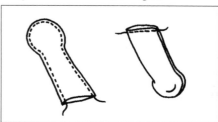

Figure 5

FEET
Sew double notched front of feet together. Clip. Reinforce edge of sole by stay-stitching around notched edges. With right sides together, sew sole to foot, and clip. (See Fig. 6.)

Turn right side out. Stuff firmly. Sew straight edge closed.

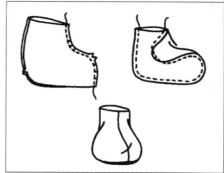

Figure 6

BODY
Place arms on body front and sew. (See Fig. 7.) Sew body pieces right sides together. (See Fig. 8.) Gather-stitch leg edges. DO NOT sew inner leg area. (See Fig. 9.)

Position feet on right side, inside leg. Adjusting gathers, pin feet to leg edge and sew. (See Fig. 10.) NOW sew inner leg and clip.

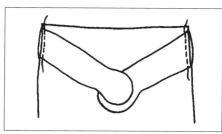
Figure 7

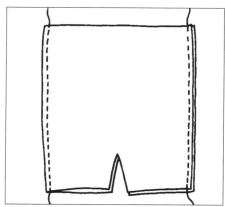
Figure 8

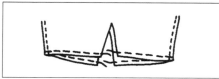
Figure 9

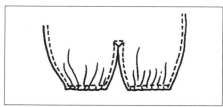
Figure 10

Turn right side out. Gather neck edge. In front, on right side, sew head to neck over tight gathers.

Loosely stuff body. Hand stitch head to neck all the way around.

Embroider eyes, going through head to give shape. Embroider nose.

BLOOMERS

Sew single notched edge of center fronts together. Clip.

Turn bottom edge under 1/4", sewing lace to that line. Zigzag thin elastic on bloomer ankles, stretching elastic to fit fabric as you sew.

Press upper edge along solid line. On wrong side zigzag elastic over fold, stretching elastic to fit fabric as you sew. (See Fig. 11.)

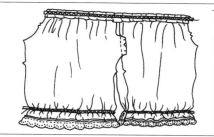
Figure 11

Stitch double notched edges together (center back seam). Clip. With right sides together sew front to back at inner leg seam. Turn right side out. (See Fig. 12.)

Figure 12

DRESS

Zigzag thin elastic on "elastic" line on sleeve, stretching elastic to fit fabric as you sew. Stitch small hem. (See Fig. 13.)

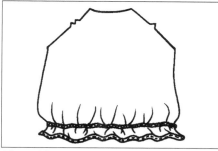
Figure 13

With right sides together, sew sleeves to front and back. Clip seams. Turning center back under, stitch small hem. (See Fig. 14.) Gather stitch neck line.

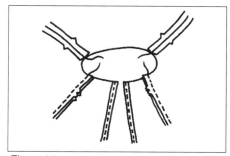
Figure 14

Press bias strip in half. With right sides together, sew bias to neck line. Pull up gather stitches to fit evenly. Slip-stitch pressed edge of bias over gathered edge.(See Fig. 15.)

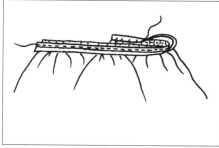
Figure 15

Sew side seams. Clip under arm. Press seams and sew small hem. (See Fig. 16.)

Figure 16

APRON

No pattern piece is given for apron. Fold apron fabric. Using folded edge as center front of apron, cut a 10"x15-1/2" piece of apron fabric. Open out apron. Sew a 1/4" hem in upper edge. Zigzag thin elastic along a straight line 1-1/4" from upper edge, stretching elastic to fit fabric as you sew. Sew a 1/4" hem on center back edge and a 1-1/2" hem at bottom of apron. (See Fig. 17.)

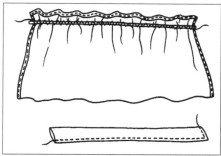
Figure 17

Fold straps in half and sew on wrong side, leaving one end open. (See Fig. 18.) Turn right side out and press. Sew straps to each side of center front placing edge of strap 2" from center front fold and along elastic casing line

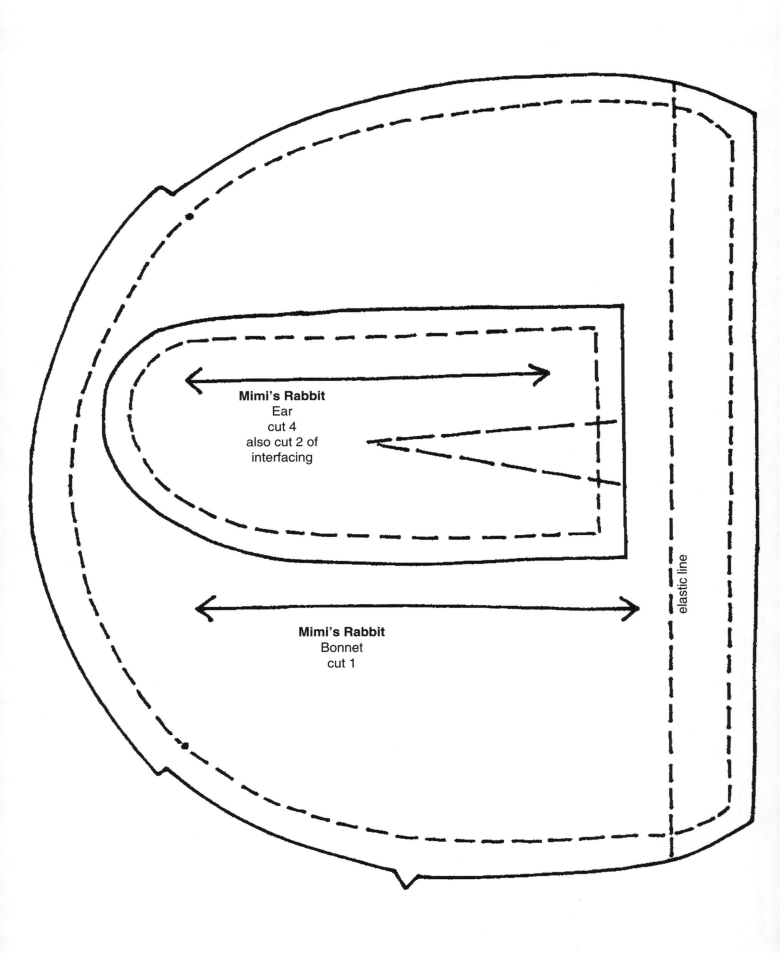

Mimi's Rabbit
Ear
cut 4
also cut 2 of
interfacing

Mimi's Rabbit
Bonnet
cut 1

elastic line

On wall: Hand-pieced Center Square Quilt, p. 60. On quilt and on back of bench: Angel Garland and Hanging Angel, p. 2. On bench starting at left of picture: Dresden Plate Pillow, p. 49; Potpourri, p. 154; Jeremiah Bear, p. 72; Scented Fire Starters, p. 120; Christmas Ball with Doily, p. 4; Basket Pillow, p. 50.

Starting with Christmas Tree Wall Hanging, p. 70; then clockwise: Crazy Quilt Pillow, p. 59; Angel and Heart Garland, p. 3; (on floor) Christus Cross-stitch Picture, p. 54; Clothespin Doll, p. 88; 24" Santa, p. 45; Poinsettia Center Table Runner, p. 160; (center) Christmas Bear Ornament, p. 4.

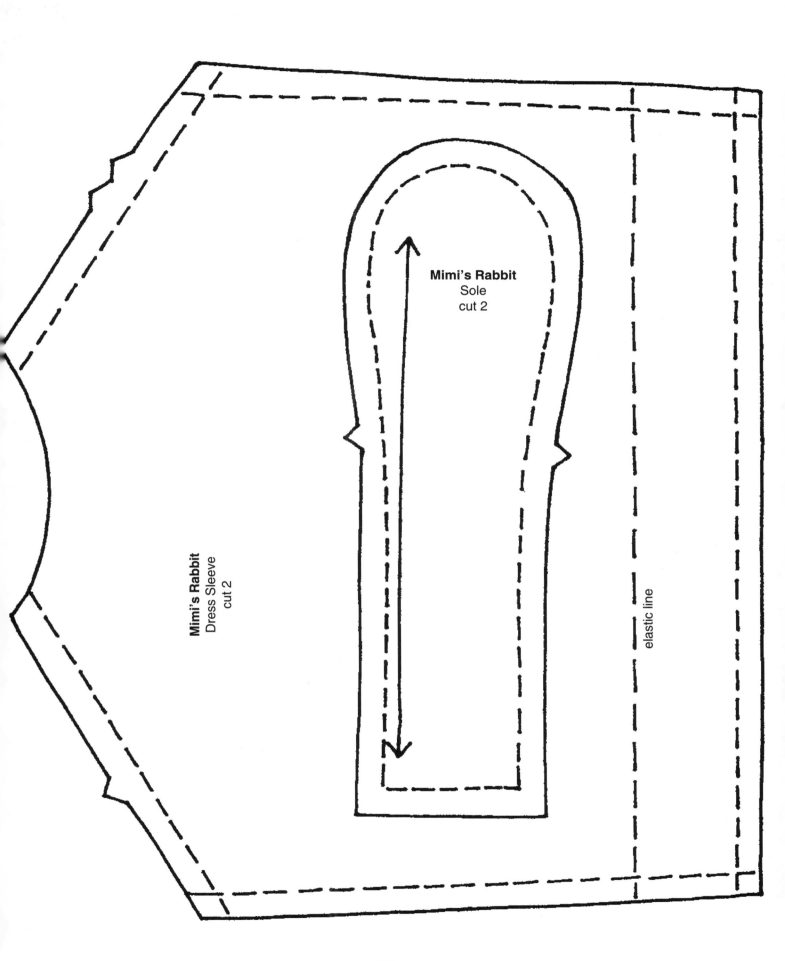

Mimi's Rabbit
Sole
cut 2

Mimi's Rabbit
Dress Sleeve
cut 2

elastic line

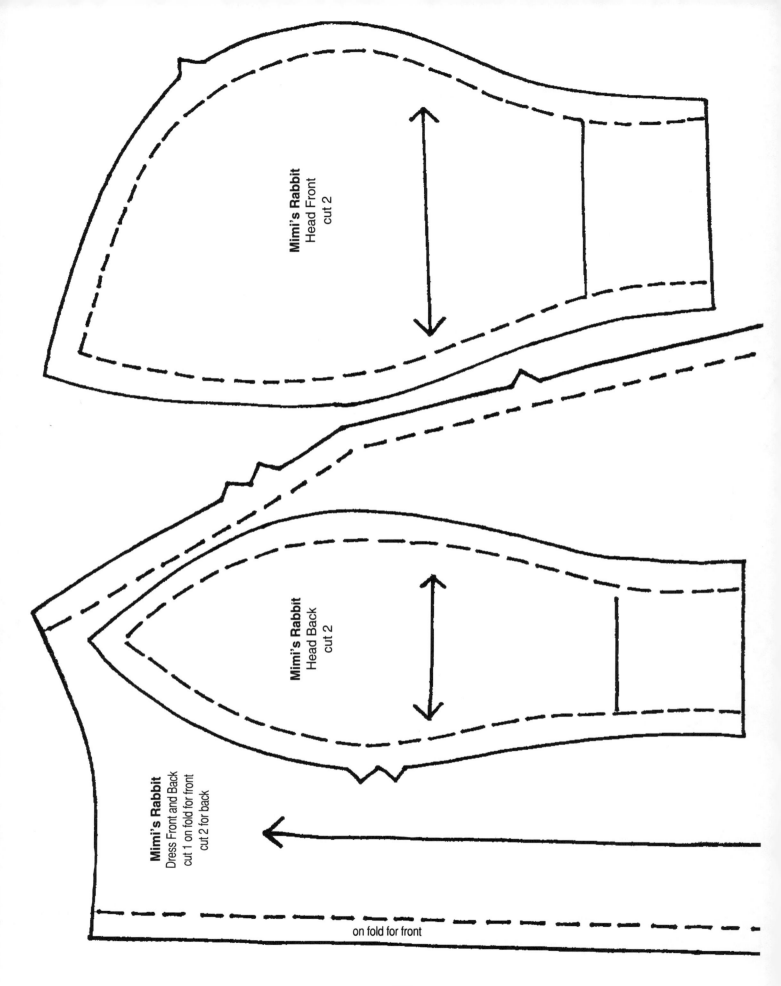

Mimi's Rabbit
Head Front
cut 2

Mimi's Rabbit
Head Back
cut 2

Mimi's Rabbit
Dress Front and Back
cut 1 on fold for front
cut 2 for back

on fold for front

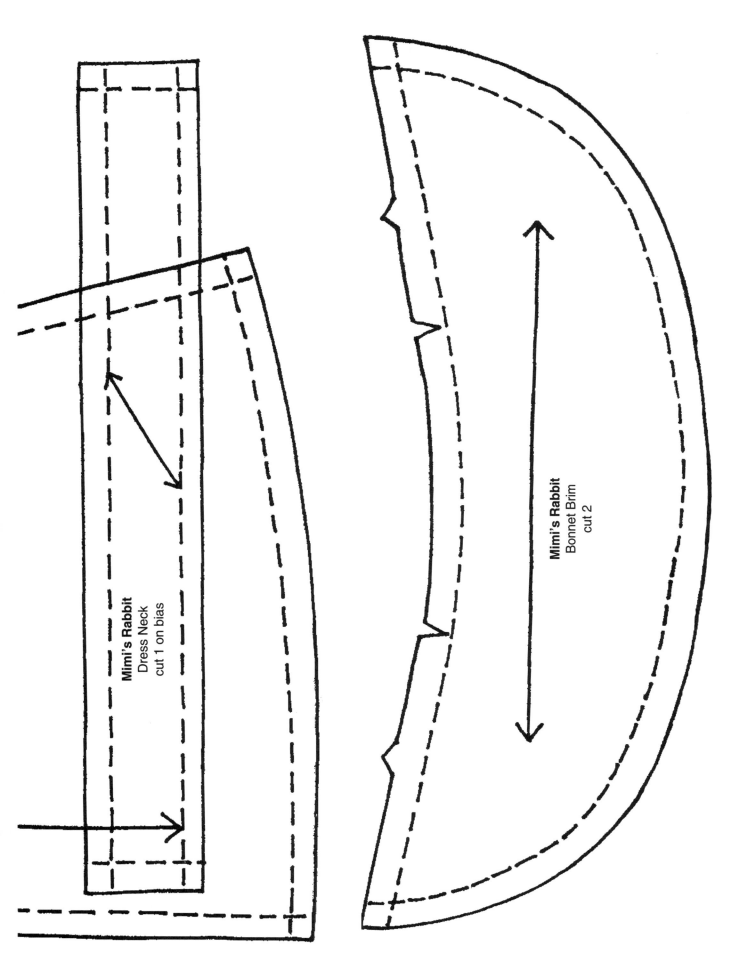

Mimi's Rabbit
Dress Neck
cut 1 on bias

Mimi's Rabbit
Bonnet Brim
cut 2

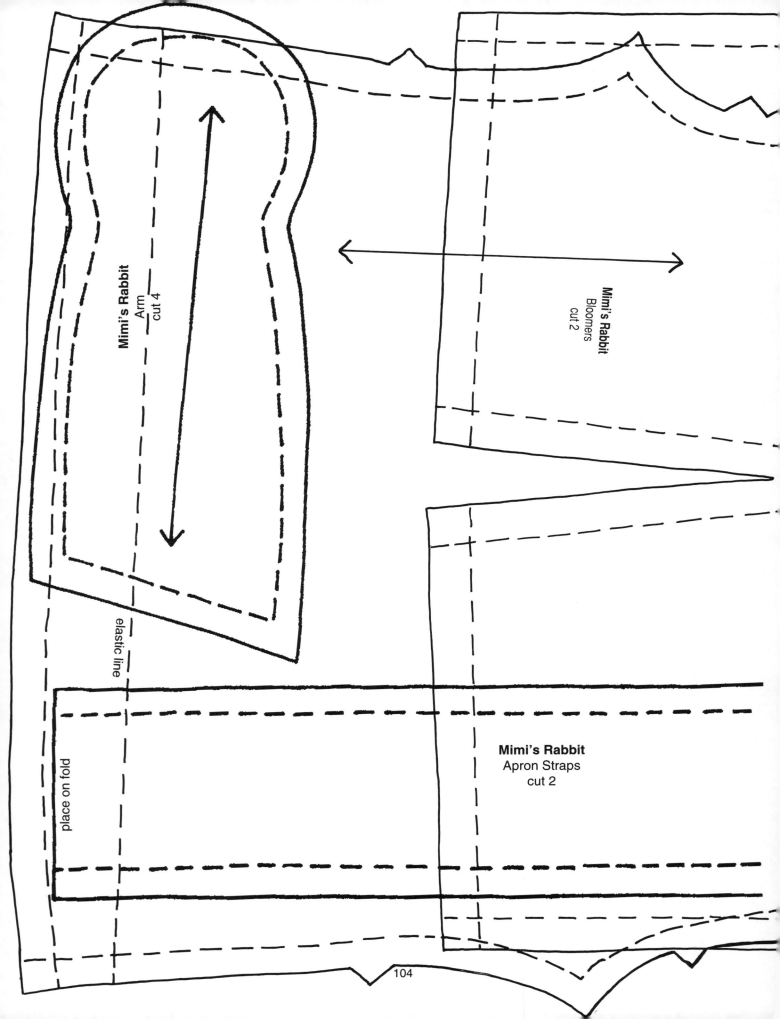

Mimi's Rabbit
Arm
cut 4

elastic line

place on fold

Mimi's Rabbit
Bloomers
cut 2

Mimi's Rabbit
Apron Straps
cut 2

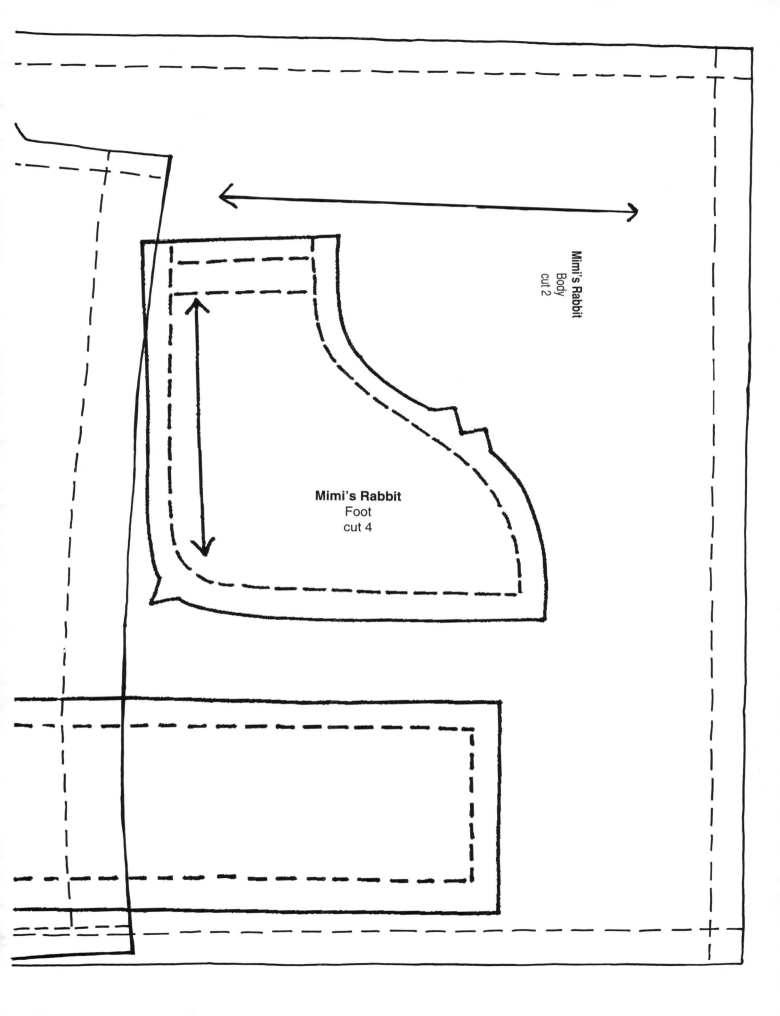

Mimi's Rabbit
Body
cut 2

Mimi's Rabbit
Foot
cut 4

at top. (See Fig. 19.) Hem the ends of the straps.

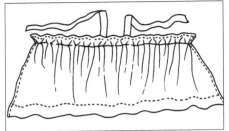

Figure 19

Sew buttonholes near center back, making holes large enough for strap to go through. (See Fig. 20.) Straps go over shoulders, cross, slip through button holes, and tie in bow. (See Fig. 21.)

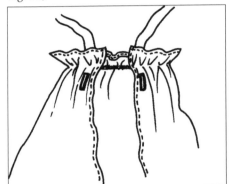

Figure 20

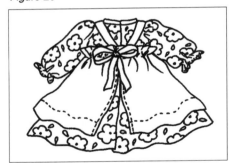

Figure 21

BONNET

Stitch under top of bonnet to form casing for elastic. (See Fig. 22.) Insert 2-1/2" piece of elastic. Stitch ends to secure elastic. Sew a small hem on bottom of bonnet.

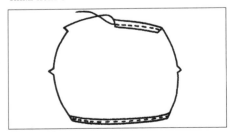

Figure 22

Zigzag thin elastic on "elastic line" stretching elastic to fit fabric as you sew. (See Fig. 23.) Gather stitch notched sides of bonnet.

Figure 23

Iron or stitch on interfacing on brim. (See Fig. 24.) Sew lace to right side of brim. (See Fig. 25.) Press under between inward notches. (See Fig. 24.) With brims right sides together sew curved edge. Clip. Turn right side out. Press. Stitch between inward notches (ear opening).

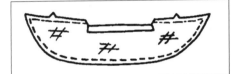

Figure 24

Figure 25

With right sides together, sew brim to bonnet, pulling up gather stitch. (See Fig. 26.) Sew tie ribbons on and you're done. (See Fig. 27.)

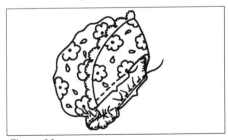

Figure 26

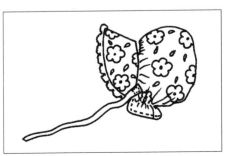

Figure 27

CAMILLE

Bonnie S. Olaveson
See picture on p. 63.

Finished doll is 17" high.

1/3 yd. muslin (body)
2/3 yd. fabric (dress, hat)
2/3 yd. coordinating fabric (sash, bow, pantaloons, puff in hat)
Matching thread
2-1/2 yds. 1/2" wide lace
1-1/2 yds. 1/8" wide elastic
Polyester fiber filling
6" doily (collar)
1 ft. crepe hair
Brown embroidery floss
Feather
1/3 yd. craft pearls
Two 1" porcelain rose buds
1 yd. 1/4" wide ribbon
10" doily (umbrella)
1/8" dowel, 7" long (umbrella)
Hot-glue gun and glue sticks

GENERAL INSTRUCTIONS
Please read all instructions before you begin. Transfer all appropriate markings from pattern pieces. All seams are 1/4" allowance. RST = right sides together.

CUTTING INSTRUCTIONS
Cut body, dress, sleeve, and pantaloons as indicated on pattern pieces.

There are no patterns for the following pieces. Measure and cut.
Skirt—5"x45"
Hat—6"x45"
Bow—9"x12" (coordinate)
Sash—9"x22" (coordinate)
Puff in hat—9"x9" square (coordinate)

BODY
With RST, stitch around arms, legs, and body. Leave open as indicated on pattern pieces. Clip curved areas, and turn right sides out.

Stuff arms and legs to stitching line. Stitch across and continue stuffing to within 1" of opening. Stuff body. Turn raw edges of openings on arms, legs and body inside. Pin and zigzag closed.

Hand stitch arms and legs to body as indicated on pattern.

EYES
Thread a small darning needle with six strands of embroidery floss. Double floss and tie a knot at the end.

Mark eye placement with a pin. Tie a French knot for each eye as follows. From back of head, put thread through to front of one eye. Wrap thread around needle three times. Push needle back through head very near the hole it was brought through. Tie a knot. Repeat for other eye.

DRESS

With RST, stitch backs to front at shoulder seams. Fold each center back under 1/4" and topstitch. Fold neck edge under 1/4". Press and topstitch. Stitch lace to neck edge.

Narrowly hem sleeve edge. Topstitch lace to edge. Stitch elastic to sleeve as line indicates on pattern. Stretch as much as you can, as you sew.

Machine gather top of sleeve. Pull gathers to fit armhole. Pin and stitch into place. Clip curved areas.

To form sleeve, with RST, start at sleeve hem. Stitch down to bottom of bodice in one continuous seam. Turn right side out.

Pin left side of center back to right side of center back, overlapping 1/4". Set aside.

Narrowly hem one long edge of skirt. Topstitch lace to skirt edge. Using a 1/4" seam, with RST stitch short edges of skirt together. This is center back. Machine gather other long edge of skirt. Pull gathers to fit waist of bodice. With RST, pin to bodice and stitch.

Place dress on Camille. To close back, stitch an X at the neck edge and also half way down center back.

To make collar, cut doily in half. (You will use only half.) Fold raw edge under. Put around neck. Hot glue at center front and center back. Hot glue porcelain rose bud at center front.

SASH

Start at large dot on center front bodice right side. Use a double thread with a knot in the end. Pull thread from wrong side of dress to right side of dress.

Put needle back into fabric 1/4" lower than where you pulled the thread to the right side. Pull through to wrong side until thread is almost tight.

Scrunch short end of sash underneath the thread as you are pulling. Extend the end of the fabric 3/8" past the

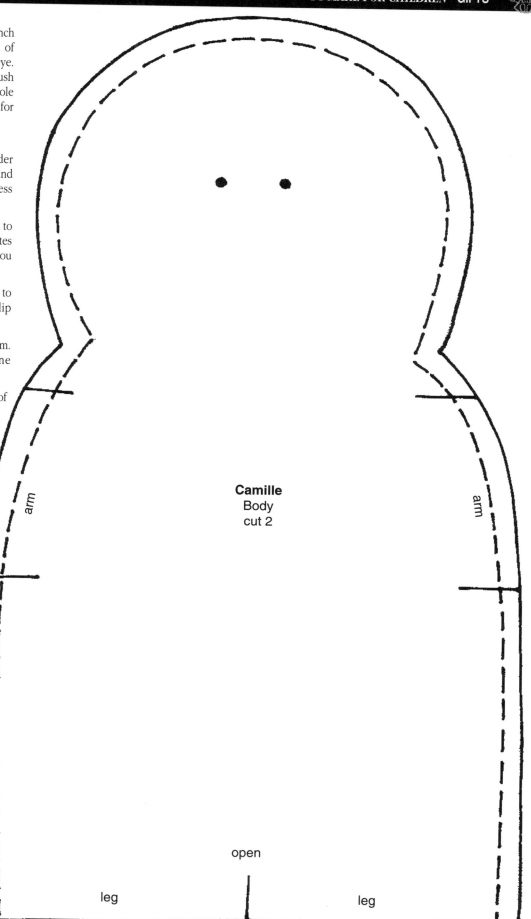

Camille
Body
cut 2

arm

arm

open

leg

leg

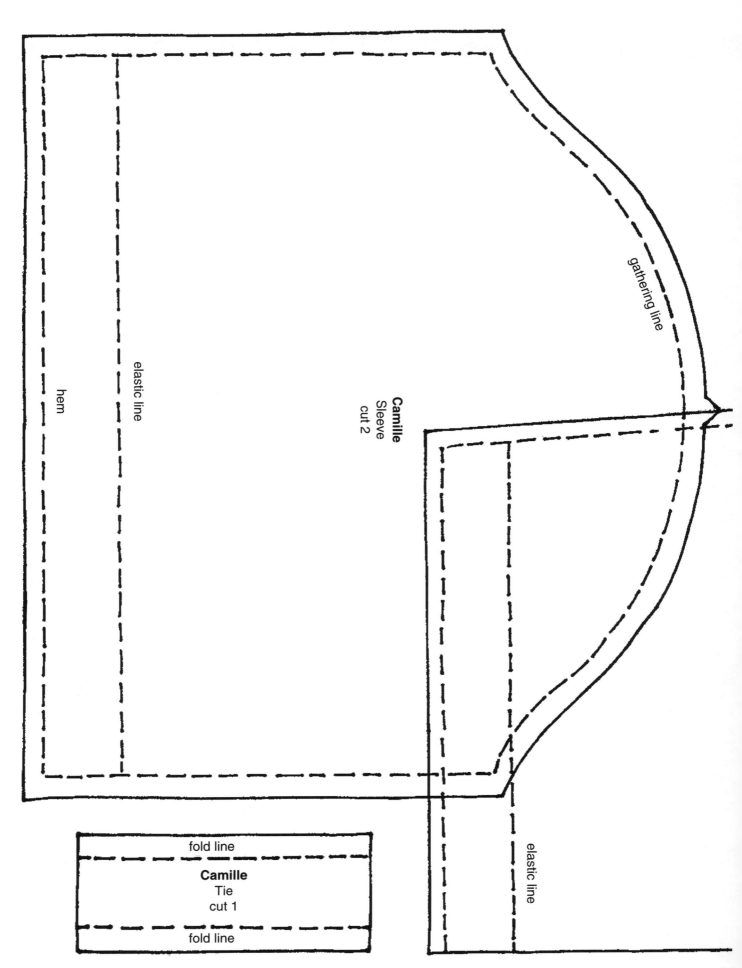

hem

elastic line

Camille
Sleeve
cut 2

gathering line

elastic line

fold line

Camille
Tie
cut 1

fold line

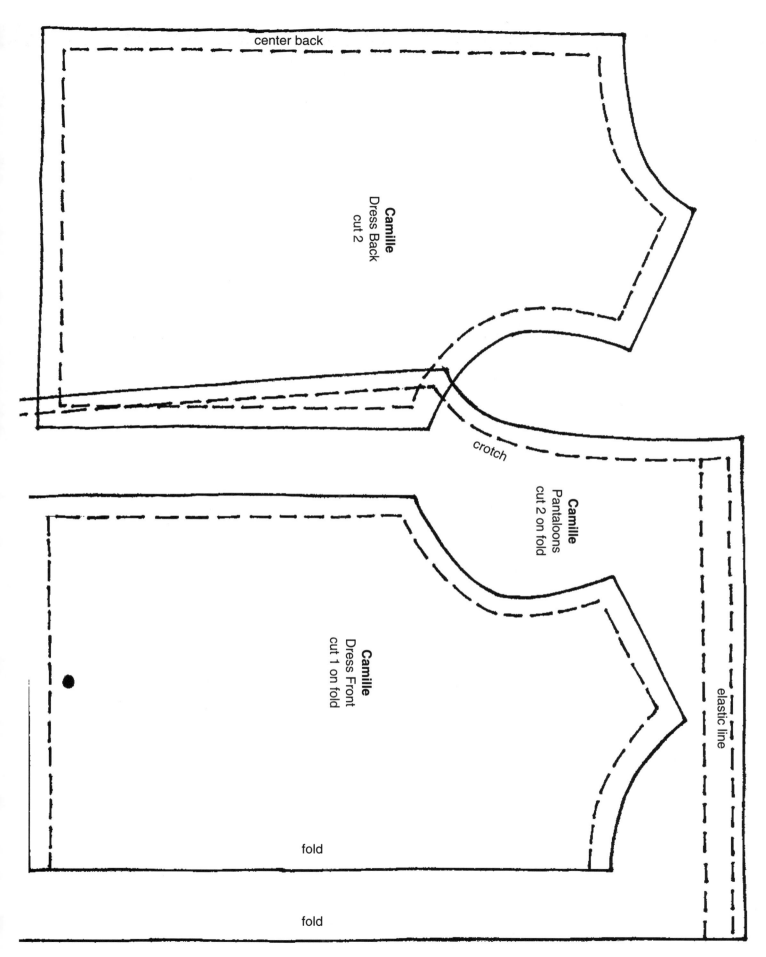

center back

Camille
Dress Back
cut 2

crotch

Camille
Pantaloons
cut 2 on fold

Camille
Dress Front
cut 1 on fold

elastic line

fold

fold

open

stitching line

Camille
Arm
cut 4

open

stitching line

Camille
Leg
cut 4

thread. Pull thread tight to make a small stitch. Fabric should be gathered up into stitch. Knot.

Continue around dress at each side seam and again at front repeating above steps.

BOW
With RST, sew a 1/4" seam along long edges of fabric. Turn to right side. You should have a tube with raw edges at each end. Fold tube in half to find center. Mark center with a pin.

Fold raw edges into the center overlapping 1/4". With a double knotted thread, hand stitch a gathering thread down center of bow. Pull tightly and knot.

Fold bow tie as pattern indicates. Wrap around center of bow. Stitch or hot glue tie together. Stitch or hot glue to front of dress. The bow should cover raw edges of sash.

To make the bow look scrunched and fuller, put both index fingers into one loop of bow. Slide fabric from inside to outside so the top looks scrunched.

PANTALOONS
With RST, stitch crotch seams together. Narrowly hem waist. Stitch elastic to waist as line indicates on pattern. Stretch as much as you can, as you sew.

Narrowly hem each leg. Stitch lace to edge. Stitch elastic to each leg as line indicates on pattern. Stretch as much as you can, as you sew.

With RST, starting at bottom of one leg, stitch down one leg and up the other in one continuous seam. Turn right side out and put on Camille.

HAIR
Unravel crepe hair and pull apart gently to fluff. It should measure at least 21" long.

Cut one piece 14" long, one piece 6" long, and one piece 1" long. The 1" piece is the bang.

Take the longest piece of hair. This is the front piece. Fold in half 6" from left end. Tie a piece of thread down 1" from fold. This will make a little loop of hair in front.

Center this piece of hair on front, making sure both sides are even. Hot glue in place. The 6" long piece is the back. Slightly tuck this piece under the front piece so the edge does not show. Hot glue into place. Take the 1" piece and divide it into two small strands. Hot glue one strand right under front loop. Arrange hair to look natural, not like three separate strands.

HAT

Fold strip of fabric in half with RST so that strip measures 3"x45" long. Stitch each short end closed with a 1/4" seam. Turn to right side. Make sure corners are pointed.

With a strong double thread, preferably buttonhole thread, hand gather long raw edge. Stitches may be as long as 3/8" to 1/2". Pull as tightly as you can.

To form hat into a circle, take a stitch in the end you started gathering, before you knot the thread. Your center hole should be no larger than a quarter. If it is, you need to pull your thread tighter. Be careful not to pull too hard, you will break the thread.

Hot glue to head, placing opening in front.

With the 9" square and using a strong double knotted thread or buttonhole thread, hand gather around square, slightly rounding the corners. Pull gathers tight, making sure the right side of fabric is out. This makes a puff. Push the middle of the circle down into the middle of the gathers. Scrunch it with your hand. Hot glue raw gathered edge to center of hat covering the hole.

Cut two 5" strands of pearls. Hot glue into loops. Hot glue to hat. Tie a loopy bow with ribbon. Glue in place. Hot glue in a feather.

UMBRELLA

Paint stick with desired color or just leave natural. When it is dry, push end of stick through center of doily. If doily does not have a ready-made hole, cut a very tiny 1/8" hole in center. Put a dot of hot glue on inside of doily to keep it from sliding down the stick.

Pull doily up around stick. Tie around with a ribbon. Put a dot of glue at gathered part of doily to hold to stick. Decorate with a loop of pearls and a porcelain rose bud.

FINISHING TOUCH

Make sure you blush Camille's cheeks. A cotton swab and powder works great. Use a small amount to start. It is easier to put more on than get it off.

MOPSY LOCKS & FRECKLES

Carole Quayle

See picture on p. 63

3/8 yd. tea-dyed or regular muslin (body, head, hands, feet)
3/4 yd. print (dress, sleeves and one bow) **or**
7/8 yd. print (dress, sleeves and two bows)
1-1/8 yds. coordinating print (ruffled slip, pantaloons, and fabric collar)

This pattern gives 2 choices of hair, face, collar, shoes. These supplies are marked with an asterisk so you won't need to purchase all items listed.

1 yd. of 1/8" or 1/16" wide ribbon (sleeves and neck)
1-1/4 yds. of 1/2" wide ruffled lace (dress skirt)
1/4 yd. of 1/2" wide elastic
1/3 yd. of 1/4" wide elastic
2/3 yd. black 1/4" wide ribbon (shoe tie)
Marking pen that washes out
Fine-tip permanent marker (black or brown, for freckles)
Pink or rose-colored pencil
Hot-glue gun and 2 glue sticks
Tacky glue
Polyester fiber filling
*Hair: 17-1/2 yds. heavy jute cord, 5- or 6-ply **or** one 8-oz. or 12-oz. mop
Face: Two 3/8" flat-top buttons and one water color brush (eyelashes)
*Collar: 1 yd. of 1/2" wide ruffled lace (self-fabric collar) **or** one 6" or 8" Battenburg or crocheted doily (round or square)
*Shoes: 1 square of black felt or 2"x12" vinyl or black acrylic paint or marker pen to paint shoe
Little Mop Doll: One 12mm wood bead
1-1/3 yd. of 1/8" wide ribbon (to tie arms, legs and ponytails)
6" of ruffled 1/2" wide lace (collar)
Excess mop strands cut from mop hair bangs

Please read all instructions before beginning. This pattern has two choices of hair, face, collar, and shoes. All seam allowances are 1/4" unless otherwise indicated. Clip all curves. Cut all pattern pieces as directed. Transfer all necessary markings to fabric. Use small stitches for pieces to be stuffed. Stitch carefully and accurately to insure proper shape of finished item.

Abbreviations
RST = right sides together
RS = right sides
RSO = right sides out
CC = crochet cotton

BODY/HEAD

RST, stitch around body and head, leaving open between marks on side body, to turn and stuff. Stuff head and body firmly. Stitch side closed.

FACE

With wash-out marker, draw face. When just right, go over markings with permanent black marker, then go over mouth with a pink or rose-colored pencil. Dot freckles over nose and on cheeks with brown marker. For drawn eye, make a cross stitch with white floss or CC (after painting the inner eye black). Go all the way through head and pull to sculpt just slightly. For button eye, place in position and stitch all the way through head with heavy thread or CC. Put a little glue behind the button eye and arrange a small bunch of eyelashes (paint brush bristles). Apply powder blush to her cheeks.

HAIR

*Mopsy Locks' Hair: See Fig. 1. Use 8 oz. or 12 oz. mop. Hot glue the twill mop strip across top of head, side to side. Take several mop strands on both sides (front and back) of twill strip and only at top of the head (for Mopsy's top knot). Hold in place with rubber band. On each side in front, pull approximately 10 strands back up and over the twill strip. Glue to strip so as to cover it. This also helps to arrange side hair. Now cut front bangs and unravel the mop strands if you like. Set aside the strands cut from bangs (for little doll). Spread Tacky glue lightly on back of head and press mop against it to hold in place. Tie hair bow around top knot on her head.

Figure 1

twill strip of mop

*Freckles' Hair: See Fig. 2. Hot glue 8 rows of jute across the back of head, beginning at the base of neck (hair line), up head two thirds of the way. Cut eighteen 32" lengths of jute. Fold each length in middle, (fold is the front of bang), and glue across top of head, with loops extending 2" over forehead (9 folded strands on either side of center of head). Be sure each strand is securely glued to top of head. Cut through bangs, fold and untwist jute and finger fluff. Untwist each of the back strands and comb with fingers. Separate in middle of back. Bring pony tails up and out to either side of head and secure with rubber bands. Tie hair bows around each pony tail.

Figure 2

FEET AND HANDS
RST, stitch around, leaving open at ends. Clip curves, turn and stuff. Stitch or glue openings closed. Set aside.

PANTALOONS
With RST, stitch center front seam. Turn raw edge of waist down 3/8" to wrong side, and gather with 9" of 1/2" elastic. Turn bottom of each leg back 2" to wrong side. Using 5" of 1/4" elastic, stretch and sew on wrong side of pantaloon, close to turned-up raw edge. RST, stitch center back seam. RST, stitch inseam from bottom of one leg to bottom of the other leg. Turn RSO and press. Insert feet into leg openings, extending 2" below bottom of pantaloon ruffle. Glue or stitch foot in place, all the way around. Stuff the pantaloons lightly from the top, no higher than crotch. Place pantaloons on doll body about 1-1/2" up from the bottom of doll (see marking on pattern piece), and glue or hand stitch in place around waist.

SLEEVE/DRESS
Fold sleeve coordinating piece lengthwise, wrong sides together. Place coordinate piece along RS of sleeve (long edge), having raw edges even and stitch. On RS, fold sleeve and coordinate back, so that only 1/4" of folded edge of coordinate is showing. Pin and turn to

wrong side and baste close to raw edges. On RS, mark center of lower sleeve with a pin. Zigzag narrow ribbon on RS of sleeve. DON'T CUT RIBBON YET! With a needle or pin, pull up a 3" loop at center of sleeve (to be tied in bow later). See Fig. 3. Now secure ribbon at

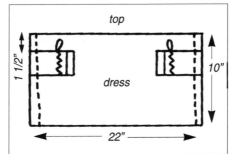

Figure 3

both ends. Fold sleeve RST, 8-1/2" sides (under arm seam) even, stitch and turn RSO, with fold of sleeve at top and seam at bottom. Gather by zigzagging over CC, through both thicknesses of fabric, gather to 1-1/2" with fold of sleeve at top, lay sleeve on RS of one dress piece, 1-1/2" down from top and pin in place. Repeat for other sleeve. Now lay other dress piece on top of first one, RST, and stitch side seams together, catching sleeve in seam (sleeve should be inside). See figure 3. Now stitch RS of narrow ruffled lace to bottom, RS of dress. Turn dress RSO and top stitch close to seam, above lace.

SLIP
RST, stitch short ends of ruffle pieces. Fold lengthwise, wrong sides together. Zigzag over CC about 1/4" from raw edges. RST, stitch one side seam. Gather the ruffle with CC to fit bottom of slip, 44" raw edges even. Stitch ruffle to slip. (See Fig. 4.) Press seam towards slip, and on RS of slip, topstitch close to seam. Stitch other side seam. With RS of dress to wrong side of slip, and having top raw edges even and side seams together, stitch all the way around top edge. Turn RSO and press seam. Starting at center front, zigzag CC 3/8" down from top, all the way around, having 2" of excess CC at both ends to work with. Back-tack at beginning and end. Press the dress and

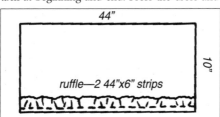

Figure 4

slip, then put on doll, gathering CC as snug as possible around doll's neck. Tie knot and dot with glue. Adjust gathers evenly around neck. On underside of dress, by hand, stitch the sleeve seam to the side seam of doll body. Stuff sleeves lightly. Place hands in sleeves, extending below ruffle about 1-1/2". Gather ruffle in with ribbon, tying bow at wrist. Stitch or glue hands in place, inside sleeve.

COLLARS
*Self-fabric collar: With RS of lace to RS of one collar piece, stitch narrow ruffled lace all the way around (with lace edge to the inside of collar). (See pattern.) Lay RS of other collar piece on RS of lace-edged one. Pin and stitch all the way around, leaving back seam open to turn RSO and press. Hand stitch closed. Sew doll-size button at top of neck and make button loop of ribbon or thread and stitch to other side of collar. Place on doll. Tack to dress at front and back. Embellish with a ribbon rose and ribbon bow at front of collar.

*Battenburg or doily lace collar: Cut hole in center, see pattern piece. Turn edge under and by hand, stitch around this edge. Stitch doll-size button to one side and make loop at other side with ribbon or thread. Put collar on doll, button and tack at front and back. Embellish with ribbon rose and ribbon bow in front of collar.

SHOES
*Fabric shoes: RST, stitch around curved lower edge of front and back of shoe piece. Clip and turn. Stitch 6" of narrow ribbon on each side of shoe. Put shoe on doll and tie in bow.

*Painted shoe: Paint shoe as shown on leg pattern piece. At each side of shoe. stitch narrow ribbon and tie in bow.

DOLLS
Dolls can hold a basket of dry flowers (glue basket to each hand) or make a small mop doll out of excess mop strands (cut from bangs). (See Fig. 5.) Glue 8 strands on back of

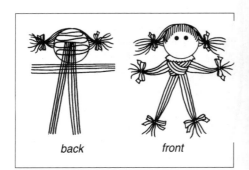

back   front

Figure 5

the bead head for body and legs (pony tails will cover). To make arms, lay 4 strands (9"-10" long) across back, below head, and tie in front (secure with glue). Tie ribbon bows around legs, 4 strands in each. Glue a small piece of ruffled lace around neck and embellish with a ribbon rose. Glue little pieces of mop strand to top front of head for bangs, then wind longer strands of mop back and forth across back of head and across top, extending out over sides for pony tails. Tie pony tails at each side with ribbon bows. Paint dots for eyes and blush checks. Mopsy Locks and Freckles can sit on a shelf, stand in a doll stand or they love to be hung on your wall to watch over you.

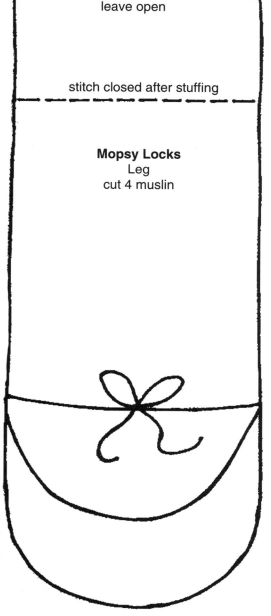

leave open

stitch closed after stuffing

Mopsy Locks
Leg
cut 4 muslin

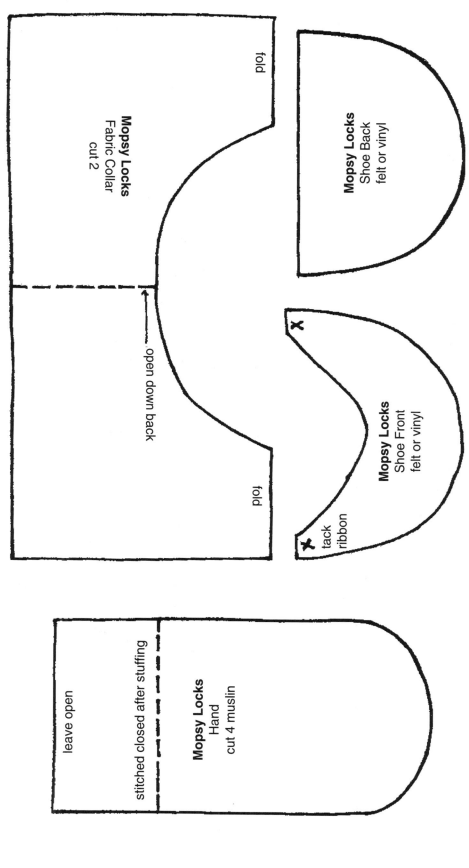

Mopsy Locks
Fabric Collar
cut 2

fold

fold

open down back

Mopsy Locks
Shoe Back
felt or vinyl

Mopsy Locks
Shoe Front
felt or vinyl

tack ribbon

leave open

stitched closed after stuffing

Mopsy Locks
Hand
cut 4 muslin

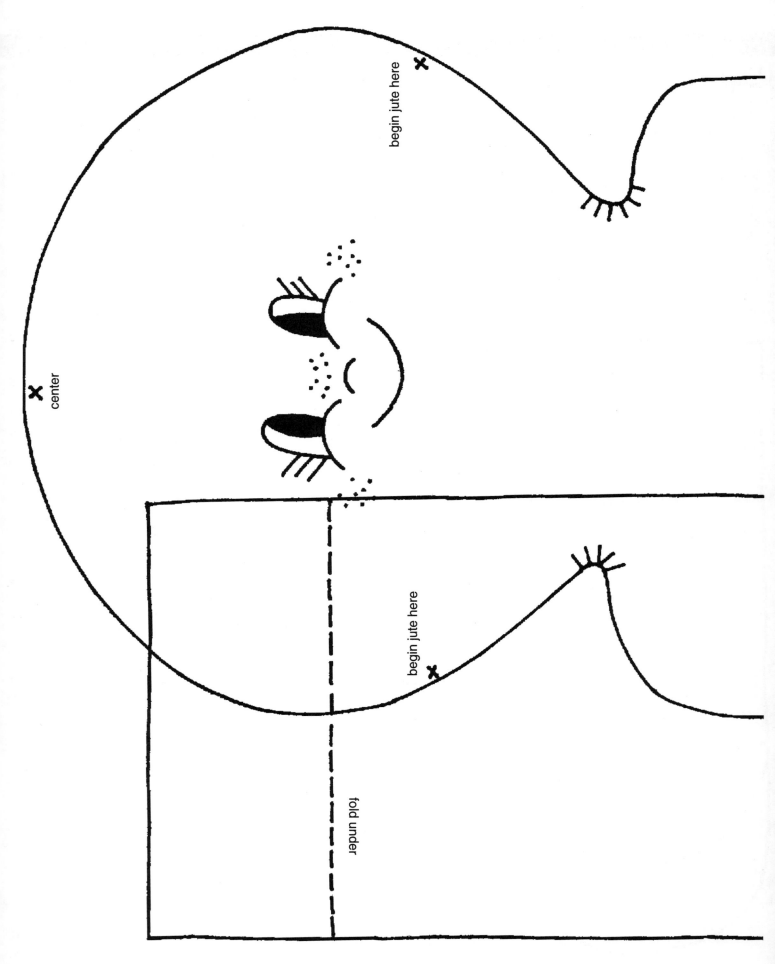

begin jute here

center

begin jute here

fold under

114

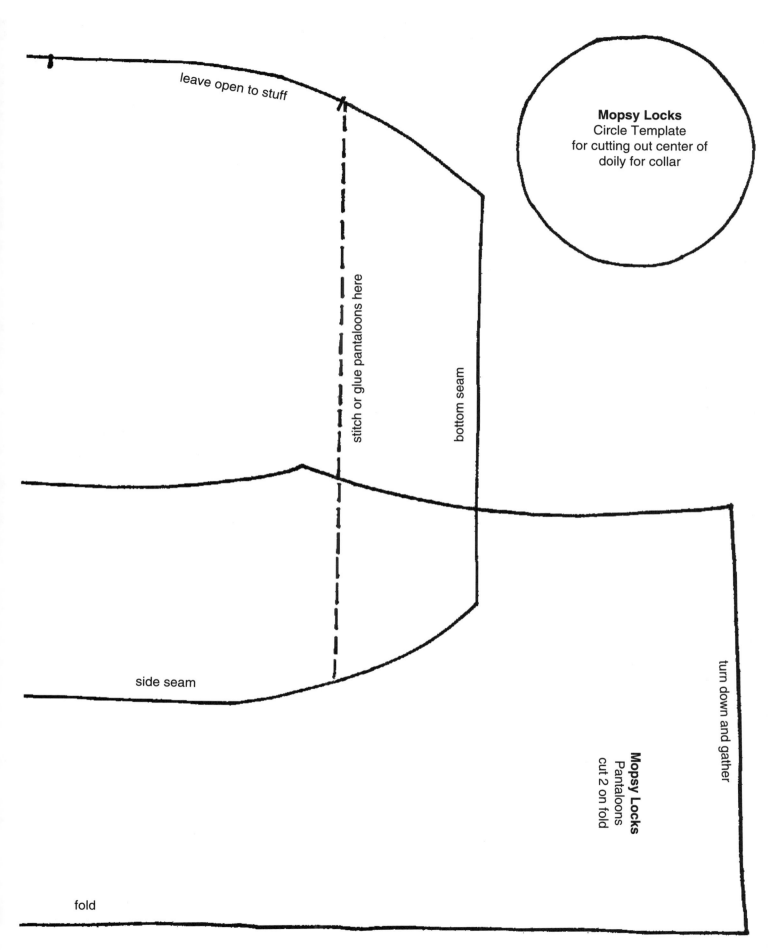

leave open to stuff

stitch or glue pantaloons here

bottom seam

Mopsy Locks
Circle Template
for cutting out center of
doily for collar

side seam

turn down and gather

Mopsy Locks
Pantaloons
cut 2 on fold

fold

NOAH'S ARK

Richard Packer

Cut out three "A" sections from 3/4" stock. Hardwood is preferred but pine works nicely. Trace through carbon paper to stock.

Trace the "B" cut-out guide in the center of two of the three "A" sections. Cut out these internal sections. (See Fig. 1.)

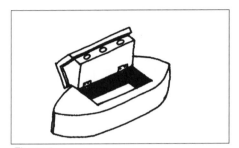

Figure 1

Glue all three "A" sections together with the uncut piece on the bottom.

Cut out two "C" sections from 3/4" stock. Glue two together. Drill three windows clear through stock. Use a 13/16" bit on a drill press or use a hand drill guide. See "C" template for window location points. Center where two "C" boards are glued together.

Cut two "E" triangles from 3/4" stock and glue to the ends of the "C" assembly as a roof support. (See Fig. 2.)

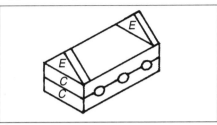

Figure 2 "C" Assembly

Cut out two "D" pieces from 3/4" stock. Cut a 30-degree bevel along one long side of each piece. Glue together and center and glue onto "E" roof supports. (See Fig. 3.)

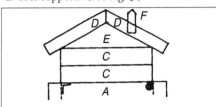

Figure 3

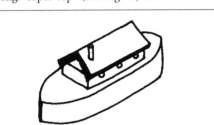

Figure 4

Make a smoke stack from a 1/2" dowel, 1-3/4" long. Taper top. (See Fig. 4.) Drill a vertical

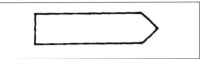

Figure 5

hole in the roof and glue stack in place. (See Figs. 5 and 3.)

Mount hinges to attach two ark sections together. (See Figs. 6 and 1.) Add a cabinet

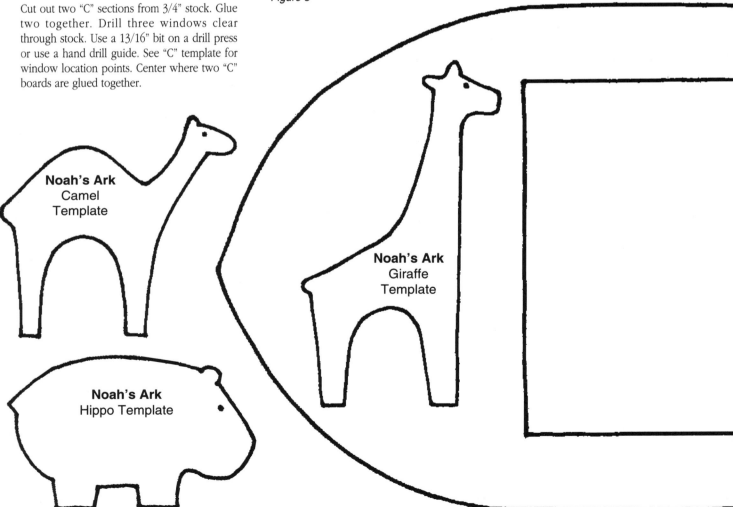

Noah's Ark
Camel
Template

Noah's Ark
Giraffe
Template

Noah's Ark
Hippo Template

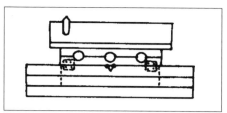

Figure 6

catch if desired or glue in a wood stop for top to rest on. (See Fig. 6.)

Cut animals from 3/4" stock and split in two for two animals or make two from 3/4" stock.

Sand sharp edges on ark and animals, then oil or paint with a non-toxic finish.

Drill eyes with a 9/64" bit for all animals.

Cut stripes on zebra with a bandsaw, hand saw or hand paint.

NOAH'S ARK PICTURE AND MOBILE

Richard Packer

The five animals can be used in both the picture and the mobile. Both make nice additions to a nursery or youngster's room. Cut out parts from patterns either by tracing through carbon paper or glue templates to stock using an adhesive similar to Scotch Spray-mount. Animals for the wall picture are 3/8" thick (3/4" cut in two). Thicknesses of other picture parts are noted.

PICTURE
Trace tree onto 3/4" stock, then rip in two for A-1 and A-2.

Cut from 3/4" stock and rip in two (clouds are same thickness as trees, sun, and animals).

Trace mountains then rip down to 1/8" thick or cut from thin hard board or plywood.

Cut sun 3/8" thick. Sun's rays are 3/8" thick and 1/8" wide. Estimate lengths when gluing in place.

Long frame members (16-3/4") are 3/4" wide and 1" thick. Make two.

Make 9" long frame members just like 16-3/4".

Back can be ply or solid stock about 1/4" thick, 16-1/2" long and 8-3/4" wide.

Use picture (Figs. 1 and 2) as a guide and glue parts together. Paint bright colors of your choice.

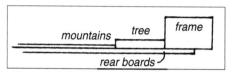

Figure 1 Cut-away side view

MOBILE
Cut out animals from 3/4" stock and use that thickness or cut down to 3/8". Drill holes in top where indicated for balance. Attach string

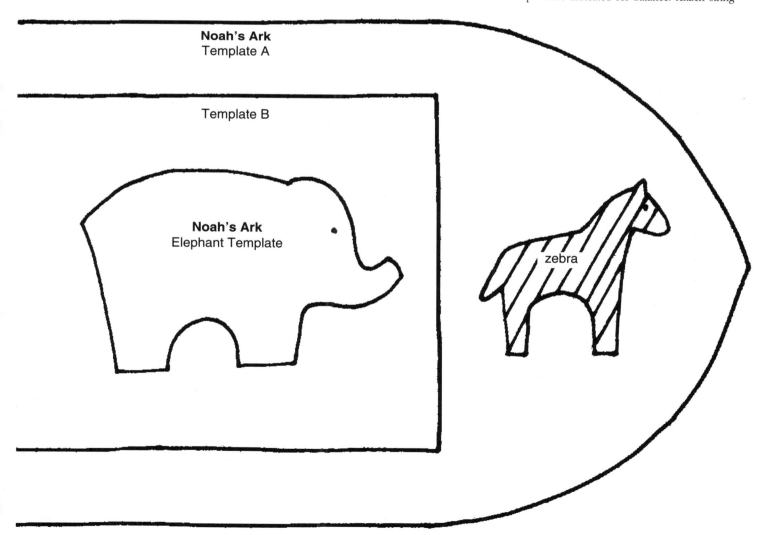

Noah's Ark
Template A

Template B

Noah's Ark
Elephant Template

zebra

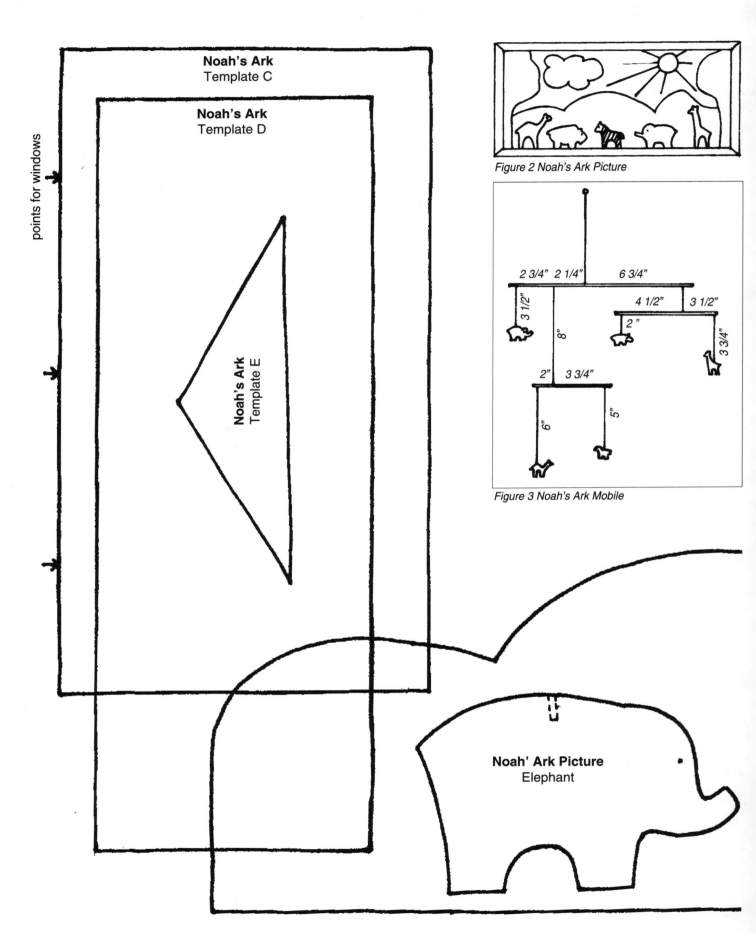

Noah's Ark
Template C

Noah's Ark
Template D

Noah's Ark
Template E

points for windows

Figure 2 Noah's Ark Picture

2 3/4" 2 1/4" 6 3/4"

3 1/2"

8"

4 1/2" 3 1/2"

2"

3 3/4"

2" 3 3/4"

6"

5"

Figure 3 Noah's Ark Mobile

Noah' Ark Picture
Elephant

118

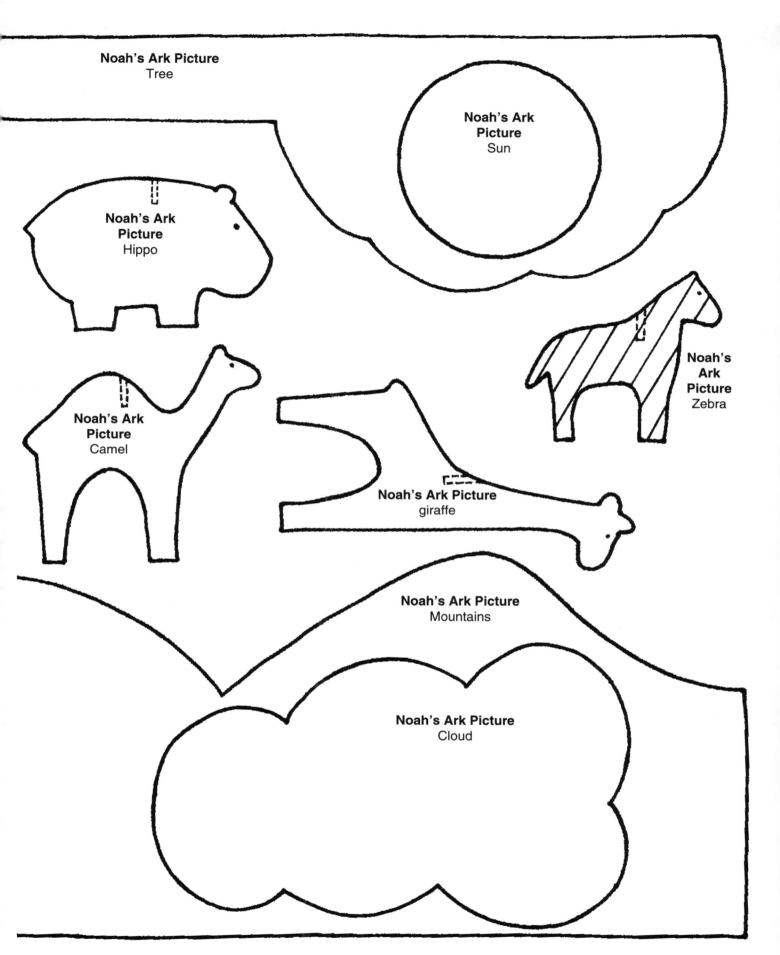

Noah's Ark Picture
Tree

Noah's Ark Picture
Sun

Noah's Ark Picture
Hippo

Noah's Ark Picture
Zebra

Noah's Ark Picture
Camel

Noah's Ark Picture
giraffe

Noah's Ark Picture
Mountains

Noah's Ark Picture
Cloud

or colored yarn as desired. Use 1/8" or 1/4" diameter dowels for the rods. Cut string to length indicated and tie to dowels. Glue other end into top of animals. Move tied sections roughly to measured points indicated in Fig. 3. Adjust until balanced. Place a spot of glue at tie points to keep from slipping. Paint animals bright, non-toxic colors. Also you can make a design of your own, perhaps with more animals.

WOODEN STICK HORSE

Richard Packer

3/4" hardwood or pine
Paint
Scotch Spray-mount

Trace through carbon paper or glue pattern directly to wood using an adhesive such as Scotch Spray-mount. Hardwood is recommended. Refer to Fig. 1 for detail.

Drill holes for handle, eyes and if desired, behind the mouth for a cord for reins. Cut mouth opening. Cut length of wood three feet long (longer for older children), 3/4" thick, 1-1/2" wide. Cut opening for shaft to assure a firm fit. Glue into place, add nail if needed for a permanent attachment. Glue 3/4" handle into place. Carefully sand sharp edge and paint or oil as desired.

SCENTED FIRE STARTERS

Julie Wilcox
See picture on p. 97

Pinecones
Paraffin
Double boiler or electric frying pan
Can (for melting paraffin)
Tongs
Red crayons with paper removed (to color wax)
Cinnamon oil (1 teaspoon per 1-1/2 lbs. of paraffin)
Newspaper

Caution: *Do not melt paraffin over an open flame or directly on burner.*

Cover work area with newspaper. Melt paraffin in double boiler over hot water or in a can placed in an electric frying pan filled with water. Add pieces of crayon to melted paraffin until desired color is obtained. Add cinnamon oil. Holding pinecones with tongs, dip cones in paraffin. Allowing paraffin to dry between coats, continue dipping cones until well coated. Allow paraffin to harden completely.

To use firestarters, place several pinecones under logs and light cones.

CLOSET SACHET

Shanon Allen
See picture on p. 62

1/4 yd. print fabric
Polyester fiber filling
3 ribbon roses
Pearls

3 yds. double-face 3/8" wide satin ribbon
6" Battenburg doily, cut in half
Hot-glue gun

Cut out 4 hearts. Slit 2 down back 2" as indicated on pattern.

Sew the half doily to the front of one heart as indicated on pattern. Sew front and back of hearts together, right sides together. Clip curves. Turn right side out through slit. Stuff with polyester fiber filling. Put slit sides of hearts together and secure with 3/8" ribbon as shown in picture. Tie at top. Make ribbon bow and hot glue to top center front on doily. Twist three ribbon roses together. Place inside center of heart. Glue loop of pearls under roses. Make a ribbon loop so sachet can hang. Scent with favorite oil or perfume.

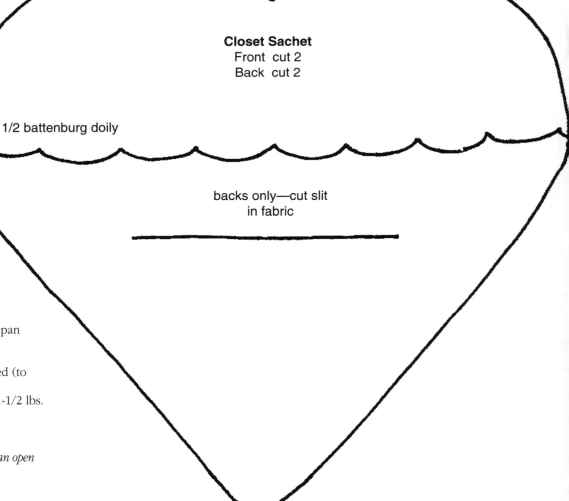

Closet Sachet
Front cut 2
Back cut 2

1/2 battenburg doily

backs only—cut slit in fabric

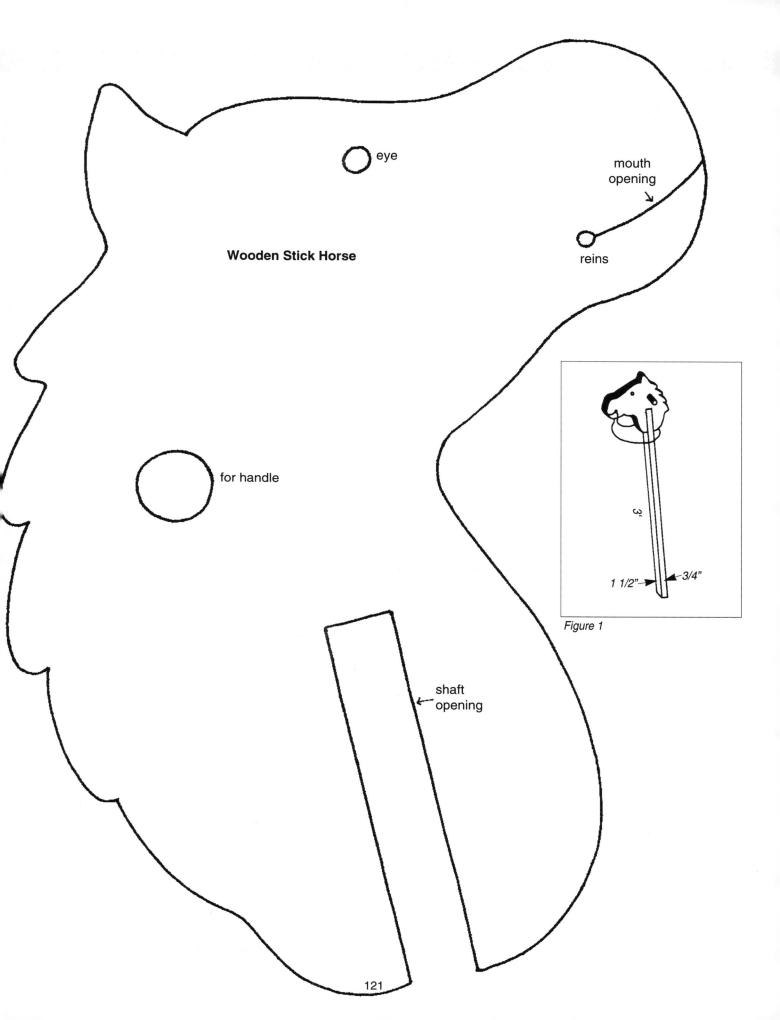

eye

mouth
opening

Wooden Stick Horse

reins

for handle

Figure 1

3'

1 1/2"   3/4"

shaft
opening

121

GATHERED FABRIC HEART

Shanon Allen

See picture on p. 62

One 9" styrofoam heart
One 28"x6" strip of printed fabric
2 yds. 1" wide craft ribbon
One yd. 1" wide gathered lace
Dried flowers
Hot-glue gun

Fold over 2-1/2" lengthwise of fabric with right side out and stitch along 2-1/2" raw edge, making a 2-1/2" tube. On outside raw edge top stitch gathered lace. (See Fig. 1.) Cut through one side of styrofoam heart. (See Fig. 2.)

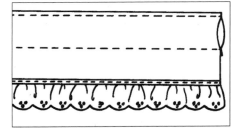

Figure 1

Carefully separate two cut edges of styrofoam heart and slide tube of fabric onto it. Tape heart back together with strong tape. Evenly distribute gathers around heart. Fold under raw edge of tube and hot glue together.

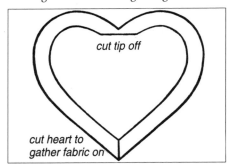

cut tip off

cut heart to gather fabric on

Figure 2

Make bow and glue to top center of heart. Embellish with dried flowers.

POTPOURRI DOLL

Sharlene Wayment

See picture on p. 62

1/8 yd. of selected calico fabric
1/2 c. rice
Polyester fiber filling
Braided wool for hair
Hot glue gun

Black acrylic paint
Crochet thread

Use 1/4" seams throughout. With wrong sides together, sew arms together and across one end. Turn. Place arms between body pieces right sides together, about 1" from top. Sew body together. Leave top open to turn and stuff. Sew head right sides together. Turn and stuff with polyester filling. Turn body right side out and fill with 1/2 c. rice. Finish stuffing with polyester filling.

Turn down top of body 1/2". Hand stitch with a large basting stitch using crochet thread about 3/8" down from folded edge. Begin at center front. Pull gathers to about the size of neck. Insert head and pull thread tight. Tie knot to secure, then a bow to finish.

Tie basket to center front of arm. Secure with hot glue to body. Unbraid about 2-3" of wool hair and glue to head. Apply blush to cheeks and dot paint eyes with black paint.

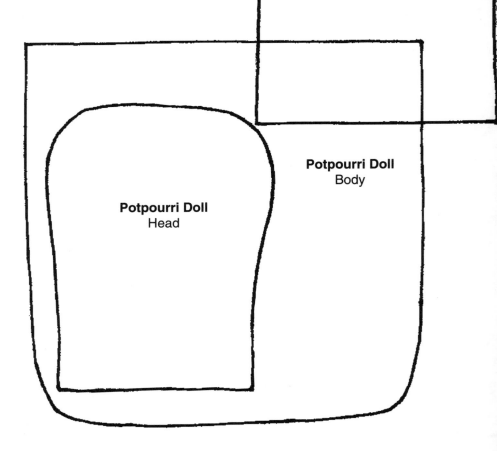

Potpourri Doll
Arms

Potpourri Doll
Body

Potpourri Doll
Head

CLOTH BASKET WITH DRIED FLOWERS

Sharlene Wayment
See picture on p. 62

1/8 yd. fabric
1/8 yd. Pellon fleece
12" piece of round basket reed
Hot-glue gun
4" doily
Two 10" pieces of 1/8" wide ribbon
Ribbon roses
Dried flowers

Sew fabric with 1/2" seam. Turn right side out. Fold top edges over 1/2".

Cut a piece of Pellon fleece from pattern piece and slide into sewn basket.

Fold doily in half and place over front fold of basket. Hot glue in place.

Soak basket reed in water until pliable. Bend and place two ends about 1" down in basket on each side. Hot glue in place. Fill basket with dried flowers and ribbon roses using hot glue to secure in place. Tie ribbon bow and center on doily. Glue in place.

WOODEN HOLIDAY TREE

Gayle Wilson
See picture on p. 133

7/8" dowel cut 24" long (center)
5/16" dowel, cut as follows:
   one 8" long
   one 13" long
   one 18" long
1/2" pine

Cut dowel to specified lengths. Drill holes through center dowel as follows: first hole 4-1/4" from top of center dowel; second and third holes 5-1/4" from first hole.

Drill small hole on top of center dowel. Glue 1" of 5/16" dowel in hole. Leave 1/2" protruding.

Make a base for the tree at least 9-10" long. Drill hole in center for large dowel. Base could be round or squared off. Stand tree in base.

Cut out decorations desired using 1/2" pine and patterns as guides. Drill holes in base to attach top decorations. Smaller decorations are cut out with holes drilled on side.

Paint and decorate decorations, if and as desired. Tree should hold at least 1 dozen cookies or other decorations.

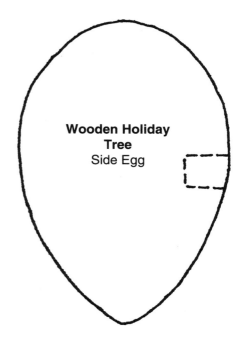

Wooden Holiday Tree
Side Egg

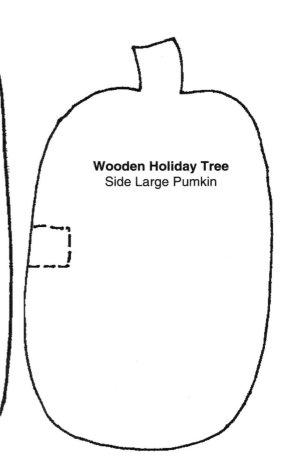

Wooden Holiday Tree
Side Large Pumkin

Cloth Basket

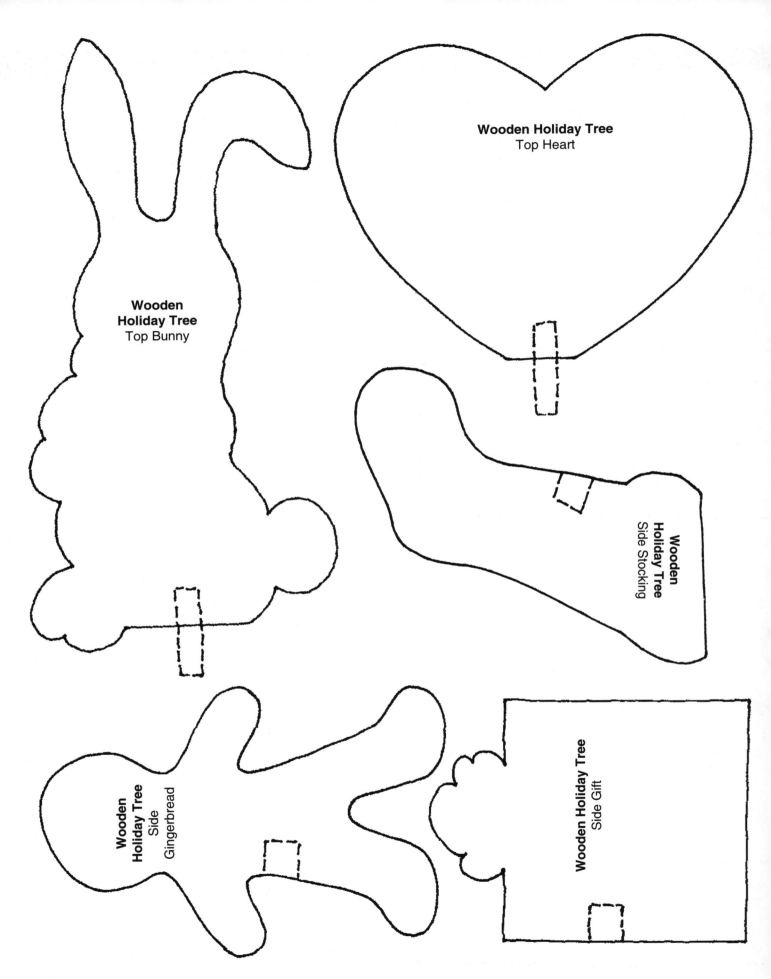

Wooden Holiday Tree
Top Heart

Wooden Holiday Tree
Top Bunny

Wooden Holiday Tree
Side Stocking

Wooden Holiday Tree
Side Gingerbread

Wooden Holiday Tree
Side Gift

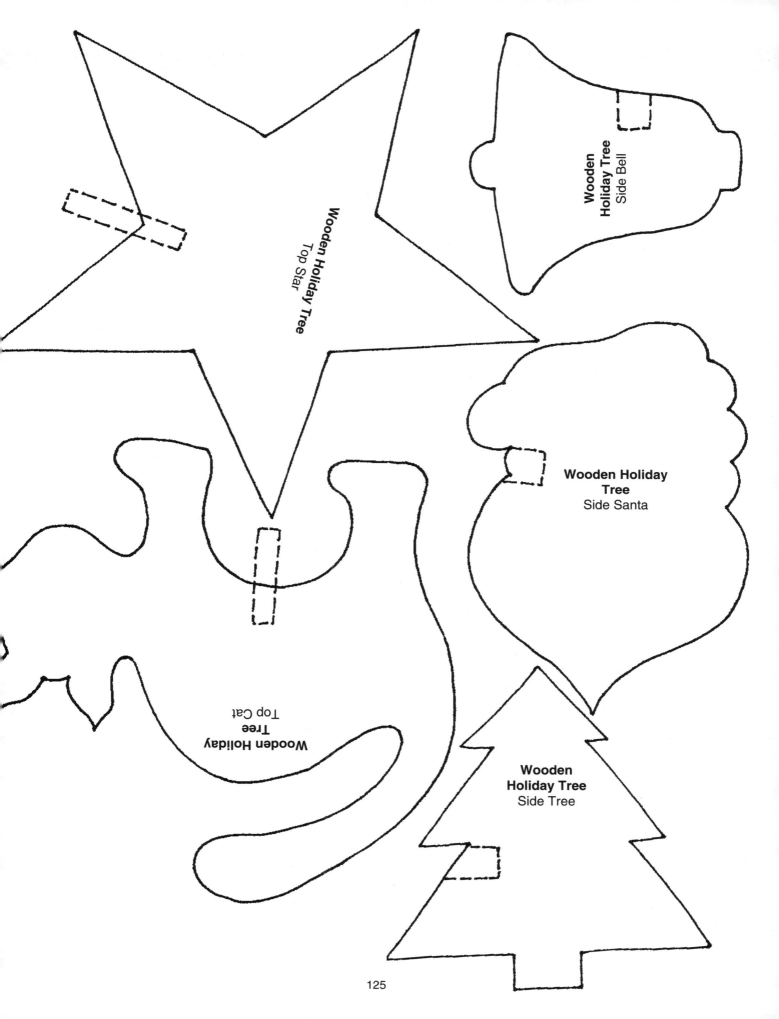

Wooden Holiday Tree
Top Star

Wooden Holiday Tree
Side Bell

Wooden Holiday Tree
Side Santa

Wooden Holiday Tree
Top Cat

Wooden Holiday Tree
Side Tree

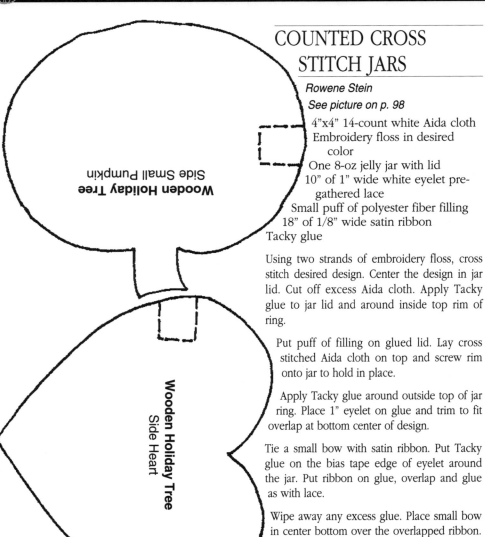

Wooden Holiday Tree
Side Small Pumpkin

Wooden Holiday Tree
Side Heart

COUNTED CROSS STITCH JARS

Rowene Stein

See picture on p. 98

4"x4" 14-count white Aida cloth
Embroidery floss in desired color
One 8-oz jelly jar with lid
10" of 1" wide white eyelet pre-gathered lace
Small puff of polyester fiber filling
18" of 1/8" wide satin ribbon
Tacky glue

Using two strands of embroidery floss, cross stitch desired design. Center the design in jar lid. Cut off excess Aida cloth. Apply Tacky glue to jar lid and around inside top rim of ring.

Put puff of filling on glued lid. Lay cross stitched Aida cloth on top and screw rim onto jar to hold in place.

Apply Tacky glue around outside top of jar ring. Place 1" eyelet on glue and trim to fit overlap at bottom center of design.

Tie a small bow with satin ribbon. Put Tacky glue on the bias tape edge of eyelet around the jar. Put ribbon on glue, overlap and glue as with lace.

Wipe away any excess glue. Place small bow in center bottom over the overlapped ribbon. Allow to dry overnight.

CANDLE HOLDER

Gayle Wilson

See picture on p. 28

1"x2" knotless pine wood
5 wooden candle cups
5 flathead Phillips 1" wood screws
Fine sandpaper
Wood sealer
2-1/2 yds 1/4" wide ribbon
Candle ring

Cut 2 pieces of wood 8" long by 1-1/2" wide. Cut a 7/8" notch in center, one at the bottom and one at the top. (See pattern.)

Smooth the bottom edges of both pieces by sanding. Drill small hole where cups are to be attached, indicated by x's on pattern. Fasten cups. Interlock the notches before fastening the center cup.

FINISHING AND DECORATING
Sand and seal the wood. Paint or stain, if desired. Tie small ribbon around each cup with bow facing out. Place candle ring of flowers around the center or attach a sprig of flowers at the base of each candle cup.

PAPER SACK GIFT WRAPPER

Carol Briggs

Choice of gift wrap paper
Ruler
Scissors
Tacky glue

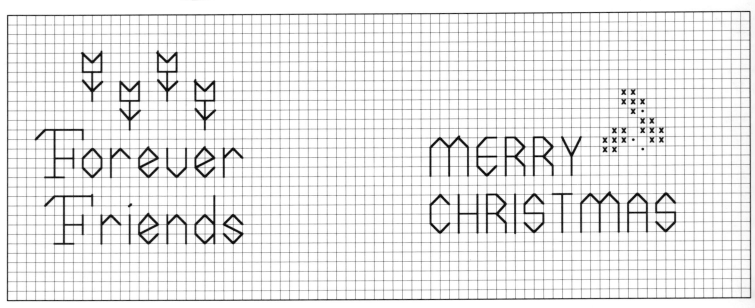

Use any kind of wrapping you want to make the sack. To find the dimensions for your sack, measure around the outside of the object you want to put in the sack. Cut the paper 2 or 3 inches longer than that measurement. For the height, measure the object and add eight inches.

Fold the length of the paper almost in half, leaving a 1/4" overhang. Fold the overhang

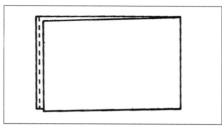

Figure 1

back over the edge and glue to close the sack. (See Fig. 1.)

To make the sides, fold the folded edge over 1/2 of the measurement you want the finished side to be. Repeat on the glued edge. (See Fig. 2.)

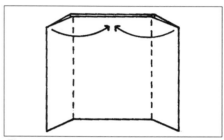

Figure 2

Open the sack and refold the edge and center so that the two folds go to the outside and the center fold goes toward the inside of the sack. (See Fig. 3.)

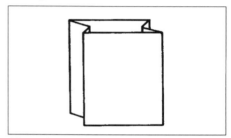

Figure 3

With the side folds in place, turn the bottom of the sack toward you and fold the corners up in a triangle shape to meet in the center. (See Fig. 4.)

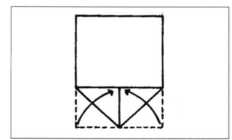

Figure 4

Also fold along the straight edge at the top of triangles. (See Fig. 5.)

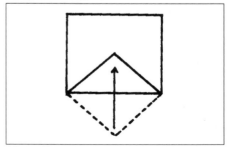

Figure 5

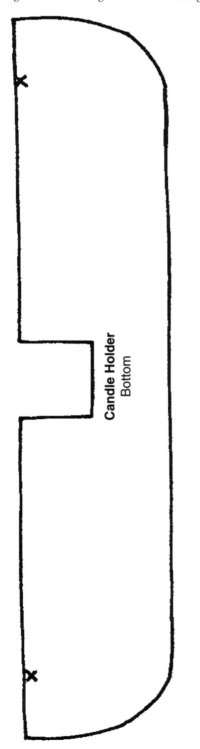

Candle Holder
Bottom

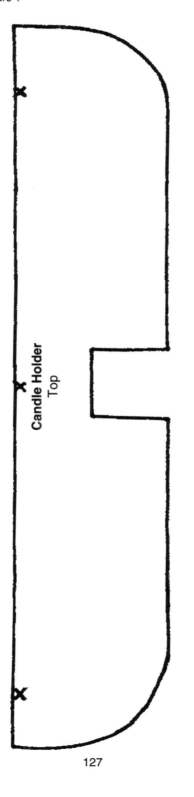

Candle Holder
Top

Open the sack. Again, you will have to refold these folds that go toward the inside of the sack so that they are repositioned toward the outside. (See Fig. 6.)

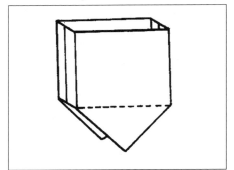

Figure 6

Now, fold the sides of the sack together, lay the sack on a flat surface and gently fold the bottom so that it lays flat and is in a hexagonal shape. (See Fig. 7.)

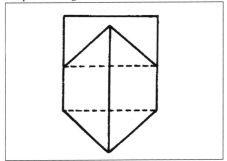

Figure 7

Fold the bottom triangle up and glue edges to bottom of sack. (See Fig. 8.) Then bring top triangle down and glue edges over first triangle. (See Fig. 9.)

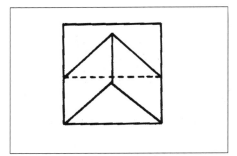

Figure 8

To finish top of sack, cut off straight or cut scallops.

When glue is dry, open completed sack. To close it, fold over top about 1-1/2 to 2 inches. Use a paper punch to punch two holes and run a ribbon through them. Tie a bow in front.

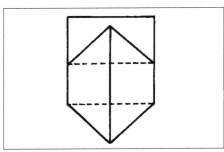

Figure 9

FABRIC BAG

See picture on p. 64

1/4 yd. fabric
Cardboard

Any decoration of the bag (stencilling, stamping, appliqué, etc.) should be done before bag is sewn together.

Cut a 14"x8" rectangular piece of fabric. Fold under 1/4" for hem on the top 14" edge of bag. Fold down another 3/4" and top stitch.

Fold in half lengthwise, right sides together, matching 8" short sides and sew 1/4" seam down side and across bottom. With seam in center of bottom, crease so that there is 1-1/2" on each side of center seam to make bottom.

Sew along the bottom triangles through both thicknesses. (See Fig. 1.) Cut a piece of cardboard (3"x3-3/4") or other sturdy paper to put in the bottom of bag to stabilize it. You

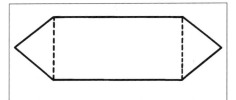

Figure 1

may want to cover this piece with contrasting fabric.

For handle, cut a 3"x9" strip. Fold in half lengthwise, right sides together. Sew, using 1/4" seam. Turn right side out and sew to the top middle portion of each side of the bag.

To stabilize bag, crease four sides of bag. Using a contrasting thread to make it more decorative, top stitch each crease 1/8" in from top to bottom.

CHRISTMAS APRON

Susan Boden
See picture on p. 28

1-1/3 yds. Christmas fabric
9-1/2" square of muslin for bib
Pellon facing
1/4 yd. "Wonder Under"
Fine-point, permanent marker

Cut fabric in pieces as follows: Skirt 24"x45"; Strap 4"x45"; Border 2-1/4"x45"; Waistband 2-1/4"x27" (cut two); Bib 9-1/2" square contrasting fabric.

BIB

Using Wonder Under, trace separate pieces of angel picture. Following Wonder Under directions in glossary, press patterns onto desired fabric. Cut out and press onto 9-1/2" bib square. Machine appliqué putting down heart piece first (wings). Use French knots for hair. Draw face on with a fine-point, permanent marker.

Note: A stencil or any other pattern that will fit onto a 9" finished square may be used in place of the angel shown.

Using the border strip, sew with 1/4" seam to top of bib section. Cut even with sides. Sew border strip on both sides of bib. Trim across top and bottom.

Using the bib/border as a pattern, cut a facing for bib.

Fold strips in half. Sew across one end and down the side using 1/4" seams. Turn and press.

Place straps next to border seams and baste. (See Fig. 1.)

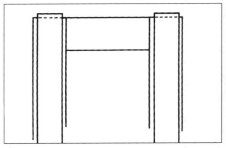

Figure 1

Pin facing to bib and sew sides and top. Turn and press.

SKIRT

Press under 1/2" along bottom. Press and pin 2" along bottom. Sew. Turn 1/4" under on each side, press. Turn 1/4" again, press and sew.

Gather along top to fit waistband. Sew to waistband. Pin bib to center of waistband, baste.

Fold a 7" scrap from the border strip in half, press. Fold each side in as with seam binding. Press and sew close to edge. Cut in 3-1/2" sections to make loops for ties.

Fold loop sections in half and sew to ends of waistband.

Pin and sew waistband facing to waistband across sides and top. Turn. Pin open section to top of skirt and hand stitch.

Press and enjoy!

BREAD CLOTHS

See picture on p. 61

1/2 yd. of selected fabric

For stenciled bread cloths use a plain fabric. To finish edge, hem with a narrow hem, cut with pinking or scalloping shears or fray fabric.

Choose a stencil of your choice and follow the stencil instructions in the Glossary. Stencil in all four corners.

Fabric stamps could also be used to decorate the bread cloth.

CUT-WORK SACHET

See picture on p. 98

One 6" cut-work doily
Matching white cotton fabric
Fabric stamp and paints

Stamp desired design onto center of cut-work doily following glossary stamping instructions.

Figure 1

Cut an 8" circle out of the white cotton fabric. Sew a gathering stitch about 1/4" away from edge of circle all the way around.

Pull thread tight to gather circle leaving enough room to fill with potpourri as follows.

Make a nest in the batting and put potpourri in nest. Fold batting around the potpourri. Stuff the nest filled with potpourri into the gathered fabric circle.

Pull tight and finish closing the opening. Knot to end. Place doily over top of stuffed circle and tack in place. (See Fig. 1.)

DOILY SACHET

See picture on p. 98

Two 4" Cluny doilies
Polyester fiber filling
Potpourri, scented oil, scented rice, etc.

Stitch around the stitching line of doily. (See Fig. 1.)

Leave open 1/2" to stuff. Stuff with fiber filling and oil, potpourri, or scented rice.

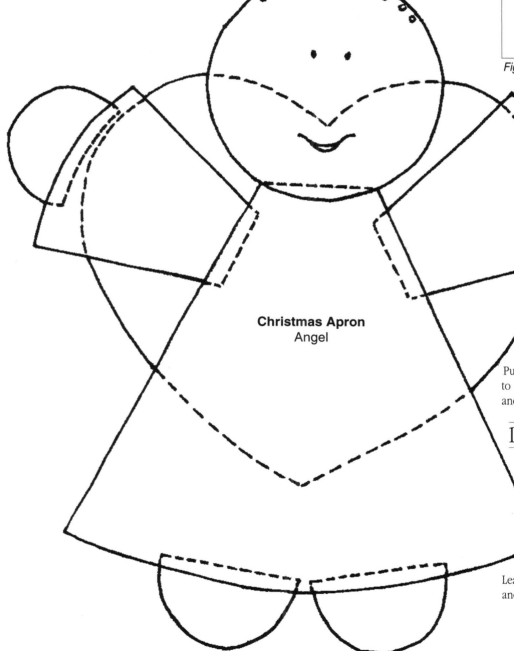

Christmas Apron
Angel

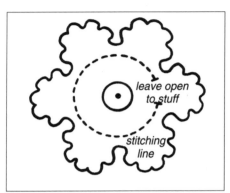

Figure 1

Sew opening closed. Embellish with ribbon, baby's breath, dried or silk flowers, beads as desired.

GATHERED DOILY SACHET

See picture on p. 98

10" or 12" Cluny doily
24" of 1/4" wide ribbon
Polyester fiber filling
Scented oils, potpourri, or scented rice

Thread ribbon through openings in doily (See Fig. 1.). Ribbon must end on the same side that you started on.

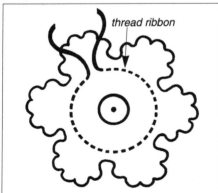

Figure 1

To gather pull ribbon (like a drawstring). Fill bag with scented stuffing, potpourri, or scented rice.

Tie the bag closed with a bow. Embellish with your favorite dried flowers, baby's breath, pearls, as desired.

STENCILED HEART

See picture on p. 133

One 8"x10" sheet of water color paper
Stencil crayon
Permanent, fine-point marker
12" of 1/4" wide ribbon

One 8" Cluny doily
Dried statice or baby's breath
Red beads or ribbon roses
Hot-glue gun or Tacky glue.

Trace template of heart onto water color paper and cut out two.

Using desired stencil, center on heart. Following stencil crayon instructions in Glossary, apply stencil.

With fine-point marker, outline design with mock quilting stitches. (See Glossary for decorative stitching ideas.)

To glue, start at one side point as marked and glue around bottom to point of heart and back to other side point mark. Place hearts together and let dry.

Tie a knot in each end of ribbon. Glue knot in between hearts at side just above where glue stops. To finish, fill with doily and statice . Place flowers or ribbon roses randomly to add color.

GRANDMA'S PADDLE

Shanon Allen
See picture on p. 63

1/3 yd. white, 14-count Aida cloth
1/4 yd. backing fabric
One paint-stirring stick or wooden spoon
Polyester fiber filling
1 yd 1" wide gathered lace
1 yd. 1/4" wide ribbon
Embroidery floss, two colors.

Cut square of Aida cloth about 2" larger than size of heart. Center design and stitch. Cut out Aida heart and backing heart.

Sew gathered lace to Aida cloth heart, raw edge of heart to gathered edge of lace, overlapping ends. With right sides together, sew backing heart to Aida heart, leaving a 2" opening at top center of heart. Clip curves and turn right side out. Stuff with polyester filling.

Place spoon or paint stick into opening and hot glue to secure. Close opening with glue. Make ribbon bow and glue to top center of heart to finish.

Stenciled Heart
Template

STRIP-QUILTED BAG

Karen Carter
See picture on p. 63

2 pieces 14-1/2"x15-1/2" of firm, plain-colored fabric (such as pant-weight material) for base (A, Fig. 1)
1 piece of same material, 44"x3-1/2" (B, Fig. 1)
2 pieces approx. 2-1/2"x18" of same material for straps (C, Fig. 1)
2 pieces bonded batting 14"x15"
Calico (or similar) material cut in strips from 2-1/2" to 3" wide in varying patterns. (Seven or eight different patterns are best.)
1 piece of calico for strip around the top of the bag, approx. 4-1/2"x36"
2 pieces of calico 2"x18" to line the straps

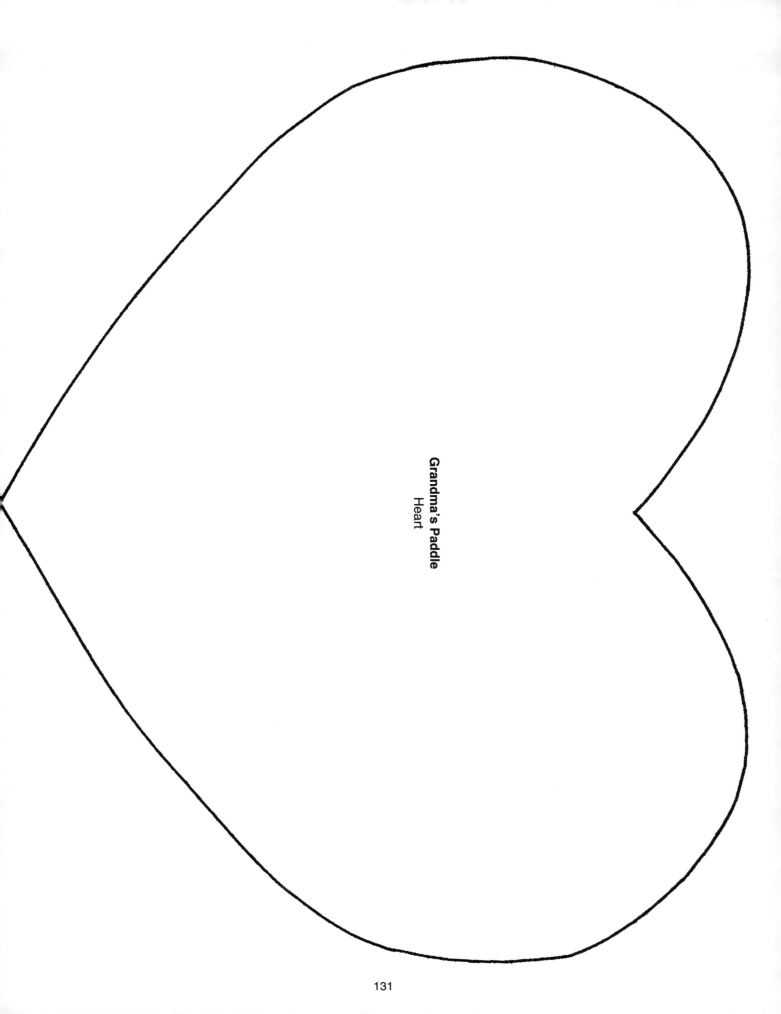

Grandma's Paddle
Heart

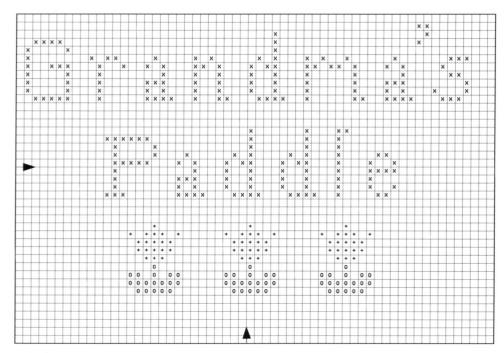

STRIP QUILTING

Lay the batting on top of the 14-1/2"x15-1/2" base. Start with a strip in the middle right sides out. (See Fig. 2.) Lay another strip of the calico right side down on top of the first strip. Stitch with the sewing machine using 1/4" seam allowance along the right edge. Turn right side out and repeat the procedure until the base pieces are covered with the strips of calico. Trim edges.

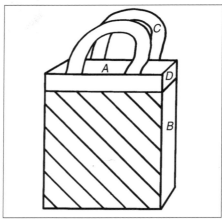

Figure 1

ASSEMBLY OF BAG

With wrong sides together, sew the strip (B, Fig. 1) to one of the pieces. Start at top of one side and sew along bottom and up opposite side. Do the same to the other strip-quilted piece so the two pieces and strip form a bag.

Seams will be on the outside. Bind the outside seams with binding cut from one of the calicos (about 1-1/2" wide by about 86" to 90"). Fold binding in half lengthwise and press. Sew raw edges to raw edge of seam. Fold binding over seam and top stitch.

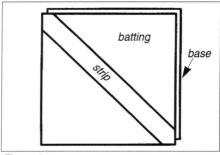

Figure 2

Make the straps by sewing the calico strapping piece to the plain piece, right sides together. Using 1/4" seam allowance, sew down both length-wise edges to form a tube. Turn right side out and press. Sew straps to sides of bag about 2-1/2" from the edges.

Cut calico piece D (Fig. 1), one inch larger than circumference of top. Fold 1/2" under on one of the short ends. Pin right side to lining around top of bag, overlapping ends of fabric with folded 1/2" piece underneath. Stitch around circumference of bag.

Turn to outside of bag and stitch down, turning under 1/4" or raw edge. Slip stitch or top stitch opening closed.

TUBE AND BAG SACHETS

See picture on p. 28

One 5"x5" piece of fabric
One 10" piece of lace
Polyester fiber filling
Two 6" pieces of coordinating ribbon
    (width of your choice)
Potpourri, scented oil, or scented rice,
    etc.

TUBE SACHET

Using the 5"x5" piece of fabric, sew lace to two parallel edges. Fold in half lengthwise with right sides together and lace at opposite ends. Stitch a 1/4" seam. Turn tube right side out.

With one 6" piece of ribbon tie a square knot 1/4" from lace edge, closing off end. Stuff half full with polyester fiber filling. Add potpourri, scented oil, or rice. Finish stuffing with polyester fiber filling. Tie off the other end.

BAG SACHET

Using double the length of size of sachet desired in the material of your choice (satin, cotton fabrics, lace, etc.), stitch lace or trimming on one long edge. Fold in half right sides together with lace edge on top. Using 1/4" seam sew down side and bottom. Turn right side out and stuff with filling and scented oil, potpourri, scented rice, etc. Tie top with bow and decorate with flowers, baby's breath, pearls, as desired.

LACE COLLARS FROM LINENS

Camille Jackson
See picture on p. 62

TABLE RUNNER COLLAR

One table runner makes two identical collars. Use pattern 1. Fold table runner in half with lace edges even. Cut in half. Each half makes 1 collar. Fold runner in half down center with lace sides even.

Measure up 8-3/4" from uncut lace edge along fold and mark. Place pattern with front neck on this mark. Cut where indicated on pattern. Press under 1/4" on all cut edges. Press under 1/4" inch again. Stitch.

Starting at top center, then clockwise: Hand and Foot Reindeer, p. 143; Wooden Holiday Tree, p. 123; Candy Train, p. 142; Tree Card, p. 146; Paper Santa Place Mat, p. 145; Children's Christmas Ornaments, p. 142; (on chair) Crayon Stocking, p. 143; (hanging from arm of chair) Christmas Necklace, p. 142; Cookie Tree, p. 143; (on corner of wagon) Stenciled Heart, p. 130; (in wagon) Christmas for the Birds, p. 142; Candy Wreath, p. 11; (on table) Christmas Heart Baskets, p. 148; Dutch Shoe, p. 147; Crayon Card, p. 143; (center rear of table) Santa Nut Cup, p. 144; Santa Mobile, p. 145.

On 2-layer dish: Caramels (top) p. 156 and Divinity, p. 157; (far right) Seven-layer Bars, p. 158;
One-Minute Cookies, p. 158; and Cherry Coconut Bars, p. 157; (lower right) English Toffee, p. 157;
(on dish at left) Raisin Bars, p. 157; Mrs. Santa's Sugar Cookies, p. 154; and Graham Cracker Squares, p. 157.

Starting with punch bowl: Wassail, p. 159; (far right) Raspberry Delight, p. 155; Cheese Ball, p. 158; (right front) No Jell-O Fruit Salad, p. 159; Baked Ham with Apricot Glaze, p. 159; Cranberry Nut Bread, p. 155.

Advent Party, p. 150

Stitch a piece of flat lace where indicated on pattern or use a round button and loop to close.

TEA TOWEL COLLAR
Use pattern 2. Fold tea towel into fourths. Place pattern on towel and cut out neck. Cut a 3-1/2" slit down center of back. Press cut edges under 1/4" then 1/4" again. Stitch. Sew flat lace at neck edges to close or use small round button and loop. If the collar sticks up on the shoulders when worn, then a small dart on the shoulders is needed.

Fold collar in half with fold along the shoulders. Mark dart on each shoulder and stitch. Dart should end just before finished neck edge.

TABLE RUNNER TIE-ON COLLAR
Use pattern 3. Fold table runner in half down the length. Measure 9-1/4" from bottom edge of lace and mark. Place pattern with center dot even with this mark. After pattern is pinned on, mark section to be cut out all the way down to other lace edge. Cut

linen edge

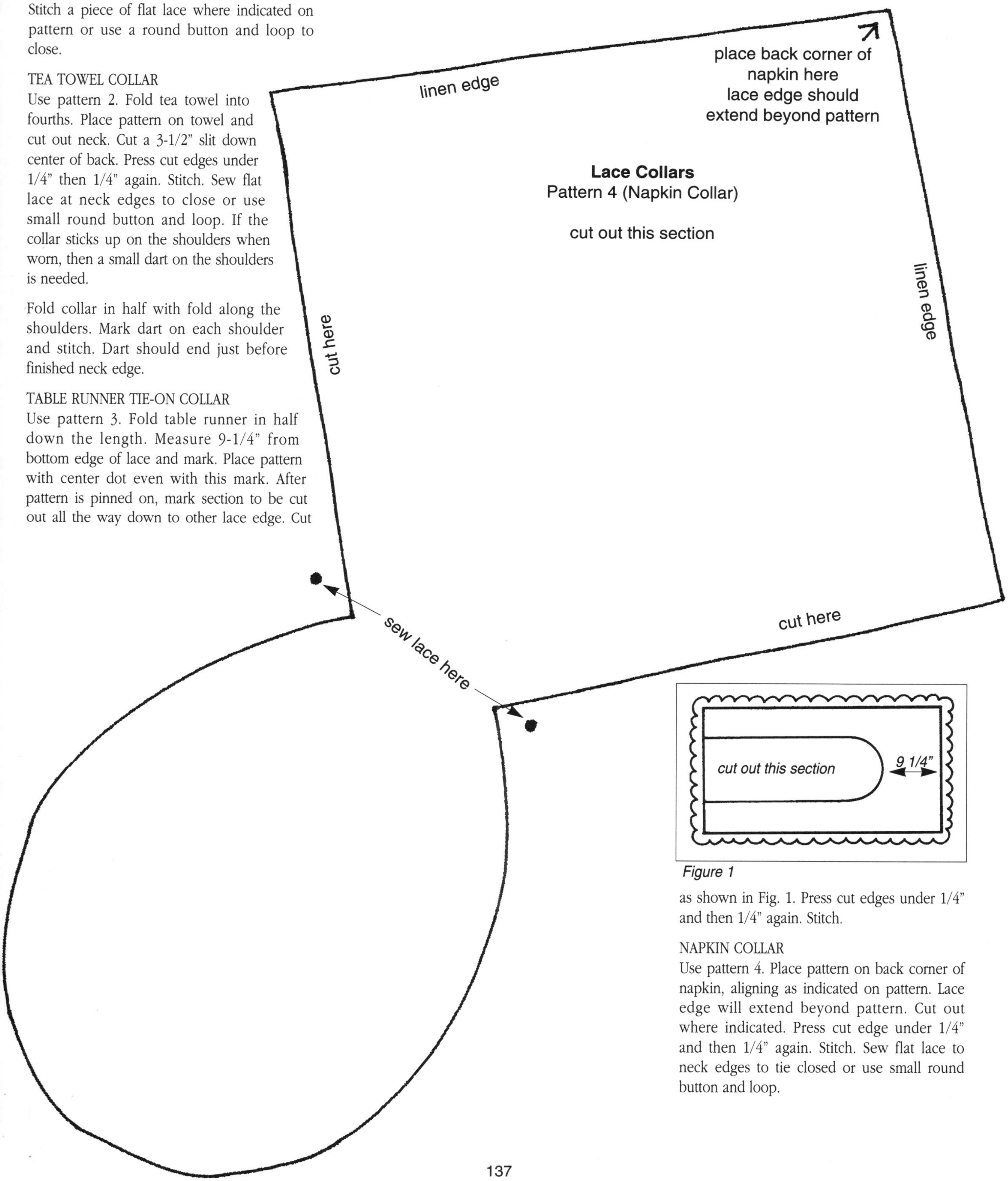

place back corner of
napkin here
lace edge should
extend beyond pattern

Lace Collars
Pattern 4 (Napkin Collar)

cut out this section

linen edge

cut here

cut here

sew lace here

cut here

cut out this section   9 1/4"

Figure 1

as shown in Fig. 1. Press cut edges under 1/4" and then 1/4" again. Stitch.

NAPKIN COLLAR
Use pattern 4. Place pattern on back corner of napkin, aligning as indicated on pattern. Lace edge will extend beyond pattern. Cut out where indicated. Press cut edge under 1/4" and then 1/4" again. Stitch. Sew flat lace to neck edges to tie closed or use small round button and loop.

back

● sew lace here

Lace Collars
Pattern 1 (Table Runner Collar)

lace edge

side

back

front fold

DOILY HAIR BOW

Take small running stitches through center of a doily. (See Fig. 2.) Pull thread tight to gather. Wrap thread around center a few times to secure and make a knot.

Place a 1-1/2" piece of 1/2" wide ribbon around center of doily to cover gathering. On back of doily fold top piece of ribbon under 1/4" and lap over bottom piece tightly. Stitch. Hot glue bow to barrette.

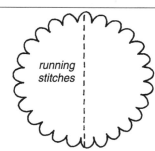

Figure 2

center neck opening

Lace Collars
Pattern 3 (Table Runner Tie-On Collar)

cut out this section

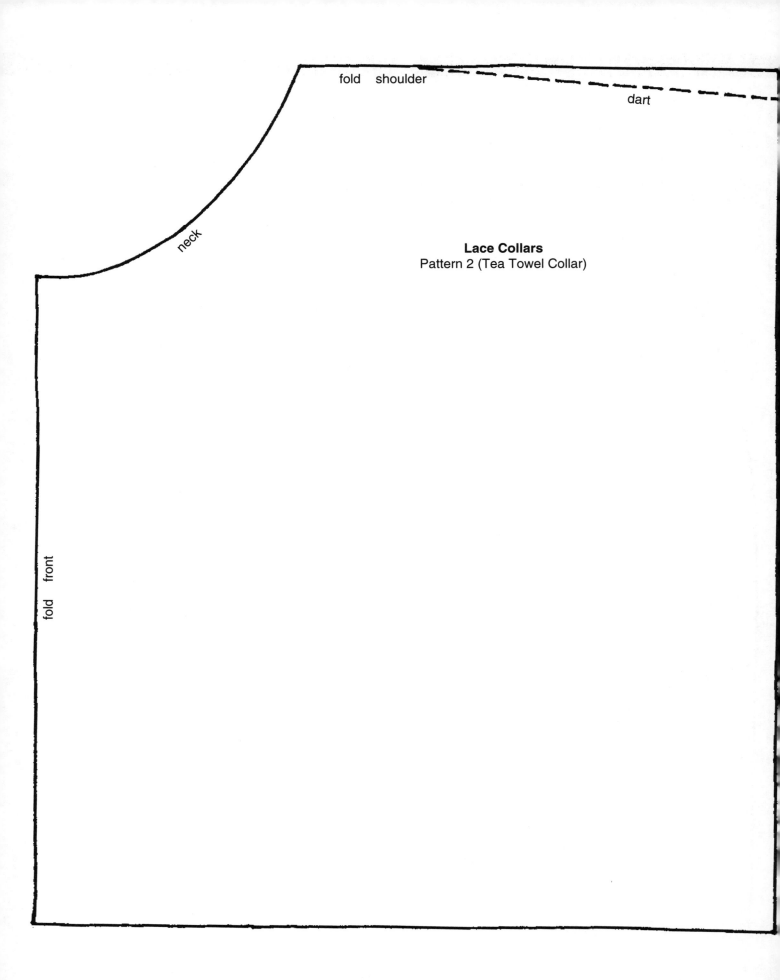

fold   shoulder

dart

neck

Lace Collars
Pattern 2 (Tea Towel Collar)

fold   front

COUNTDOWN

FOURTEEN PROJECTS

TO DO WITH CHILDREN

TO COUNT DOWN

THE LAST TWO WEEKS

TO CHRISTMAS

CANDY TRAIN

See picture on p. 133

3 small pkgs. of Big Red gum
4 small pkgs. of Dentyne gum
1 pkg. of Lifesavers
Small bag of regular M&Ms
Small bag of red licorice (Nibs)
1 Hershey Kiss
1 pkg. of Rollos
1 pkg. of Miniature Peanut Butter
    Cups
1 pkg. Starlight mints
1 pkg. Andes Mints
Frosting in a tube

ENGINE
Use one package of Big Red gum to form the base of the train. With purchased frosting in a tube or glue (if you are not going to eat the train), glue parts together. Place roll of Lifesavers on top of the gum. Use M&Ms for front wheels and Starlight mints for back wheels. Use a yellow M&M for the engine light. A wrapped Hershey Kiss is the smoke stack and the white paper label is the smoke. A Rollo and an Andes mint form the back and a miniature Peanut Butter Cup cut in half is the grate in front of the engine. (See Fig. 1.)

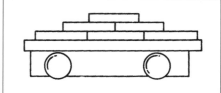

Figure 1

SECOND CAR
Use Big Red for the base. Glue Dentyne to Big Red and layer Andes mints on top. Use M&Ms for the wheels. (See Fig. 2.)

Figure 2

CABOOSE
Use Big Red and Dentyne as base as in second car. Then use single unwrapped Dentyne to form the sides and end of the caboose. Build up middle of caboose with unwrapped single pieces of Dentyne. Use Andes Mints to form

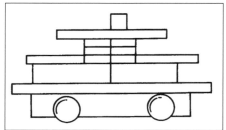

Figure 3

the roof and a small piece of red licorice to form chimney. (See Fig. 3.)

Young children may want to make a simpler engine. (See Fig. 4.)

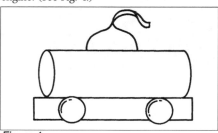

Figure 4

This train would be especially attractive with a Gingerbread House or the cookie Christmas Tree in this book.

CHILDREN'S CHRISTMAS ORNAMENTS

Deanna Hartvigsen
See picture on p. 133

Craft plastic
Christmas fabric

Children's Ornament

Tacky glue
Scribbles paints
Pearl cotton

Using pinking shears, cut round pieces of Christmas fabric.

Cut craft plastic 1/2" smaller than fabric circles and adhere edges with Tacky glue.

Draw designs, pictures, etc. on plastic with Scribbles paints. Let dry for 48 hours.

When dry, thread small loop with pearl cotton to hang ornament.

CHRISTMAS NECKLACE

Deanna Hartvigsen
See picture on p. 133

3 miniature spools, 1/2" in length
1/4" wide ribbon
1/4" wide strip of Christmas fabric
Tacky glue or hot-glue gun
1 yard rattail ribbon.

Cut ribbon in small strips and glue on two spools. Place fabric on third spool and glue thread spools onto on rattail ribbon. Tie ends together.

CHRISTMAS FOR THE BIRDS

V. DuPaix
See picture on p. 133

In Sweden, people decorate a tree outside for the birds. This festive idea helps children learn about giving, even to the wild animals. We suggest that you explain that birds and other wild animals must struggle to find food during the cold winter months.

Peanut butter
Honey
Milk
Pine cone
Bird seed
Ornament hanger
Ribbon.

Mix peanut butter, honey, and milk to a mixture of "pancake batter" consistency. Attach a wire ornament hook to the wide end of the pine cone. Dip the cone in the peanut butter mixture, then roll in bird seed.

Hang one or more of these by a festive ribbon from a tree outside. Then watch each day as the birds show their appreciation!

COOKIE TREE

See picture on p. 133

One recipe of
Mrs. Santa's
Sugar Cookie
dough, (p. 154)
Green frosting
Yellow frosting
(optional)
M&Ms
Red licorice laces
Other candy as desired to
trim the tree.

Roll dough to 3/8" thickness.
Cut out stars in graduated
sizes and bake. Frost
with green frosting.
Layer cookies
together,
offsetting
stars

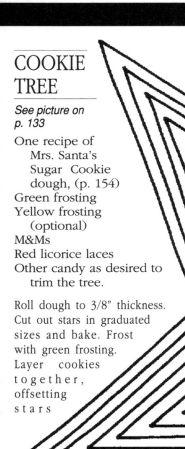

Cookie Tree
Star

with largest at bottom and smallest at top.
Stand the smallest star upright. You may want
to frost this one with yellow frosting. Use
M&Ms, red licorice laces, and other candies to
trim the tree.

HAND AND FOOT REINDEER

Melanie Van Der Hoeven
See picture on p. 133

15"x24" piece of butcher paper
Finger paints or acrylic paints
    (brown, yellow, blue)
1" red pompon
Waxed paper
Coat hanger
Staples or tape

Cut a piece of waxed paper large enough to
put paint on. Lay butcher paper on a flat
surface. Spread a layer of brown paint on
waxed paper. Press child's bare foot in brown
paint and then on the center of the butcher
paper.

Cut another piece of waxed paper and put a
layer of yellow paint on it. Press child's hands

in
the
paint
and
then on
the but-
cher paper
with heel
part of the
hands next to
toes. Let it dry.

Paint blue eyes on
the reindeer and put
glue on a pompon
for its nose. Fold the
top over a coat hanger and staple or tape to
hold in place. Write *Merry Christmas* at the
bottom and you have a cute Christmas wall
hanging.

CRAYON CARD

See picture on p. 133

Waxed paper
Crayons

Iron
Brown paper
Regular or construction
    paper
Paper punch
18" of 1/4" wide ribbon.

Cut two pieces of waxed paper
9"x12". With a knife, scrape crayons
to get shavings. Keep shavings in
color piles.

Lay one piece of waxed paper over a
piece of brown paper. Sprinkle on
crayon shavings in random fashion or in
desired design.

Place other piece of waxed paper on top
of crayon shavings. Put another piece
of brown paper on top. With hot
iron, melt both sides of
waxed paper and
crayons together.
Do not move
i r o n

while on brown paper. To be sure entire area
is melted, pick up iron and replace it, using
vertical motion. Let cool and trim with scissors.

Fold in half with construction paper inside.
Then using hole punch, make 2 holes in the
folded side of the card, making sure it goes
through both the waxed paper and the
construction paper.

Lace ribbon through holes and tie bow on
outside (front) of card. Write your message
inside on the construction paper.

CRAYON STOCKING

See picture on p. 133

3/8 yd. of muslin
Crayons
Brown paper

From muslin cut two stockings using pattern
(cut with pinking shears).

Using crayons, decorate the muslin stocking
you have chosen as the front with your
favorite Christmas ideas.

Place the designed stocking between two
pieces of brown paper (a paper bag will

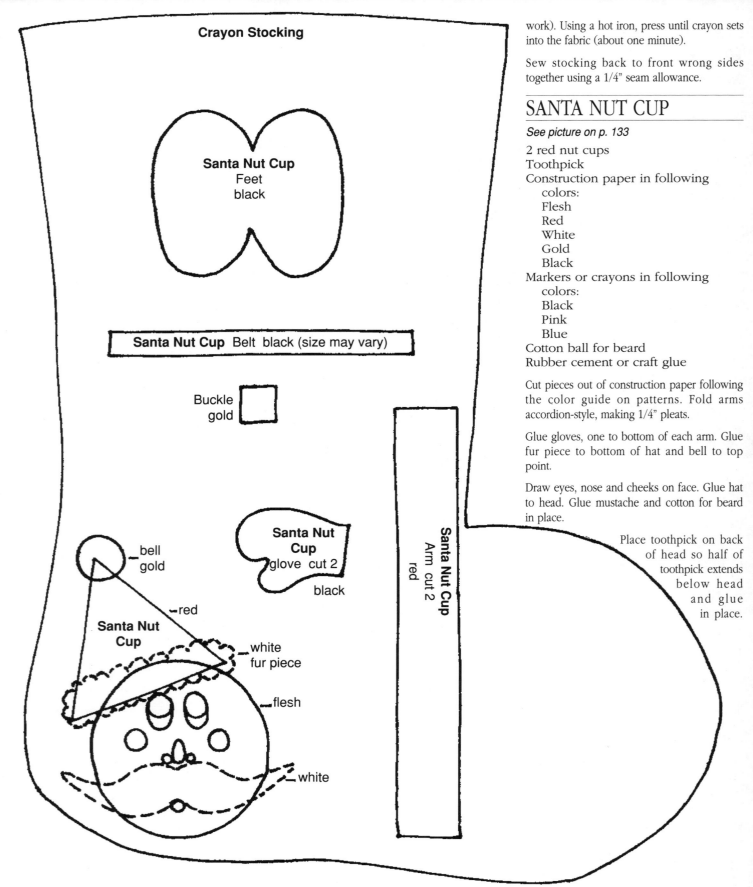

Crayon Stocking

Santa Nut Cup
Feet
black

Santa Nut Cup Belt black (size may vary)

Buckle
gold

bell
gold

Santa Nut Cup
glove cut 2
black

Santa Nut Cup
Arm cut 2
red

red

Santa Nut Cup

white
fur piece

flesh

white

work). Using a hot iron, press until crayon sets into the fabric (about one minute).

Sew stocking back to front wrong sides together using a 1/4" seam allowance.

SANTA NUT CUP

See picture on p. 133

2 red nut cups
Toothpick
Construction paper in following
    colors:
    Flesh
    Red
    White
    Gold
    Black
Markers or crayons in following
    colors:
    Black
    Pink
    Blue
Cotton ball for beard
Rubber cement or craft glue

Cut pieces out of construction paper following the color guide on patterns. Fold arms accordion-style, making 1/4" pleats.

Glue gloves, one to bottom of each arm. Glue fur piece to bottom of hat and bell to top point.

Draw eyes, nose and cheeks on face. Glue hat to head. Glue mustache and cotton for beard in place.

Place toothpick on back of head so half of toothpick extends below head and glue in place.

144

In center bottom of first cup, poke toothpick down so that the head is resting on cup. Glue arms, one to each side of first nut cup.

Glue feet to bottom of second cup, extending toes out beyond cup bottom.

Glue buckle to center of belt. Place buckle in center of second cup making sure feet are forward.

Glue belt in place cutting any extra length of belt in back, if necessary.

SANTA MOBILE

See picture on p. 133

Red, white, and black construction paper
Mobile may be made in various sizes according to the space in which you want to hang it.

Trace two of each pattern piece onto selected color of paper. Fold pieces in half and then place two like pieces together.

Using a long running stitch on the sewing machine, sew down the middle of the pieces on fold line. Sewing order, top to bottom: Pompon, hat,

Santa Mobile
Belly

Santa Mobile
Beard
white

Santa Mobile
Mustache   white

Santa Mobile
Pompon
white

Santa Mobile
Hat
red

Santa Mobile
Boots
black

Tie off threads at the end. (Do not backstitch as it will weaken the paper.)

Fold pieces in half to form an X and make the mobile dimensional. (See Fig. 1.)

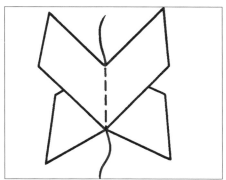

Figure 1

mustache, beard, belly, and boots. Leave about 10 inches of thread at the top of the mobile to hang it, and one to two inches between the pieces. Do not cut threads in between.

PAPER SANTA PLACE MAT

See picture on p. 133
11"x16" butcher paper
Construction paper in the following colors:
   Flesh
   Red
   Pink
   Black
   White
   Blue
   Yellow
Rubber cement or white glue
Fine-point, permanent black marker

Trace templates onto construction paper. Follow the colors written on pattern pieces. Cut out pieces. Center on butcher paper and glue in place following diagram. Edge of placement may be decorated in any manner desired. Using fine-point marker, draw mock stitches. (See Fig. 1.) Sparkle in eyes may be added using white chalk.

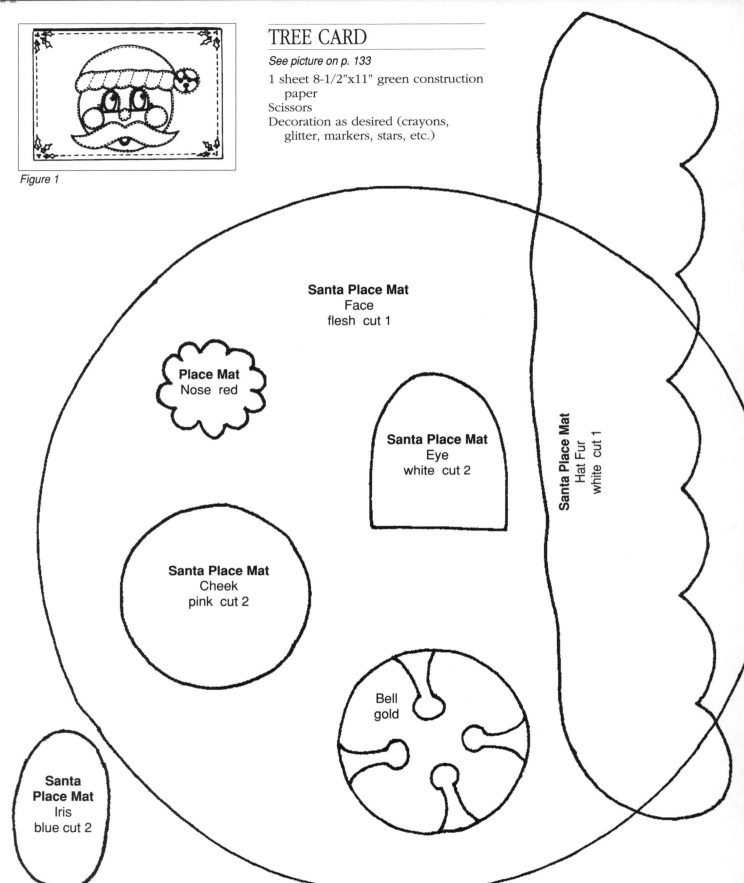

Figure 1

TREE CARD

See picture on p. 133

1 sheet 8-1/2"x11" green construction
    paper
Scissors
Decoration as desired (crayons,
    glitter, markers, stars, etc.)

Santa Place Mat
Face
flesh cut 1

Place Mat
Nose red

Santa Place Mat
Eye
white cut 2

Santa Place Mat
Hat Fur
white cut 1

Santa Place Mat
Cheek
pink cut 2

Bell
gold

**Santa
Place Mat**
Iris
blue cut 2

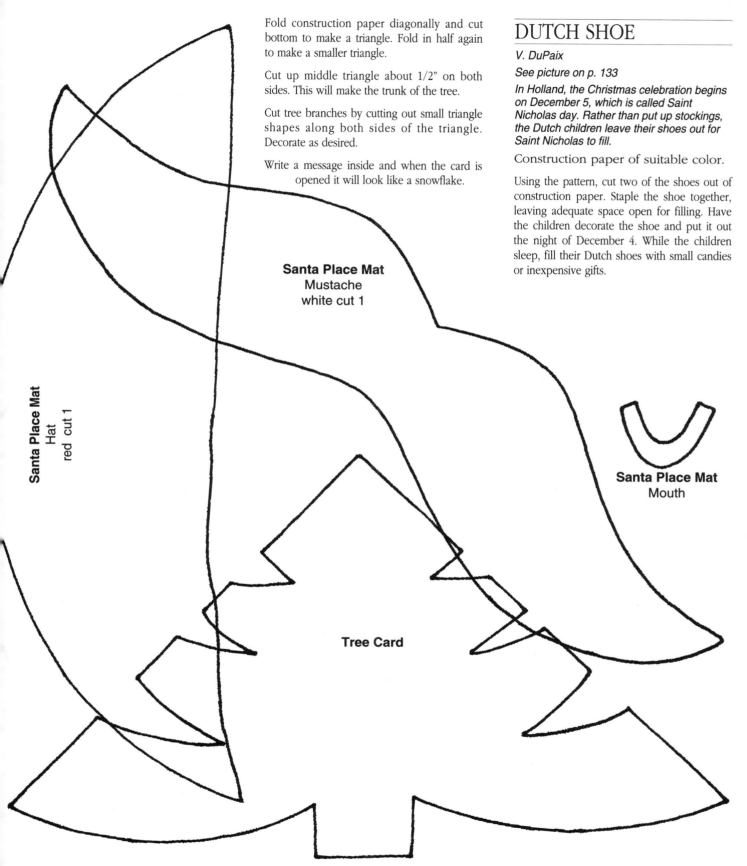

Fold construction paper diagonally and cut bottom to make a triangle. Fold in half again to make a smaller triangle.

Cut up middle triangle about 1/2" on both sides. This will make the trunk of the tree.

Cut tree branches by cutting out small triangle shapes along both sides of the triangle. Decorate as desired.

Write a message inside and when the card is opened it will look like a snowflake.

DUTCH SHOE

V. DuPaix

See picture on p. 133

In Holland, the Christmas celebration begins on December 5, which is called Saint Nicholas day. Rather than put up stockings, the Dutch children leave their shoes out for Saint Nicholas to fill.

Construction paper of suitable color.

Using the pattern, cut two of the shoes out of construction paper. Staple the shoe together, leaving adequate space open for filling. Have the children decorate the shoe and put it out the night of December 4. While the children sleep, fill their Dutch shoes with small candies or inexpensive gifts.

Santa Place Mat
Mustache
white cut 1

Santa Place Mat
Hat
red cut 1

Santa Place Mat
Mouth

Tree Card

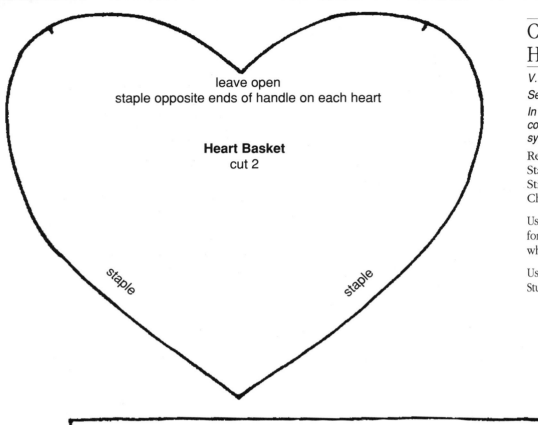

leave open
staple opposite ends of handle on each heart

Heart Basket
cut 2

staple

staple

CHRISTMAS HEART BASKETS

V. DuPaix

See picture on p. 133

In Europe and especially in the Scandinavian countries, hearts are a festive Christmas symbol.

Red construction paper
Stapler
Stickers, felt-tip markers, sequins, etc.
Christmas tissue

Using pattern, cut two hearts and one handle for each basket wanted. Staple hearts together where shown. Staple handle to V in hearts.

Using whatever is desired, decorate baskets. Stuff baskets with decorative Christmas tissue.

Heart Basket
Handle cut 1

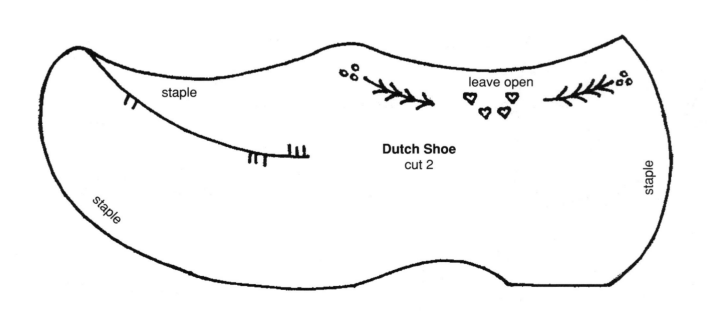

staple

leave open

Dutch Shoe
cut 2

staple

staple

ENTERTAINMENT

PARTY IDEAS

RECIPES

TABLE TREATMENTS

ADVENT PARTY

Ann Danzig
See picture on p. 136

Advent parties are celebrated on the four Sundays before Christmas. Four items are essential to an Advent Party: music, food, the advent wreath, and scripture reading.

Try to bring as much atmosphere to each party as possible. Dim the lights and burn candles. Burn a Christmas scent in a potpourri pot to create a festive aroma.

If you have invited guests, it is fun to give them gifts or treats before they depart. Each Sunday's events should contribute to a relaxed spiritual evening that will invite the spirit of Christmas into your home early in the season. If necessary, keep foods simple and easy. Prepare ahead as much as possible in order to invite and sustain the true spirit of the Sabbath.

ADVENT WREATH

This wreath is made of green boughs and is either set on a table or hung horizontally. It is most festive hanging with red ribbon from the ceiling. It must support four candles placed at equal distances around the wreath.

On the first Sunday one candle is lit and burned one quarter of the way down. On the second Sunday, the first candle and a second candle are lit and each is burned another quarter of the way down (this takes the first candle down half way). On the third Sunday, the first two candles and a third candle are lit and each is burned an additional quarter of the way down. On the fourth and last Sunday, all the candles are lit and all are allowed to burn all the way down.

The first advent Sunday frequently falls on the last Sunday of November, so plan well ahead so that you will be prepared with at least your advent wreath hung.

FOOD

A nice meal should be prepared using foods that are special to those gathered. Be sure to use any special Christmas china or linens you may have. The following recipes are popular in our family.

ROULADEN

1 lg. round steak
1 lb. bacon strips
1 lg. onion, chopped
Dill pickles sliced in thin strips or
   chopped

Mustard
Salt and pepper
Cotton string

Pound the round steak on a cutting board until very thin. Cut into 5"x5" pieces. Spread with mustard, salt and pepper. Place two to three pieces of bacon on the round steak pieces. Sprinkle with onion and chopped pickle, or if dill strips are used, place two or three of them on the steak pieces with the onion. Roll the pieces tightly and tie with cotton string at each end to hold together.

Grease a pan and brown the meat on all sides. Add 1 to 1-1/2" of water and simmer for four or five hours or until tender. Add water as needed. Remove strings and serve. Gravy can be made from juices if desired. Serve with boiled or mashed potatoes.

PIROSHKI

Dough:
2-1/2 c. white flour
1 c. soft butter
1/2 to 3/4 c. cold water
1 egg

Blend flour, butter, and egg. Add enough cold water to make a dough that holds together.

Filling:
1 lb. lean ground beef
1 finely chopped onion
1 lb. bacon
1 tsp. chopped caraway seed
   (optional)
Salt and pepper to taste

Cook bacon until crisp, then break into small pieces. Brown ground beef and onions in frying pan. Add other ingredients.

Roll dough out on floured surface to about 1/8" thickness. Cut in 3" to 4" circles and fill with approx. 1 tsp. filling. Fold in half and seal. Place on greased cookie sheet and brush with beaten egg. Bake for 25 min. or until brown in a 400-degree oven.

These are wonderful served with cranberry sauce and your favorite homemade soup.

SAUERBRATEN

1-1/2 lb. beef roast
1 c. wine vinegar
1 tsp. salt
2 c. water
1 lg. onion, cut in large pieces
5 peppercorns
2 juniper berries

Combine all ingredients except roast in sauce pan. Bring to boil. Simmer for 15 min. Pour over roast and cover. Marinate in refrigerator for two to three days, turning meat occasionally. Drain meat and strain marinade. Cook the beef as you would a roast beef, browning first in shortening and then adding the strained marinade as liquid. Simmer three to five hours until tender. Add liquid as needed. Thicken the juice with gingersnap crumbs and use for gravy over potatoes.

MUSIC

Christmas music is a vital part of an Advent Party. It helps create a warm atmosphere. Play Christmas carols softly in the background throughout the evening. Invite your guests to prepare some music if they are musically inclined. One evening it would be especially lovely to play the music from the Messiah and follow along in the scriptures. This will require some earlier preparation to find and mark the scriptures. It is a wonderful way to invite the true spirit of Christmas into your home.

SCRIPTURES

The following groups of scriptures are suggested for the four Advent Sundays.

Scriptures Used in the Messiah:

Isaiah 40:1-5	Psalms 69:19
Haggai 2:6-7	Lamentations 1:12
Malachi 3:1-3	Isaiah 53:8
Isaiah 7:14	Isaiah 40:9
Isaiah 60:1-3	Isaiah 9:6
Psalms 16:10	Psalms 24:7-10
Luke 2:8-14	Hebrews 1:5-6
Zech. 9:9-10	Psalms 68:10, 18
Isaiah 35:5-6	Isaiah 40:11
Rom. 10:15, 18	Matthew 11:28-29
John 1:29	Psalms 2:1-4, 9
Rev. 19:6	Isaiah 53:3-4
Job 19:25-26	Psalms 22:7-8
1 Cor. 15:20-22	

The Christmas Story:

Luke 1:27-42	Luke 2:1-20
Matthew 2:1-12	

Attributes of Christ:

Forgiving	John 8:1-11
Healing power	Mark 2:1-12
Prayerful	Matthew 6:9-13
Performs miracles	Matthew 14:14-21
Loves children	Mark 10:13-16
Teaches	Matthew 13:33-52
Resists temptation	Matthew 4:1-11
Respects temple	John 2:13-22
Is baptized	Matthew 3:13-17
Suffered for our sins	Luke 22:40-46
Is the Messiah	John 8:23-32
Is the Light of the world	John 8:12
Commands the elements	Matthew 14:22-33

Prophecies of the Coming of Christ:

Job 19:25	Psalms 24:7
Psalms 102:16	Isaiah 40:3, 5
Isaiah 45:23	Ezekiel 21:27
Malachi 3:2	Haggai 2:7
Matthew 16:27	

A DICKENS OF A PARTY!

John M. Hartvigsen

The small novel A Christmas Carol *has made Dickens's name synonymous with Christmas. Credited with reviving the celebration of Christmas, his little book contains a rich sampling of Christmas traditions. Draw from these traditions to create a Christmas party that would warm even Scrooge's heart! There are many adaptations of the story, but start by reading the original book. It is short and easy reading. The reading may not only give you some ideas for your party, it will bring joy to your entire celebration of Christmas.*

DECORATIONS

Use plenty of evergreens. Pine garlands and holly form the basic decorations. Surprisingly, the Cratchits didn't have a Christmas tree. Christmas trees did not become common in Britain until after Scrooge's time.

Cut out construction paper figures to represent a plum pudding: an oval for the plate, a brown circle for the pudding. Stud the pudding with black paper punches for the raisins. Top it with holly leaves and berries.

A ponderous chain ". . . of cashboxes, padlocks, ledgers, deeds, and heavy purses wrought in steel" bound Marley's ghost. Make colorful chains from construction paper and attach silhouettes of the cash-boxes and the other symbols of Marley's miserly life.

Scrooge's door knocker changed into Marley's face. On the door leading to the party, display a door knocker also transformed into Marley's face. This ghostly door knocker can be made as elaborately as you like. A cloth sculpture made from a stuffed nylon could be a decoration you'll keep. It can also be made simply out of construction paper cut-outs or an old Halloween mask. A pair of wire spectacles on the forehead will complete the specter. Marley's face seemed so real to Scrooge that as he looked at the back of the door "he half-expected to be terrified with the sight of Marley's pigtail sticking out into the hall." Make Marley's pigtail and hang it on the back of the door opposite his face hung on the front. See how many guests notice.

GAMES

Several games are mentioned in *A Christmas Carol*. Dickens loved to play party games. Although these games are old, modern versions are still common today.

BLINDMAN'S BUFF

A blindfolded guest must catch another person and guess whom he's caught. Those players hiding might be told to position themselves and then freeze silently in place. They might stand, sit, or even lay on the floor. Players might alternately be told to keep moving and make different noises to attract the blindfolded player. The "blind man" might only be allowed to identify people by their hands or the shape of their heads. Many variations are possible.

YES AND NO

A guest leaves the room while the group picks some object. Upon returning he or she must guess the object selected. This is done by asking questions that may be answered by either "yes" or "no." Whoever guesses correctly by asking the fewest number of questions is the winner.

FORFEITS

Each player is given three pieces of wrapped candy. The players sit on chairs in a circle. The blanks in a series of sentences are completed using words that begin with consecutive letters of the alphabet. If a player cannot add the needed word, a piece of candy is forfeited. After all three pieces of candy are forfeited, the player takes his or her chair and leaves the circle. The last two players left in the game are the winners and divide the forfeited candy.

Examples of the series of sentences are shown below:

I love my love with an "a" because he is <u>available</u>.

I love my love with a "b" because she is <u>beautiful</u>.

I love my love with a "c" because he is <u>courteous</u>, and so on.

Another version of forfeits comes from a movie adaptation of *A Christmas Carol*.

The minister's cat is an <u>amiable</u> cat.

The minister's cat is a <u>boisterous</u> cat.

The minister's cat is a <u>colorful</u> cat.

With this second version, players may clap in time to establish a four-count rhythm. On count one and two the hands are clapped against the knees. The hands clap together on count three. On count four the hands clap on the knees again.

The minister's / cat is a / <u>boisterous</u> / cat.

   clap 1   / clap 2   / clap 3   / clap 4

The person adding the new word must keep time in giving the answer or it is a miss.

FOOD

At Fezziwig's Ball, guests ate "cold roast" and "cold boiled." A tray of assorted, thin-sliced delicatessen meats is the modern equivalent. Oranges and apples cut in slices and sections add an authentic and festive touch. Garnish with green parsley and maraschino cherries. Add rolls, spreads, mustard, horseradish, and other sandwich fixings.

Mrs. Fezziwig also served mince pies. Buy the pies or make your own favorite recipe.

At the end of *A Christmas Carol*, Scrooge invites Bob Cratchit to share a bowl of "Smoking Bishop" with him to celebrate Christmas. "Smoking Bishop" was a hot punch made of spiced red wine and orange juice. It received its name from its purple color. The following two recipes substitute cranberry juice for the red wine. The first is a hot punch that warms the body and spirit after caroling on a cold evening. The second is a cold punch that gets its steaming appearance from dry ice.

SMOKING BISHOP
(hot punch)
1 qt. cranberry juice
1 qt. orange juice
6 whole cloves
1 stick of cinnamon, 3" long
4 whole allspice corns
1/2 c. sugar
Orange slices

Heat everything except orange slices slowly until sugar dissolves. Garnish with orange slices. Serve in cups or mugs. Serves 12.

STEAMING BISHOP
(cold punch)
2 c. water
2 c. sugar
1 qt. cranberry juice
2 c. water
1 c. orange juice
Juice of 1/2 lemon
Orange slices

Boil first 2 c. of water and sugar together for five minutes. Cool. Mix rest of ingredients adding sugar syrup to taste. Add orange slices for garnish. Chill. Just before serving, add one pound of dry ice to the bottom of the punch bowl. Stir until ice is gone. Serves 12.

PLUM PUDDING

Plum pudding is a centuries-old English tradition of Christmas. Contrary to what might be expected, it contains no plums, but is full of raisins and currants (called plums in Dickens's day). The name could also refer to the fact that the pudding swells or "plums up" during cooking. The pudding originated as a soup or porridge made from cereals, fruits, and meat. It symbolized the good things of the earth provided by God for our food.

"In half a minute Mrs. Cratchit entered— flushed, but smiling proudly— with the pudding, like a speckled cannonball, blazing in ignited brandy, and bedight with Christmas holly stuck into the top.

"Oh, a wonderful pudding! Bob Cratchit said, and calmly too, that he regarded it as the greatest success achieved by Mrs. Cratchit since their marriage."

Plum pudding may be too rich and heavy for modern tastes. To keep the spirit of this dessert, try Plum Pudding Custard Ice Cream.

PLUM PUDDING CUSTARD ICE CREAM

1-1/2 c. scalded milk
3/4 c. sugar
1/2 c. cold milk
1 whole egg and 2 egg yolks, slightly
   beaten
1 pt. cream
1 Tbsp. vanilla
1/4 Tbsp. salt
1/4 c. mixed candied fruit, chopped
   fine
1/4 c. currants
1/4 c. dry macaroon crumbs

Add the scalded milk to the sugar and cold milk. Stir mixture over hot water to cook for eight minutes. Add eggs. Cook over hot water for an additional two minutes. Then add rest of ingredients. Mix well. Freeze in ice cream freezer. Scoop into a round-bottomed stainless steel bowl and smooth to conform to shape of bowl. Cover top with heavy-duty aluminum foil. Harden in the freezer. Loosen from bowl by dipping in hot water for a few seconds. Invert on plate and remove. Garnish top with a sprig of holly leaves using red cinnamon candies in place of berries. Makes 3 pts.

It took the visit of three ghosts to teach Ebenezer Scrooge how to keep Christmas well. Share with your guests the memories of Christmas Past, the joy of Christmas Present, and the hope of Christmas Yet to Come.

CHRISTMAS MORNING FAMILY BRUNCH

Julie Wilcox

Christmas morning, family, warm wishes, and love—a perfect combination for celebration! Families gather for sharing and create memories that last for years to come.

INVITATIONS

A collage of pictures from Christmases past create the perfect cover for an invitation. Pictures of Grandpa standing near the old Model A in the snow, Grandma baking her famous apple pie, Mom and Dad on their first Christmas day together, and brothers and sisters gathered around the Christmas tree—all invoke memories never to be forgotten and ideal to use on the cover of an invitation to be sent to precious family members. Inside, you may want to use the following:

Old photos and letters collecting the dust

*And time honored memories from attics and
   such*

*Remind us of loved ones who down through
   the years*

*Brought us memories of Christmas, love and
   good cheer.*

Time never changes the heart or the sound

Of family carols and children around

To dish out the merry-tide cheer and the glee

Of true Christmas spirit so precious to me.

> Let's celebrate
> Christmas morning together.
> Time: 10:00 a.m.
> Place: Home with Mother and Dad

FAMILY GIFTS

One month prior to Christmas, family members draw names. The name they choose will be the person they are to present a gift to on Christmas morning. Be sure to include the children.

As the days get closer to Christmas, everyone creates a personalized "gift" for the relative whose name he or she has drawn. A $3.00 limit is placed as a limit for expenditures. If Dave likes music, a recorded tape of his favorite country/western songs (featuring the singing voice of the person giving the gift) makes a perfect gift. Does Aunt Shirley love a beautiful flower garden? Why, a basket full of seeds! Aaron loves M&Ms—so how about a whole shoeboxful, individually wrapped!

When Christmas morning comes around, the family gathers around the family room and opens up the gifts one at a time. Laughter, teasing and fun make this creative gift-giving among brothers and sisters (and cousins) a tradition to last throughout the years.

BRUNCH BUFFET

Food becomes a Christmas tradition in every home. Families create their favorite dishes for the perfect Christmas morning buffet. A blend of breakfast casseroles, fruit, bread and delicious jellies satisfies all appetites.

> Bacon-Chestnut Wraps
> Sausage and Apple Appetizers
> Sausage Casserole
> Cheesy Potatoes
> Cranberry Salad
> Peach Cobbler
> Pumpkin Muffins
> Date Nut Bread
> Apricot-Pineapple Jam
> Cinnamon-Apple Jelly
> Chocolate Egg Nog
> Cinnamon Santa Sticks

CENTERPIECE

The centerpiece is a collection of colorful fruits. Apples, oranges, nuts and twigs of evergreen adorn a round wooden tapered cone to complement the buffet. Nails attached to the cone hold the apples and oranges to the cone shape. Nuts and evergreen fill in the spaces between the arrangement of fruits. The cone is topped off with a medium-sized pineapple for a crowning effect. Traditional candlesticks with tapered candles complete the setting.

BACON-CHESTNUT WRAPS

1 lb. sliced bacon
60 whole chestnuts, drained
1 bottle Hunt's Original Flavored
   Barbeque Sauce
1/2 c. honey

Cut each slice of bacon into thirds. Wrap a piece of bacon around each chestnut, securing with a toothpick. Bake at 375 degrees for 30 min. Drain fat. Mix barbeque sauce and honey together. Pour over wrapped chestnuts and bake an additional 15 min. Serve in warming tray. Makes about 60 appetizers.

SAUSAGE AND APPLE APPETIZERS

2 Tbsp. butter or margarine
1 lg. onion, chopped
1/2 c. apple jelly
1/2 c. brown sugar, firmly packed
2 lbs. cocktail-sized smoked sausages
3 apples, peeled, cored, and sliced

1 Tbsp. cornstarch
2 Tbsp. warm water

In a large skillet, melt butter over medium high heat. Add onion and sauté, stirring constantly, until onion is golden. Stir in apple jelly and brown sugar. Add sausages and reduce heat to medium low. Cook, stirring occasionally, 20 min. or until mixture begins to thicken. Combine cornstarch and water and stir into mixture in pan. Cook 2 to 3 min. more or until mixture thickens. Serve warm. Makes about 30 appetizers.

SAUSAGE CASSEROLE
1 lb. browned sausage
8 slices bread, crust removed and cubed
1 c. grated cheese
3-1/2 c. milk
8 eggs
1/2 tsp. salt

Layer bread, cheese, and sausage in 8-1/2"x11" pan. Mix together milk, eggs and salt. Pour over the layered mixture. Bake uncovered at 325 degrees for 1 hour. Serve warm. Serves 20.

CHEESY POTATOES
6 medium potatoes, cooked, peeled and sliced
1 pt. sour cream
1 can cream of mushroom soup
1 c. grated sharp cheese
1 small onion, chopped

Mix together sour cream, soup, cheese and onion. Fold sauce into potatoes. Pour into casserole dish. Cover top with plenty of extra cheese. Bake at 350 degrees for 1/2 hour. Serves 20.

CRANBERRY SALAD
1 c. water
2 c. sugar
4 c. cranberries
2 c. mini-marshmallows
2 apples, sliced
3 c. orange sections
3 bananas, sliced
1/2 c. pecans

Combine water and sugar; boil until syrupy. Add cranberries and cook until cranberries burst. Remove from heat and let stand 10 min. Chill. Add remaining ingredients to cranberries and chill thoroughly. Serve on lettuce leaf. Top with whipped cream dressing, if desired. Serves 28.

PEACH COBBLER
3 c. fresh or frozen peaches, sliced
1 Tbsp. lemon juice

1/4 tsp. almond extract
1 c. sifted flour
1 c. sugar
1/2 tsp. salt
1 egg, beaten
6 Tbsp. margarine, melted

Preheat oven to 375 degrees. Butter 10"x6" baking dish. Place peaches on bottom. Sprinkle with lemon juice and extract. Sift together dry ingredients. Add egg and mix with fork or hands until crumbly. Sprinkle over peaches. Drizzle with melted margarine. Bake 35 to 40 min. This is also excellent made with blueberries or other fresh fruit.

PUMPKIN MUFFINS
2 c. Bisquick
1/2 c. sugar
1/2 tsp. cinnamon
1/4 tsp. nutmeg
1/4 tsp. cloves
1 egg
3/4 c. milk
2 Tbsp. salad oil
1/2 c. cooked pumpkin

Preheat oven to 400 degrees. Mix dry ingredients together. Add remaining ingredients and mix. Pour into greased muffin tins and bake 20 min. Makes 16 muffins.

DATE NUT BREAD
1-1/2 c. water
1 c. chopped dates
2 tsp. baking soda
1 Tbsp. shortening, melted
3/4 c. sugar
1/2 tsp. salt
1/4 tsp. baking powder
1 tsp. vanilla
1 egg, beaten well
2-1/4 c. flour
1 c. chopped nuts

Simmer water and dates together for 3 min. Cool slightly, then add soda. Combine remaining ingredients except nuts; mix until smooth. Add date mixture and nuts. Blend well. Pour into two medium loaf pans, which have been greased and lightly floured. Bake at 350 degrees for about one hour, or until loaf tests done. Remove from oven and let stand in pan for 10 min. Turn out onto rack to complete cooling. Makes two loaves. Serve with softened cream cheese.

APRICOT-PINEAPPLE JAM
3 c. apricots
One 20-oz can crushed pineapple
1/2 lemon, sliced and quartered
4 c. sugar

Rinse apricots. Simmer, covered in 1 c. water until tender. Mash apricots; add pineapple, lemon and sugar. Simmer, stirring frequently until thick and clear, about 45 min. Ladle into hot, sterilized jars; seal. Makes about six half-pint jars.

CINNAMON-APPLE JELLY
3 lbs. tart apples
3 c. sugar
1 drop oil of cinnamon
6 drops red food coloring

Wash fruit; do not pare or core. Cut in eighths, removing blemishes. Barely cover with water; simmer until soft. Strain juice through jelly bag. Measure 4 c. juice into large kettle. Add sugar; stir till dissolved. Bring to full rolling boil over high heat. Boil hard till syrup sheets off spoon, about 8 degrees above boiling point of water. Remove from heat; skim off foam quickly. Add cinnamon and coloring. Pour into hot, sterilized glasses. Seal immediately with paraffin. Makes three half-pint jars.

CRANBERRY COFFEE CAKE
Cake:
1/2 c. butter or margarine, softened
1-1/2 c. granulated sugar
2 eggs
1-1/2 tsp. almond extract
1 tsp. vanilla extract
2 c. all-purpose flour
1 tsp. baking powder
1 tsp. baking soda
1 tsp. salt
1 c. sour cream
1 c. whole-berry cranberry sauce
Glaze:
1 c. confectioner's sugar
3 Tbsp. milk
1/2 tsp. almond extract

Preheat oven to 350 degrees. For cake, cream butter and sugar in a large bowl. Beat in eggs and extracts until well blended. In another bowl, combine flour, baking powder, baking soda, and salt. Add flour mixture to creamed mixture, alternating with sour cream. Pour half of batter into a greased 9-inch tube pan. Spoon cranberry sauce over top of batter. Top with remaining batter. Bake 55-60 min. or until a toothpick inserted in center of cake comes out clean. Cool in pan 10 min. For glaze, combine ingredients in a small bowl, blending well. Remove warm cake from pan and drizzle with glaze. Serves 20.

CHOCOLATE EGGNOG
Mix equal amounts of chocolate milk and egg nog in a large beverage bowl. Serve in

decorated Christmas mugs with Cinnamon Santa sticks.

CINNAMON SANTA STICKS
Cinnamon sticks, 6" long
Acrylic paints: Red, Flesh, Black, and
    Pink
Small paint brush
Small stiff paint brush
Duncan Snow Accents

For hat, paint 1/2" of one end of stick red. For face, paint 3/4" below hat flesh; paint eyes black and cheeks pink. Use stiff brush and Snow Accents to paint beard, eyebrows, and hat trim. Use cinnamon sticks to stir Chocolate Egg Nog, hot chocolate, apple cider, or herb tea.

HOMEWARMING THANK-YOU GIFTS
There's no place like home and the very special love of mom and dad. Gifts to say thank-you to mom and dad are treasured for years to come.

MEMORY ALBUM
Pictures and Christmas memories are recorded and displayed in a memory album. The album holds a collection of hand-written memories from the children, grandchildren and close relations. Favorite Christmas thoughts and stories, pictures of mom and dad as children in the winter snow, grandparents fondly remembering their children's cheerful reactions to new-fallen snow or Christmas baking are a delight to younger generations. Reflections of Christmases past in a single collection make a perfect homewarming gift from children to parents.

CHRISTMAS CROSS-STITCH
Have daughters and daughters-in-law pass a Christmas cross-stitch sampler from one to another, each stitching a portion of a beautiful sampler, to be given to mom on Christmas Day. Their combined efforts will be cherished by everyone.

Suggested thoughts for sampler:
All hearts come home for Christmas.
Peace on Earth
May your days be merry and bright
Glory to God
Joy to the World
Let Saints and Angels Sing

YULE LOG

Pieter J. Lingen, Mark J. Johnson
See picture on p. 64
The traditional Yule Log is a wonderful way to enjoy the Christmas season. The Yule Log

originated in Norway hundreds of years ago. During the winter months in Norway, the sun shines for only a brief time. Norsemen were led to believe that by burning a log the sun would not die. It became the custom to burn logs of tree-trunk size during the winter months. The custom evolved to burning the log on Christmas Eve at a family gathering. The hostilities of the year were forgotten, bringing the family together.

Some families decked their yule log with greenery, ribbons, and paper flowers, singing yuletide songs as they dragged the log home.

It was traditional to recite a prayer such as the following when the yule log was lighted. "May the fire of this log warm the cold; may the hungry be fed; may the weary find rest, and may all enjoy Heaven's peace."

One yule log, approx. 2 ft. long, and
    5" in diameter, with rounded
    edges and interesting features
    such as knots, twisted grain, and
    weathering
3 yds. ribbon
Green pine branches
Berries, pine cones, holly leaves, a
    candle, and other decorations as
    desired

Tie a large ribbon bow. The size of the bow will determine how much other decoration will be needed to make the log look good. If using a candle, drill a hole about two inches deep next to where the ribbon will go. Make sure the hole is wide enough for the candle. Tie some ribbon around the log and let the ends hang down. Glue or tie the bow to the ribbon. Glue greenery and holly around the bow, concealing the ends under the bow and ribbon. Continue to add decorations and branches as desired. Be creative and have fun!

POTPOURRI

Julie Wilcox
See picture p. 97
1/2 c. dried apple slices (cut into
    small pieces)
1/2 c. whole cranberries
Four cinnamon sticks
One whole nutmeg (broken into
    small pieces)
2 Tbsp. each whole cloves and
    allspice

Allow apples and cranberries to dry for several days. Mix all ingredients together. To simmer potpourri, place 1/2 c. of mixture and 2 c. of water in a small saucepan or potpourri crock.

Place pan over low heat and simmer several hours. Add more water as needed.

MRS. SANTA'S SUGAR COOKIES

Grace Bagley
See picture on p. 134
1 c. butter
1-1/2 c. white sugar
2 tsp. vanilla
3/4 tsp. salt
3 eggs, well beaten
1 c. sour cream with 1 tsp. lemon
    juice
1-1/2 tsp. baking soda
6 c. flour

Cream butter and sugar together well. Add vanilla, salt and eggs. Mix thoroughly. Add sour cream and baking soda. Mix. Add flour. Roll and cut into desired shapes. Dough may be chilled for easier handling if desired. Bake at 400 degrees for about 7 or 8 min. or until light brown. Do not overbake. Makes about 4 doz. medium-sized cookies.

Icing:
3 c. powdered sugar
1/4 c. soft butter
1 tsp. vanilla

Stir ingredients together and add enough hot water until icing is of spreading consistency. Add food coloring to all or portions, as desired.

TEXAS FUDGE CAKE

Tracy Lee Tyler
2 sticks margarine
4 Tbsp. cocoa
1 c. water
1/2 tsp. salt
2 c. sugar
2 c. flour
2 eggs, well beaten
1 tsp. baking soda
1/2 pt. sour cream

Combine flour, sugar, salt and soda in large mixing bowl. Stir margarine, cocoa and water together and heat until they come to a boil. Pour in bowl with dry ingredients. Mix well. Add beaten eggs. Stir sour cream before adding to mixture. Stir well. Pour into a large, greased cookie sheet. Bake at 375 degrees for 20 min. Pour icing over warm cake.
Icing:
1 stick margarine
2 Tbsp. cocoa

6 Tbsp. milk
1-lb. box powdered sugar
1 tsp. vanilla

Bring margarine, cocoa and milk to boil. Remove from heat. Pour into bowl and add remaining ingredients. Beat with mixer. Pour over warm cake. Sprinkle with chopped nuts if desired.

TEXAS FLAT CAKE

Pieter Lingen

2 c. flour
2 c. sugar
1 c. butter
1 c. water
1/4 c. cocoa
1/2 c. buttermilk or sour milk
2 eggs
1 tsp. baking soda

Mix flour and sugar with fork. Bring butter, water, and cocoa to boil. Add buttermilk, eggs, and soda. Add flour and sugar. Beat. Bake at 375 degrees in a 9"x13" greased pan about 25-30 min.

Frost when cool.

FROSTING:
Boil 1/2 c. butter with 6 Tbsp. cream or milk, and 1/4 c. cocoa. Add 1 tsp. vanilla and 3 c. powdered sugar. Beat until smooth.

RASPBERRY DELIGHT

Rexalee Jolley
See picture on p. 135

Crust:
2 c. flour
1/2 c. brown sugar
1 c. margarine or butter
1/2 c. chopped nuts

Mix together and place in 9"x13" pan. Bake 15 min. at 375 degrees. Cool a little, then break into crumbs. Set aside.

Raspberry mixture:
1 pkg. raspberry Danish Dessert mix
One 10-oz. pkg. frozen raspberries

Prepare Danish Dessert according to directions on package. Break up frozen raspberries and add to Danish Dessert juice and all.

Cream cheese mixture:
One 8-oz. cream cheese at room
    temperature
1 tsp. vanilla
1 c. powdered sugar
2 pkg. Dream Whip

Mix Dream Whip according to directions on package. Mix together with cream cheese, vanilla and powdered sugar.

Assembly:
Leave half of crumbs in pan. Cover with cream cheese mixture. Sprinkle with other half of crumbs. Cover with raspberry mixture. Cover and let stand in refrigerator for at least eight hours. Serves 12 to 15.

POOR MAN'S FRUIT CAKE

Carol Ferguson

2 c. raisins
4 c. water
1 tsp. soda
1 c. shortening
2 c. sugar
5 c. flour
1 Tbsp. cinnamon
1/4 tsp. allspice
1/4 tsp. cloves
1 tsp. salt
2 level tsp. baking powder
4 - 6 Tbsp. cocoa
1 c. chopped nuts

Boil raisins and water together for 20 min. Remove from heat. Add soda, shortening and sugar. Mix well. In separate mixing bowl sift flour, spices, salt, and baking powder. Add cocoa. Pour raisin mixture into a second mixing bowl. Add sifted dry ingredients. Mix together. Add 1 c. chopped nuts. Bake in loaf pan at 350 degrees for 15 min. and 325 degrees for 45 min. Frost with chocolate frosting. Drop cookies may also be made with this recipe.

GINGERBREAD

Cherie Dalton

2-1/2 c. sifted flour
1 tsp. baking powder
1-1/2 tsp. baking soda
1 tsp. ginger
2 tsp. cinnamon
1/2 c. butter (at room temperature)
3/4 c. brown sugar
2 eggs
3/4 c. molasses
1 c. buttermilk

Preheat oven to 350 degrees. Grease and flour a 13"x9"x2" pan. Sift flour and sift again with spices. Cream butter and sugar together. Add eggs one at a time. Mix well after each addition. Blend in molasses. Add dry

ingredients, alternating with buttermilk. Mix well after each addition. Pour into pan. Bake 35-40 min. until toothpick comes out clean. Serve warm with whipped cream on top.

CRANBERRY NUT BREAD

See picture on p. 135

Sift together:
2 c. flour
1 c. sugar
1/2 tsp. baking soda
1-1/2 tsp. baking powder
1 tsp. salt

Add:
7/8 c. orange juice
2 Tbsp. melted margarine
1 egg

Mix together with a spoon just until dampened.

Add:
3/4 c. chopped pecans or walnuts
1-1/2 c. chopped cranberries

Mix just until blended. Bake in greased and floured loaf pan(s) at 350 degrees. One 9-5/8"x5-1/2"x2-3/4" loaf will take one hour. Two 7-3/8"x3-5/8"x2-1/4" pans will take 45 minutes.

A 12-oz. bag of cranberries makes 2-1/2 recipes, but you can skimp a little and make it do for 3 recipes. A 16-oz bag of cranberries is plenty for 3 recipes. Cool the loaves on wire racks. Wrap in foil and freeze in Zip-loc bags.

FRESH PUMPKIN PIE

1-1/2 c. mashed pumpkin
3/4 c. sugar
1/2 tsp. salt
1-1/4 tsp. cinnamon
1 tsp. ginger
1/2 tsp. nutmeg
1/2 tsp. cloves
3 slightly beaten eggs
1-1/4 c. milk
1 6-oz. can evaporated milk
1 uncooked 9" pie shell

Mix ingredients together. Pour into pie shell. Bake at 400 degrees for 50 minutes.

APPLE-BERRY GINGER PIE

3 c. (12 oz.) cranberries
3/4 c. apple juice
1-1/3 c. sugar

1/3 c. cornstarch
3 c. cooking apples, peeled, cored, and chopped
1/2 tsp. ground ginger
Pastry dough
Powdered sugar

In a medium saucepan, cook cranberries and apple juice, uncovered, over medium heat 5 to 8 min. or until cranberries begin to burst; stir occasionally. Combine sugar and cornstarch; stir into hot cranberry mixture. Cook and stir until mixture is thickened and bubbly. Remove from heat. Stir in apples and ginger. Set aside.

Roll out pastry dough forming a circle about 15" in diameter. Place in 9-inch pie plate easing to fit. Do not stretch pastry. Trim to 1-1/2" or 2" beyond edge of pie plate.

Spread cranberry mixture evenly in pastry-lined pie plate. Bring crust up over filling, pleating to fit. Cover edge of pie with foil to prevent overbrowning. Bake at 375 degrees about 15 min. Remove foil from pie. Bake for 30 to 35 min. more or until pastry is golden. Cool on wire rack. Before serving sprinkle with powdered sugar. Makes 8 servings.

HOLLIDOLLIES

Melanie Van Der Hoeven

10 or 11 crushed graham crackers
1 stick of butter
1 c. semi-sweet chocolate chips
1 c. coconut
1 c. chopped walnuts
1 can Eagle brand condensed milk

Melt butter in 8"x12"x2" pan. Spread crushed graham crackers in bottom. Sprinkle coconut, nuts, and chocolate chips on top. Spread can of condensed milk over all. Bake at 325 degrees for 30 minutes or until lightly brown on top.

SHAGGY DOGS

Karla Gerome

1/2 c. margarine
1 c. chocolate chips
2 eggs, well beaten
1 lb. powdered sugar (about 3-1/2 c.)
One 10-oz. bag of mini-marshmallows
Coconut

Melt margarine and chocolate chips over low heat. Beat eggs and add to mixture. Add powdered sugar. Beat thoroughly. Add marshmallows. Quickly roll in coconut. Place on buttered tray. These will keep in a cool place for several days.

CHOCOLATE CLUSTERS

Deanna Hartvigsen

2 Tbsp. butter
1/4 c. milk plus 2 tsp.
1 pkg. dry chocolate fudge frosting mix
1-1/2 c. salted peanuts

Heat butter in milk over low heat until butter melts and mixture just begins to simmer. Remove from heat. Stir in frosting mix. Stir contantly with rubber scraper over low heat until smooth and glossy, 1 to 2 min. Do not overcook!! Stir in peanuts or other nuts. Drop by teaspoonful onto waxed paper.

FIVE-MINUTE FUDGE

Susan Petersen

2 Tbsp. butter
2/3 c. undiluted evaporated milk
1-2/3 c. sugar
1/2 tsp. salt
2 c. mini-marshmallows (4 oz.)
1-1/2 c. chocolate chips
1 tsp. vanilla
1/2 c. chopped nuts

Combine butter, milk, sugar, and salt in saucepan over medium heat, stirring constantly. Bring to boil. Cook 4 to 5 minutes, stirring constantly. Remove from heat. Stir in marshmallows, chocolate chips, vanilla and nuts. Stir vigorously for about 1 minute (until marshmallows melt and blend). Pour into 8" square buttered pan. Cool. Cut into squares.

VIENNESE CHOCOLATE WHIRLS

Gaynor Van der Hoeven

8 oz. softened butter or margarine
1/2 c. powdered sugar
1/2 tsp. vanilla
1 c. flour
1/4 c. Nestle's Quik
1/2 c. corn meal
12 oz. Hershey bar

Cream the butter and sugar together until light and fluffy. Add vanilla and beat well. Sift flour, Quik, and corn meal over mixture and whisk until smooth. Fill a large piping bag with a 3/4" star tip and pipe the shapes onto two greased baking sheets. Bake in preheated oven for about 25 min. or until golden brown.

Leave for 2-3 min., then lift onto wire tray to cool. Melt chocolate. Then dip half of each biscuit into the chocolate and cool until set on waxed paper. Line up the biscuits with chocolate ends all facing the same direction. Cover the chocolate with waxed paper and cover the other ends with powdered sugar icing. Store in airtight containers for up to 2 or 3 days.

CHEATIN' FUDGE

1 can Eagle brand condensed milk
1/2 c. chopped nuts
1/2 lb. Hershey bar (broken in squares)
1 tsp. vanilla

Cook milk at high temperature, stirring constantly. Boil while stirring until thick. Dump chocolate, nuts, and vanilla into milk and melt together. Pour mixture into an 8"x8" pan. Let cool. Cut in squares.

PEANUT BRITTLE

Doris Peterson

2 tsp. vanilla
1 tsp. baking soda
2 c. sugar
1 c. light Karo syrup
2 c. raw peanuts
2 Tbsp. butter

Grease a large cookie sheet. Mix vanilla and soda in a cup to remove lumps in soda. In a heavy skillet on high, cook sugar, syrup, and peanuts. When sugar dissolves, add butter. Continue to cook on high, stirring constantly, to the hard crack stage or when color changes to dark amber. Quickly add vanilla and soda mix. Remove from heat and beat vigorously until soda mixture is well mixed in. Pour out on buttered cookie sheet and spread quickly. Cool and break into pieces.

CARAMELS

Ann Danzig
See picture on p. 134

1-1/3 c. Karo syrup
1/2 lb. butter
1 pt. cream
2 c. sugar
Nuts (optional)

Combine ingredients in heavy sauce pan on high. Heat, stirring constantly. Bring to boil; continue boiling for seven minutes. Turn heat to medium and cook to soft ball stage. Add nuts if desired. Put in square buttered pan.

Refrigerate for 2 hours, then warm to room temperature. Cut and serve.

CHINESE NOODLE CANDY

One 6-oz. pkg. butterscotch chips
2 Tbsp. peanut butter
One 12-oz. pkg. cashew nuts
One 5-oz. can Chinese noodles

Melt chips over hot water, do not boil. Add peanut butter. Add nuts and noodles. Spoon onto buttered cookie sheet and cool.

DIVINITY

Betty Gillett
See picture on p. 134

3 c. sugar
3/4 c. light Karo syrup
3/4 c. water
Dash of salt
3 egg whites
1-1/2 tsp. vanilla
Walnuts (optional)

Mix sugar, syrup, water, and salt together. Cook on medium heat until 250 degrees on candy thermometer. At this time beat egg whites until they are stiff. Continue cooking syrup until 265 degrees on candy thermometer. Remove from heat and add slowly to egg whites while beating on high speed. Add vanilla. Beat until candy loses its gloss. Add nuts and drop by teaspoons on waxed paper.

ENGLISH TOFFEE

Melanie Van Der Hoeven
See picture on p. 134

1 c. sugar
2 Tbsp. water
1 c. butter
1/2 c. slivered almonds
1 c. chocolate chips
1/2 c. chopped walnuts

Cover the bottom of a cookie sheet with tin foil. In a heavy saucepan on medium-high, bring sugar, water, and butter to a boil. When it starts to boil, stir in slivered almonds. Continue stirring in same direction for 7-10 min. (until the mixture is the color of a brown paper bag). Remove immediately from stove and pour onto tin foil. DO NOT SCRAPE PAN! Spread chocolate chips on top. Sprinkle chopped walnuts on top. Gently press walnuts down. When set, break into pieces. NOTE:

Candy turns out best when made on a clear day. Always stir in the same direction and never take spoon out.

ROLL COOKIES

1/2 c. butter or margarine
1 c. sugar
1 egg
2-1/4 c. flour
1/2 tsp. salt
2 Tbsp. milk
1/4 tsp. nutmeg
1/2 tsp vanilla
2 tsp. baking powder

Cream butter; add sugar gradually. Add beaten egg. Mix and sift dry ingredients and add alternately with milk. Add flavoring. Chill dough 1 hour. Roll part of the dough at a time to 1/8" in thickness. Cut with floured cookie cutter. Bake on greased baking sheet 10 to 12 minutes at 375 degrees. Yields 48 cookies.

NUT COOKIES

1/2 c. butter or margarine
1 c. brown sugar
1/2 c. milk
1 egg
1/2 c. walnuts
1/2 c. chopped dates
1/2 c. raisins
2 tsp. baking powder
1/2 tsp. salt
1 tsp. cinnamon
1/2 tsp. cloves
1/2 tsp. nutmeg
2 c. flour

Cream butter or margarine and add sugar gradually. Add beaten egg. Add fruit and nuts. Add milk and dry ingredients alternately. Drop from spoon on greased baking sheet. Bake at 375 degrees for 10 to 12 minutes. Yields 36 cookies. (Dates may be omitted or a cup of chocolate chips added.)

RAISIN BARS

Nan Gulbransen
See picture on p. 134

1 c. raisins (covered with water and cooked 5 min.)
1-1/2 c. water, including raisin liquid
1/2 c. shortening
2 eggs
2 c. plus 2 Tbsp. flour
1 tsp. cinnamon
1 tsp. soda
1 tsp. vanilla

Cook raisins in water. Drain and add water to equal 1-1/2 c. liquid. Combine sugar, shortening, eggs, and flour. Mix all ingredients. Spread on greased cookie sheet and bake 15 to 20 minutes at 375 degrees. Ice with a thin icing.

GRAHAM CRACKER SQUARES

Ann Danzig
See picture p. 134

2 eggs
1 c. sugar
3/4 c. butter
1 tsp. vanilla
30 graham cracker 3x3 squares, crushed
2-1/2 c. mini-marshmallows
1-1/2 c. chopped nuts
4 Tbsp. coconut

Beat eggs in a saucepan. Add sugar and butter. Cook over low heat until thickened. Set aside to cool. Add vanilla, graham cracker crumbs, marshmallows, nuts, and coconut. Mix thoroughly. Put in a 13"x9" pan. Chill 2 hrs. and cut in squares. Coat with powdered sugar. (Squares may be frozen and powdered with sugar just before serving.)

CHERRY COCONUT BARS

Carol Briggs
See picture on p. 134

Pastry:
1 c. flour
3 Tbsp. powdered sugar
1/2 c. butter
Dash salt

Mix all pastry ingredients together until crumbly. Spread evenly in an 8" pan and press down. Bake for 25 minutes in 350-degree oven. Remove from oven and spread filling over pastry. Bake again for 25 minutes. Let cool and serve.

FILLING:
2 eggs, slightly beaten
1 c. sugar
1/4 c. flour
1/2 tsp. baking powder
1/4 tsp. salt
1 tsp. vanilla
3/4 c. nuts, chopped
1/2 c. coconut
1/2 c. Maraschino cherries, cut in half

CARAMEL APPLE WALNUT SQUARES

Ann Brown

1-3/4 c. unsifted flour
1 c. quick-cooking oats
1/2 c. firmly packed brown sugar
1/2 tsp. baking soda
1/2 tsp. salt
1 c. cold margarine or butter
1 c. chopped walnuts
20 unwrapped caramels
One 14-oz. can sweetened
  condensed milk (NOT evaporated
  milk)
One 20-oz. can of apple pie filling or
  topping

Preheat oven to 375 degrees. In large bowl, combine flour, oats, sugar, baking soda, and salt. Cut in margarine until crumbly. Reserve 1-1/2 c. crumb mixture. Press remainder on bottom of 13"x9" baking pan. Bake 15 minutes. Add walnuts to reserved crumb mixture. In heavy saucepan, over low heat, melt caramels with sweetened condensed milk, stirring until smooth. Spoon apple filling over prepared crust; top with caramel mixture, then reserved crumb mixture. Bake 20 minutes or until set. Cool. Serve warm with ice cream. Makes 10 to 12 servings.

PUMPKIN COOKIES

Christie Lott

2 c. flour
1 c. uncooked quick oats
1 tsp. baking soda
1 tsp. cinnamon
1 c. butter
1 c. packed brown sugar
1 c. sugar
1 egg, slightly beaten
1 tsp. vanilla
1 c. solid pack pumpkin

Preheat oven to 350 degrees. Combine flour, oats, baking soda, cinnamon. Set aside. In another bowl, cream butter with sugars until light and fluffy. Add vanilla and mix well. Alternately stir in flour mixture and pumpkin. Mix well. Drop 1/4 c. batter at a time onto lightly greased cookie sheet. Mold into pumpkin shape. Bake 20 minutes. Remove and cool. Makes 20 pumpkins.

SEVEN-LAYER BARS

See picture p. 134

Place each of the following ingredients except milk as a layer in a 9"x13" pan. Do not stir.
1/2 c. butter, melted in pan
1-1/2 c. graham cracker crumbs
1 6-oz. pkg. chocolate chips
1 6-oz. pkg. butterscotch chips
1 c. coconut
1 c. chopped nuts
1 can Eagle brand condensed milk

After all layers are in place, top with 1 can Eagle brand sweetened condensed milk. Bake at 350 degrees for 30 minutes. Cut and remove while warm.

MY FAVORITE COOKIES

Nan Gulbransen

2 c. brown sugar
1 c. white sugar
4 eggs
1 lb. margarine
2 tsp. baking powder
2 tsp. baking soda
6 c. flour
2 tsp. cinnamon
2 tsp. vanilla
Two 12-oz. pkg. chocolate chips (1
  pkg. can be mint flavored)
3 c. nuts (optional)

Mix margarine, sugars. Add eggs and cream together. Sift dry ingredients and add to mixture. Add chips and nuts. Bake at 350 degrees for 10 to 12 minutes.

ONE-MINUTE COOKIES

Nan Gulbransen
See picture p. 134

2 c. white sugar
1/2 c. shortening
1/2 c. milk
3 c. quick-cooking oats
1 c. coconut
6 Tbsp. cocoa
2 c. mini-marshmallows
Pinch of salt
1 tsp. vanilla

Boil first 3 ingredients about 1 min., then add rest. Mix together thoroughly and drop on waxed paper.

DEANNA'S BROWNIES

Deanna Hartvigsen

1 c. butter
3 squares unsweetened chocolate
4 eggs
2 c. sugar
1-1/3 c. flour
1 tsp. vanilla
Salt
1 c. nuts

Melt butter with unsweetened chocolate. Beat eggs with sugar until very stiff. Add remaining ingredients. Bake at 350 degrees for 25 min. They should be chewy.

GRACE'S BROWNIES

Grace Bagley

2 c. white sugar
3/4 c. cocoa
2 tsp. vanilla
1/2 tsp. salt
1 c. margarine
4 eggs
2 c. flour
1-1/2 c. chopped walnuts

Combine first five ingredients. Mix well. Add eggs. Mix well. Add flour and nuts. Mix well. Bake on cookie sheets (with sides) at 350 degrees for about 20 min. or until toothpick comes out clean. Frost with chocolate frosting.

HACIENDA DIP

Ann Brown

Two 8-oz. pkgs. cream cheese,
  softened
1/2 c. salsa
Dash of onion salt

Mix cream cheese, salsa and salt until well blended. Spread cheese mixture in microwavable pie plate or bowl. Microwave on high 3 to 4 minutes or until thoroughly heated, stirring every 2 minutes. Use corn chips and raw vegetable pieces as dippers. Makes 2 cups.

CHEESE BALL

See picture on p. 135

Two 5-oz. jars Kraft Old English
  cheese
One 4-oz. pkg. bleu cheese
One 3-oz. pkg. cream cheese
2 Tbsp. finely grated onion
1 tsp. Worcestershire sauce
1/2 c. chopped fresh parsley

1 c. chopped pecans or walnuts

Have cheeses at room temperature. Mix cheeses, onion, Worcestershire sauce together with electric mixer. Add 1/2 c. nuts and 1/4 c. parsley. Form into ball. Line small Pyrex bowl with foil. Put ball into bowl with foil. Wrap foil completely over ball to cover. Chill overnight. One hour before serving, sprinkle remaining parsley and nuts on a piece of waxed paper. Roll cheese ball in the parsley and nuts to cover the outside. Serve with a knife and crackers. Freezes well. (If you use dried parsley instead of fresh, use about 1 tsp. in the ball and about 1-1/2 tsp. on the outside.)

BAKED HAM WITH APRICOT GLAZE

Grace Bagley
See picture on p. 135

One pre-cooked ham, 4 to 6 lbs.
1/3 c. A-1 steak sauce
1/4 c. honey
1 c. firmly packed brown sugar
1/2 c. apricot nectar
2 Tbsp. apricot preserves or apricot jam or orange marmalade
2 tsp. lemon juice

Bake the ham according to directions. Combine remaining ingredients in sauce pan. Heat until syrupy, about 8 to 9 min. This can be used to baste the ham or serve warm at the table with the ham.

WASSAIL

Ann Danzig
See picture on p. 135

1-1/2 c. sugar
3 c. water
3 cinnamon sticks
4 whole cloves

Simmer 15 minutes to an hour, and add:
1 c. orange juice
4 c. apple cider
2 qts. water
1 c. lemon juice
2 c. pineapple juice

Reheat, but avoid boiling.

NO JELL-O FRUIT SALAD

Doris Peterson
See picture on p. 135

1 can Eagle brand sweetened condensed milk

8 oz. Cool Whip
One 11-oz. can mandarin oranges
One 17-oz. can fruit cocktail
One 20-oz. can cherry pie filling
2 c. mini-marshmallows

Mix together milk and Cool Whip. Drain oranges and fruit cocktail. Fold into Cool Whip mixture. Add cherry pie filling and marshmallows. Mix thoroughly and refrigerate overnight.

ORANGE JELL-O SALAD

Tracy Lee Tyler

One 6-oz. pkg. orange Jell-O
3 c. hot water
One 6-oz. can frozen orange juice concentrate
One 20-oz. can crushed pineapple
Two 11-oz. cans mandarin oranges

Mix all ingredients until Jell-O dissolves. Let set. Serve with whipped cream topping.

PINK POPCORN

Betty Gillett

2 c. sugar
2/3 c. milk, half & half, or cream
1 Tbsp. light Karo syrup
1/4 tsp. salt
1 Tbsp. vanilla
1 or 2 drops red food coloring.

Mix ingredients together in saucepan. Cook until slightly firm (230 degrees). Pour over 6 qts. popcorn. Stir to coat. Pour on waxed paper. (Does NOT make good popcorn balls.)

PEANUT BUTTER POPCORN

Carol Briggs

3 c. popped corn
1 c. sugar
1/2 c. honey
1/2 c. Karo light syrup
1-1/2 c. almonds (optional)
1 c. peanut butter
1 tsp. vanilla

Keep popcorn and nuts warm in a 250-degree oven. Butter sides of 1-1/2 qt. heavy saucepan. Combine sugar, honey, and corn syrup in pan. Bring to boil, stirring constantly. Boil hard for 2 min. Remove from heat and stir in peanut butter and vanilla. Pour immediately over popcorn mixture, stirring to coat well. Spread on waxed paper or greased surface of cookie sheet. Cool. Break in pieces.

CARAMEL CORN

Martha Whitehead

8 qts. popped corn
2 c. brown sugar
1 c. margarine or butter
1/2 c. light Karo syrup
1 tsp. vanilla
1/2 tsp. baking soda
1 c. peanuts (optional)

Bring brown sugar, margarine or butter, Karo syrup and vanilla to a boil. Boil for 5 min. Remove from heat, add soda, stir. Pour over popped corn. Add 1 c. peanuts if desired. Mix well. Bake in oven one hour at 250 degrees. Stir 3 or 4 times while baking.

DIPPED PRETZELS

Two 9-oz. pkgs. small, butter-flavored pretzels
1 lb. white chocolate

Melt chocolate in microwave or double boiler until smooth and creamy. Dip unbroken pretzels on one end.. Cool on waxed paper.

SOFT PRETZELS

1 pkg. dry yeast
1/2 c. warm water
1/2 c. sugar
1-1/2 tsp. salt
2 c. milk, scalded and cooled to room temperature
1/4 c. salad oil
5-1/2 to 6 c. all-purpose flour, unsifted
3/4 tsp. baking powder
3 Tbsp. salt
2 qts. boiling water
1 egg white, slightly beaten
Coarse salt

In large bowl, dissolve yeast in warm water. Stir in sugar, 1-1/2 tsp. salt, milk, and oil. With wooden spoon, gradually mix in about 2-1/2 c. flour. Cover and let rise in warm place until bubbly (about 40 min.). Sift 3 c. of flour with baking powder and add to dough. Mix with a wooden spoon, then turn out dough on a lightly floured board. Knead for about 5 min. or until dough is no longer sticky, adding a little more flour if necessary.

Roll out and pat dough into a 9"x15" rectangle. Cut dough into strips that are 1/2" wide and 15" long. With palms, roll each strip back and forth on the board into a strand about 20" long. Twist each into pretzel shape as desired. Let rise, uncovered, for 30 min.

Dissolve the 3 Tbsp. salt in boiling water. With a slotted spoon, lower one pretzel at a time into boiling water; after about 2 seconds, lift out, wipe the bottom of the spoon on paper towels to drain briefly, then set pretzels on a liberally greased baking sheet, arranging 1/2" apart. Brush with egg white and sprinkle lightly with coarse salt.

Bake in 400-degree oven for 20 min. or until crust is golden brown. Serve warm or transfer to a rack to cool. Makes 18.

Try them spread with a little mustard!

CHRISTMAS PLACE MATS

Nan Gulbransen

HOLLY BERRY PLACE MAT
See picture on p. 27

White place mats (store bought or
   hand made)
Scrap of green fabric for leaves
Scrap of red fabric for berries
7"x7" piece of bonded batting
Polyester fiber filling

Cut four holly leaves (for each place mat) from the green fabric. Cut two from the bonded batting. Cut three circles from the red for berries.

Using 1/4" seam allowance, place a pair of leaves right sides together, with batting leaf on the bottom. Stitch all around outside edge, leaving an opening for turning near the stem. Clip curves and corners. Turn.

Whipstitch opening shut. Machine topstitch with green thread as indicated on pattern.

To sew berries, run a gathering stitch around the outside edge. Stuff and draw up tightly. Hand stitch the three berries to the top of the leaves. Stitch to place mat.

HOLLY LEAF PLACE MAT (FABRIC)
See picture on p. 28

1/2 yd. fabric for each place mat
18"x22" Pellon fleece
Scraps of red fabric for berries
1/4 yard "Wonder Under"

Cut out place mats following directions on pattern. Cut two of green material and one of fleece for each place mat. With right sides together and fleece on top, using 1/4" seam allowance, sew all around edges leaving 3" open to turn. Clip curves. Turn right side out. Press. Whipstitch opening closed.

Cut three red berries for each place mat. Cut three pieces of Wonder Under same size as berries and iron onto green holly leaf. Follow Wonder Under directions in Glossary. Zigzag edges of red berries.

HOLLY LEAF PLACE MAT (PAPER)
14"x21" piece of green
   construction paper for
   each place mat
Small piece of red paper
   for berries
Rubber cement or craft
   glue

Cut out place mats and berries following directions on pattern (same as for fabric place mats).

Glue berries in place with rubber cement or craft glue.

POINSETTIA TABLE RUNNER
See picture on p. 100

18-1/2"x44" quilted fabric
Pellon fleece
Scraps of yellow fabric for
   poinsettia center

Cut 10 large poinsettia petals (pattern on p.164) of red fabric and 5 of fleece. Cut 6 medium poinsettia petals of red fabric and 3 of fleece. Cut 4 small poinsettia petals of red fabric and 2 of fleece. Using a 1/4" seam allowance and with right sides of material together and fleece on top, sew all around edges, leaving an opening to turn. Clip curves and corners. Turn right side out and press. Slip stitch opening closed. Topstitch center vein on petals.

For leaves, cut 6 each of large and small leaves out of green fabric and 3 large and small of fleece. Proceed as for petals. Cut five circles of yellow fabric for center of poinsettia. Baste around edge of circle 1/8" from edge. Pull thread in tightly

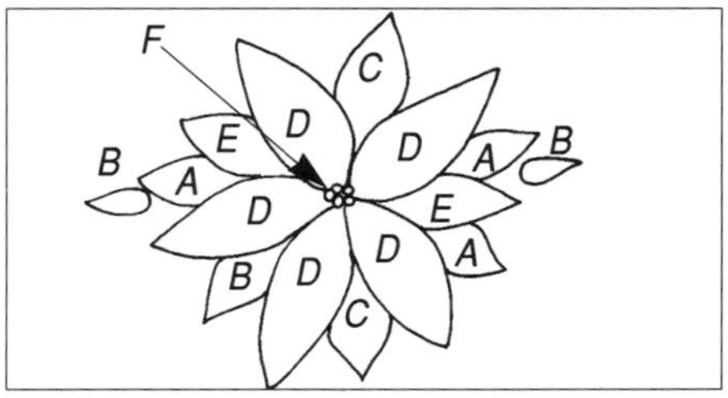

Figure 1

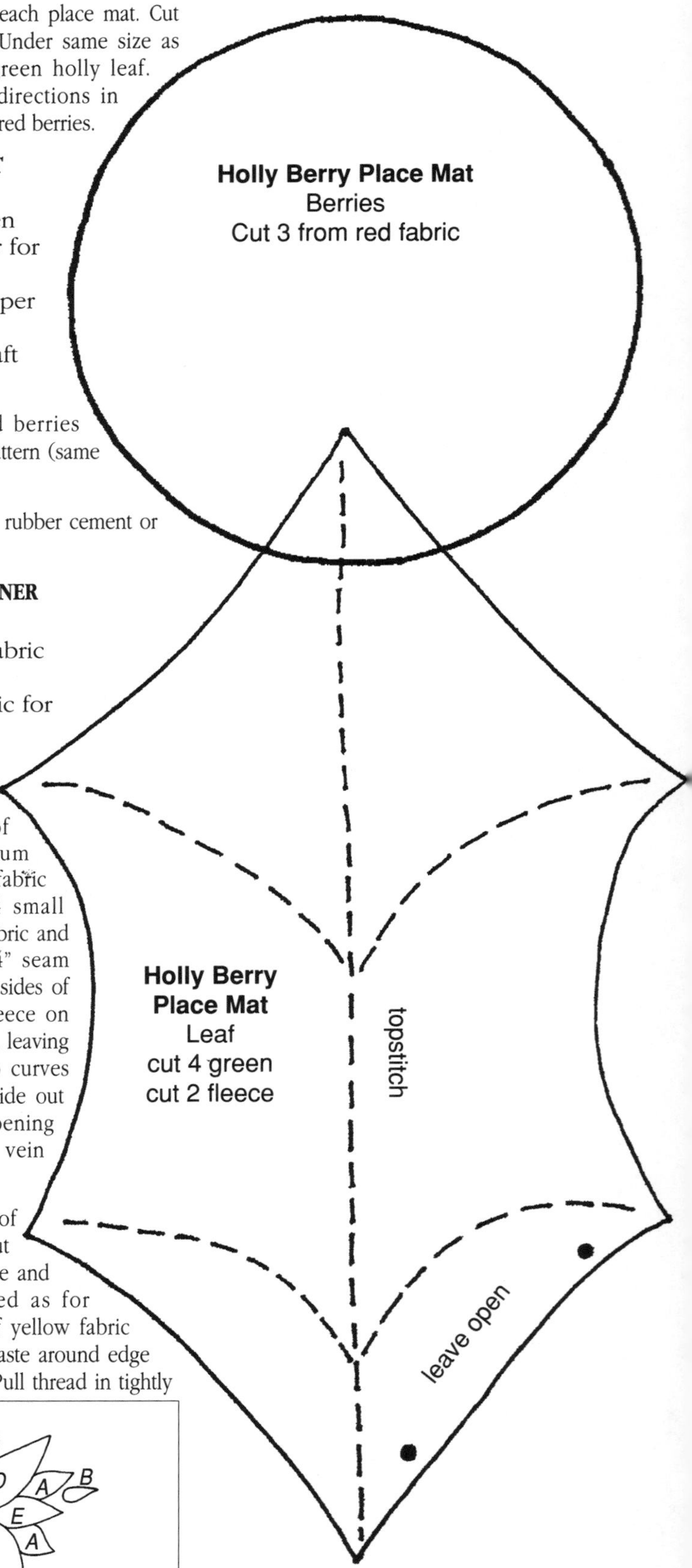

Holly Berry Place Mat
Berries
Cut 3 from red fabric

Holly Berry Place Mat
Leaf
cut 4 green
cut 2 fleece

topstitch

leave open

to form a circle. Center on runner following Fig.1 for placement.

CHRISTMAS PRESENT PLACE MATS
See picture on p. 64

1/2 yd. red fabric
1/2 yd. Christmas print fabric
1/2 yd. Pellon fleece

Cut the following:
One 14"x22" piece of Pellon fleece
Two 14"x22" pieces of red fabric

From Christmas print, cut:
One 18"x18" square
One 2"x22" strip
One 2"x14" strip
One 2-1/2"x7" strip

On top red piece, place 2" strips as shown and machine appliqué in place. (You may use Wonder Under to keep the strips in place while you appliqué them on.) (See Fig. 1.)

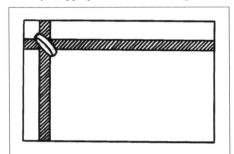

Figure 1

Fold the 2-1/2"x7" strip in half lengthwise, right sides together, and sew along one end and the raw edges using a 1/4" seam. (See Fig. 2.)

Figure 2

Turn right side out and overlap ends 1/2". Stitch closed. Place ring on a diagonal at crossing point of strip. (See Fig.1.)

Place two red pieces right sides together. Place the Pellon fleece on top and stitch all layers together, leaving a 6" opening to turn. Trim corners. Turn and slip stitch opening closed.

Turn under all edges of the 18"x18" square piece of Christmas print to form a narrow hem. Stitch. To finish, fold napkin in half and fold as a fan. Place through the ring on place mat to form bow on package.

BOW NAPKIN RING

See picture on p. 62

One 8-1/2"x3" strip of fabric for bow
One 6-1/2"x3" strip of fabric for ring
One 3"x2" strip of fabric for center loop
Aleene's fabric stiffener

Dampen fabric and saturate with stiffener. Allow to dry for 2 to 3 minutes.

Ring: Fold long sides into middle wrong sides together and fold in half lengthwise again. Set aside.

Bow: Fold long sides into middle wrong sides together. Fold long edges to center and then fold short ends together overlapping 1/2". Flatten the circle so that the overlapped edges are in the center and it forms a bow loop on each side. Scrunch the center together to gather.

Overlap the ends of the ring strip to form a circle. Attach the bow on top of the overlap. Fold center bow piece long side to middle and in half lengthwise again. Wrap the small center bow part twice around, overlapping underneath. Start on top side and end underneath, pinning in place. Support opening with tin foil or waxed paper. Allow finished product to dry completely (overnight).

TREE PLACE MATS AND NAPKIN RINGS

See picture on p. 61

1/2 yd. green fabric (back of mats)
1/2 yd. red fabric (front of mats)
1/8 yd. each of four different green fabrics (trees)
1/8 yd. light background fabric
1/2 yd. Pellon fleece
1/4 yd. "Wonder Under"
1/2 yd. red fabric (napkin)
1/8 yd. beige or yellow (stars)
Scraps of red fabric (hearts)

Materials are sufficient to make two place mats and napkin rings.

Trace pieces of tree pattern to paper side of Wonder Under (star, heart, trunk, and body of tree). Repeat for all three trees of each place mat. Roughly cut out the traced pieces and with rough side of Wonder Under down on the WRONG side of the fabric, iron the Wonder Under on. Carefully cut out each piece and lay aside.

Cut out a 4-1/2"x14" piece of beige background fabric. Peel the paper off the backs of the tree pieces and place the tree, trunk first, then star and heart on the light background fabric so that they are evenly spaced. Leave an extra 1/4" at the top and bottom. Iron these pieces on.

Set your sewing machine to a fine satin stitch about 1/16" in width (loosen top tension on sewing machine to get a better stitch). A tight blind hem stitch may also be used to appliqué the pieces. Stitch around all pieces to secure them in place.

Cut a 14"x14-1/2" piece of red fabric for the rest of the top of the place mat. Using a 1/4" seam allowance, sew this piece and the tree piece together. Lay the top of the place mat on the Pellon fleece and cut to the same size. Cut the bottom piece for the place mat 1" bigger all the way around.

Pin all three pieces together, centering with wrong sides together. Topstitch around place mat about 1/8" in from edge of place mat.

To bind the place mat, turn under the raw edge of the back green fabric and bring to the front. Pin in place and slip stitch or topstitch on the sewing machine.

Napkin: Cut an 18" square piece of fabric and turn under 1/4" on all edges. Stitch.

Napkin ring:

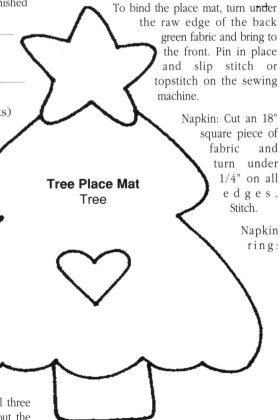

Tree Place Mat
Tree

Trace tree, trunk, and star on paper side of Wonder Under. Roughly cut out the traced pieces and iron onto WRONG side of selected fabrics. Carefully cut out traced pieces. Cut out one whole tree from green fabric. This will include the star and trunk. Cut out one whole tree of Pellon fleece. Cut out heart in center of tree on all pieces.

Remove paper from the back of Wonder Under pieces. Iron onto a green piece of fabric. Be careful about placement of pieces so that they will match the Pellon fleece and the green tree that have already been cut out. Trim excess fabric from these pieces and pin all three trees wrong sides together (green plain, Pellon, and the pieced tree). Satin stitch around the edge of tree, star, and heart, joining all three pieces together.

Cut a piece of green fabric 2-1/2"x4". Fold in half lengthwise right sides together and stitch a 1/4" seam on the long side. Turn to right side and iron. Satin stitch ends and then straight stitch ends to opposite wrong sides of the tree. This will form a loop that the napkin can go through.

Holly Leaf Place Mat
Piece 2

Holly Leaf Place Mat
Berries
cut 3 red

place on fold

overlap pattern here

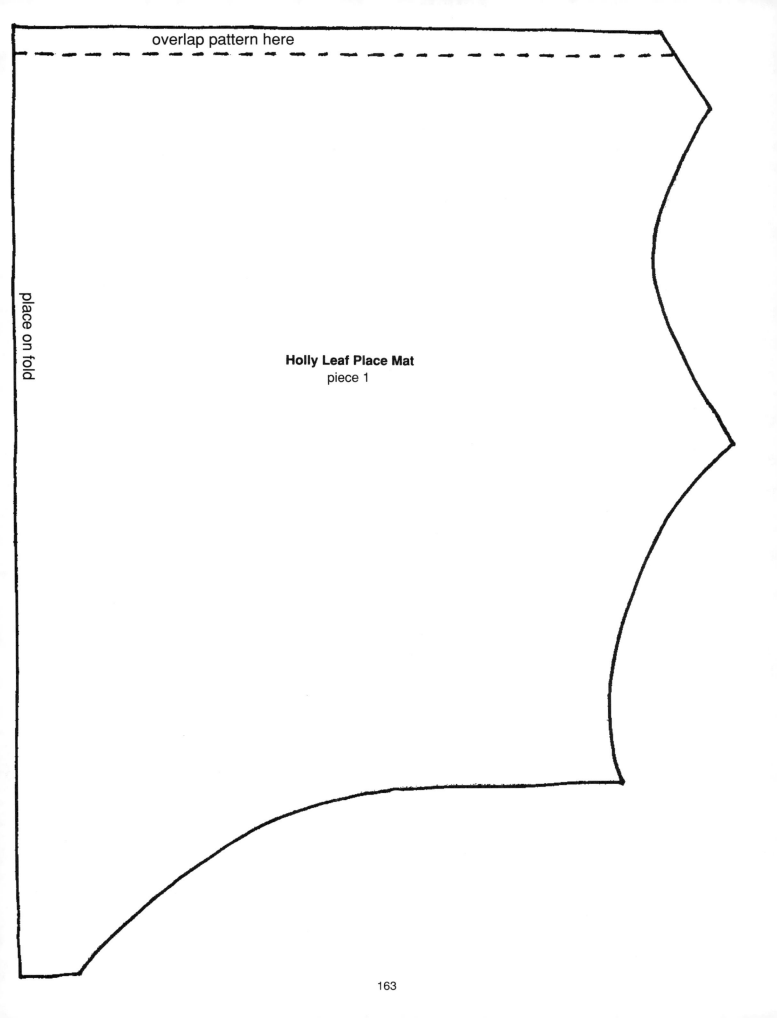

overlap pattern here

place on fold

Holly Leaf Place Mat
piece 1

163

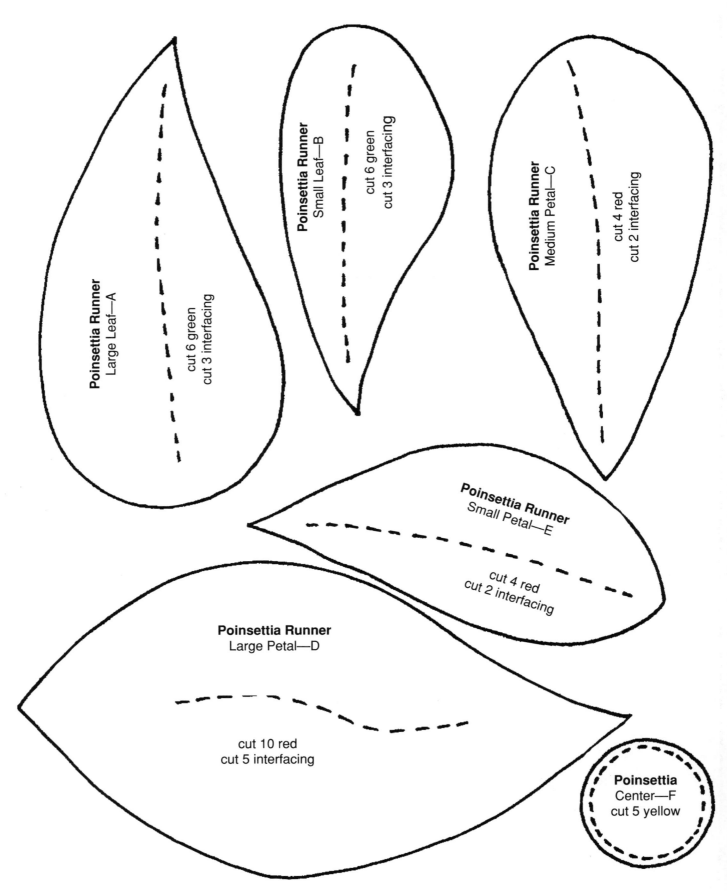

Poinsettia Runner
Large Leaf—A

cut 6 green
cut 3 interfacing

Poinsettia Runner
Small Leaf—B

cut 6 green
cut 3 interfacing

Poinsettia Runner
Medium Petal—C

cut 4 red
cut 2 interfacing

Poinsettia Runner
Small Petal—E

cut 4 red
cut 2 interfacing

Poinsettia Runner
Large Petal—D

cut 10 red
cut 5 interfacing

Poinsettia
Center—F
cut 5 yellow

GLOSSARY

PAINTING TECHNIQUES

STAMPING AND STENCILING

SEWING TERMS AND STITCHES

WONDER UNDER INSTRUCTIONS

PAINTING TECHNIQUES

WASH:
Mix paint on a brush using about 90% water. Paint the whole area specified evenly showing no wood. If color isn't dark enough, paint another coat. Too light is better than too dark.

FLOATING:
Use a damp, flat, very wide brush. Blot it on a paper towel. Sideload the brush with paint at least 1/4 up to 1/2 deep. For tiny areas, load just a small corner of the brush.

Blend it back and forth on the palette several times to get a softened blend. Paint on the edges indicated.

STYLUS:
A tool with small ball points on each end, used to trace patterns for tole or dot painting.

CROSS-STITCH EMBROIDERY

COUNTED CROSS STITCH:
Work one cross stitch to correspond to each colored square on the chart. For horizontal rows, work stitches in two journeys (see Fig. 1.) For vertical rows, complete each stitch as shown in Fig. 2. When pattern calls for backstitches in same square as cross stitches, work backstitches on top of cross stitch.

BACKSTITCH:
Backstitching is usually done for outline detail and should be worked after rest of design has been completed. (See Fig. 3.)

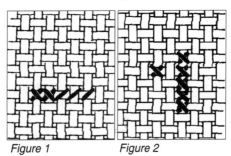

Figure 1   Figure 2

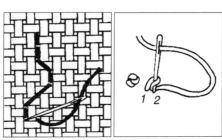

Figure 3   Figure 4

FRENCH KNOT:
Bring needle up at 1. Wrap thread as many times as pattern instructs or as desired around needle and insert needle at 2, holding end of thread with non-stitching fingers. (See Fig. 4.)

Tighten knot, then pull needle through fabric, holding thread until it must be released. Size of knot may be adjusted by using fewer or more strands of floss, or by varying number of times thread is wrapped around needle (usually no more than three).

RUNNING STITCH:
Make a series of straight stitches with stitch length equal to the space between stitches.

CRAZY QUILT DECORATIVE STITCHERY

Use the chart below to select and perfect the decorative stitches that will add the finishing touches to crazy quilt work.

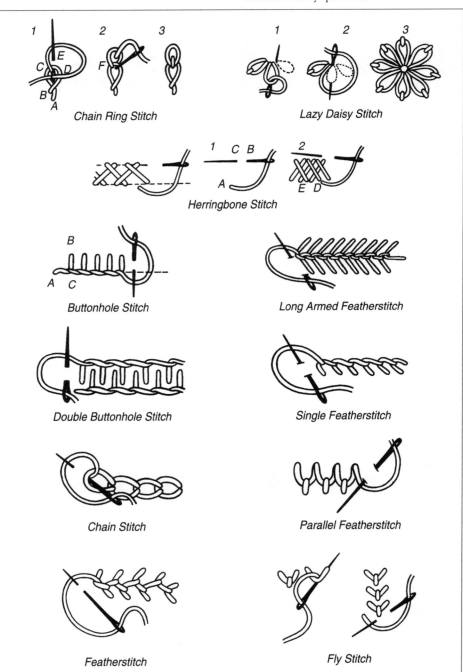

Chain Ring Stitch   Lazy Daisy Stitch

Herringbone Stitch

Buttonhole Stitch   Long Armed Featherstitch

Double Buttonhole Stitch   Single Featherstitch

Chain Stitch   Parallel Featherstitch

Featherstitch   Fly Stitch

STENCILING

To make your own stencil, you will need the following:
1 sheet of Mylar
1 permanent fine-tip black pen
Exacto knife

Trace design on Mylar with black pen. Place design on a hard surface, cut out stencil by following pen design with the Exacto knife. You may need to go over it more than once.

To use the stencil, you will need the following:
Metal, paper, or plastic stencil
Stiff stencil brush (sizes vary from 5/8" to 1/4")
Oil stencil crayons in choice of colors
Masking tape

Before starting, be sure the surface you desire to stencil is clean (wall, fabric, wood, etc.) Carefully position stencil on surface and tape in place. If using one color only, do not tape over the stencil. If using more than one color, tape over the sections not being used.

Peel or rub off self-healing coating from the crayon. Outline the stencil, being careful not to get crayon on the item being stenciled. Using an inward stroke, brush across stencil onto the item.

To obtain darker colors, repeat the painting steps. To shade, lighten the stroke as you get to the center of the stencil.

Before using another color, brush out all extra color on brush onto a scrap piece of fabric. DO NOT clean in water!

Allow paint to dry 24 hours. Clean stencil and brush after each use.

FABRIC STAMPS

A few helpful hints for using fabric stamps:

1. Prewash fabric. Do not dry fabric with a fabric softener sheet in the dryer.

2. Select a lightly colored fabric.

3. Dampen felt pad and place on a plastic plate.

4. Work black fabric ink into the pad.

5. Select a firm, flat surface on which to work and protect the surface with waxed paper or cardboard.

6. Test the stamp on paper or a scrap of fabric.

7. Allow to dry five minutes.

8. Heat set design with a hot iron on cotton setting for five minutes. Keep iron moving.

9. Paint design with favorite colors of textile paint.

10. Allow paint to dry for 24 hours. When washing painted garment, turn it inside out. Iron painted portion on the wrong side.

11. Clean rubber stamps with mild soap and water. Do not immerse stamps in water. Store in a cool, dry place.

SEWING TERMS

APPLIQUÉ:
Appliqué work is basically a sewing craft consisting of overlaying one fabric with another to create a design. Light- to medium-weight, smooth-surfaced fabrics are easiest to handle. Avoid loosely woven or extremely bulky fabrics as they are very difficult to manage. Before using any fabrics, press out all wrinkles and creases. Appliqués may be hand-stitched, machine-stitched, or ironed into place with fusible webs. (See "Wonder Under" instructions.)

BIAS:
A line diagonal to the grain of a fabric; a line at a 45-degree angle to the selvage.

NAP:
A hairy or downy surface. To check direction of nap, rub fabric from top toward bottom with hand and take note of appearance of fabric. When cutting patterns from fabrics with a nap, be sure the nap is running in the same direction for all appropriate pieces.

RUFFLES:
To create proper ruffles, measure all sides of item to which ruffle will be attached. Multiply that figure by three for a full ruffle. Divide that figure by 45. Now multiply that number by the width of your ruffle. This will give you the amount in inches of fabric needed. Double this amount if ruffle is to be folded to make a two-sided ruffle.

STRAIGHT OF GRAIN:
Parallel to the bound or selvage edge of fabric.

IN-THE-DITCH:
Quilt or stitch from right side of piece as close to the "ditch" created by previously stitched seam as possible.

MITERING CORNERS:
Directions given are for mitering corners on quilts, but technique may be applied to any area where a mitered corner is desired.

If you do not wish to fold the miters in the corners, you can sew the miters in your binding. To do this, the binding is applied to each side of the quilt separately. Each strip of binding is cut four inches longer than the quilt side. As you place your binding on the edge of the quilt, allow 2" to extend at each side.

Sew the binding on to all four sides of the quilt, stopping 1/4" from the ends (or the width of your binding seam) and back tacking (Figure 1). Fold the binding out from the edge of the quilt, overlapping the two strips at right angles. If you are applying traditional binding, fold the second seam allowance now.

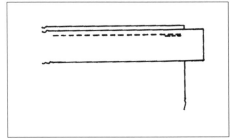

Figure 1

Mark each strip where they cross—point A (Figure 2). On the wrong side of the binding,

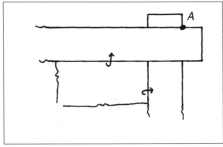

Figure 2

draw a line from point A into the corner seam—point B (Figure 3). Place your ruler along the stitching line and make a mark at

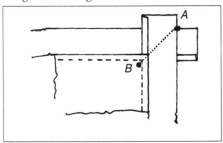

Figure 3

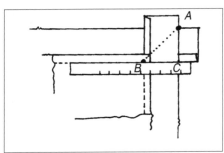

Figure 4

the folded edge of your binding, directly across from the corner seam—point C (Figure 4). Lay your ruler so that it touches point C

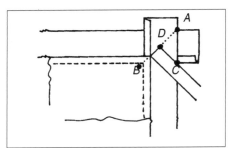

Figure 5

and the diagonal line. Draw a line from point C to the line - point D (Figure 5).

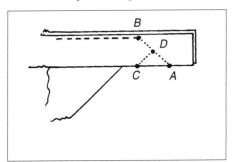

Figure 6

Place the binding strips right sides together, matching points A together (Figure 6). Sew

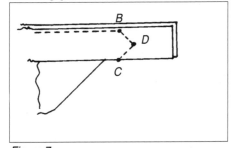

Figure 7

from B to D to C (Figure 7). Trim the seam to 1/4" and finger press it open. Turn the binding over the edge to the back of the quilt, forming miters on the front and back (Figure 8).

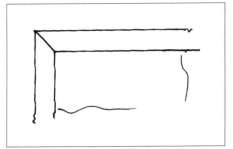

Figure 8

WONDER UNDER

Trace pattern to the paper side of Wonder Under. (Be sure to do all pattern pieces the same way—either face up or down. They are not reversible!) Cut around traced pieces to separate. Choose fabric for pieces and iron Wonder Under to the wrong side of chosen fabrics (paper side up). Carefully cut pieces out along the traced line. Remove the paper back and position pieces as desired. Then iron them on.

OTHER INSTRUCTIONS FOR PUFF STOCKING, P.58

Fig. 3 shows where to attach lace and piping to toe piece. Fig. 4 details pleating and lace placement for satin cuff.

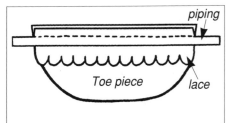

Figure 3

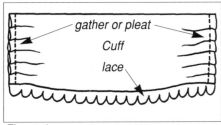

Figure 4